All Pro Baseball Group

Drills and Instruction for Coaching Youth Baseball

third edition

by Major League coach Ron Wotus
and players Erik Johnson and Joe Millette

International Standard Book Number 0-9718202-0-1

Revised 2012

Introduction

Managers, coaches and players, All Pro Baseball Group would like to welcome you to our instructional program. Preseason and in-season training has become an integral part of youth baseball, and we are honored to help you provide that experience for your players. Since the late 1980s, our staff has worked closely with numerous youth leagues to make the game of baseball an enjoyable and educational experience.

In addition to more than 55 years of combined professional experience, we bring to our program a deep love of the game and a keen desire to improve the experience for all youth participants. Our goal is to educate and refresh your knowledge of the game. Our philosophy is to motivate and build players' self-esteem and character while developing their skills in a positive environment.

This manual is designed to guide you at practice and enhance your knowledge. It is also intended to give you a simplified and fun way to teach. The manual is organized to be user-friendly. Each specific subject includes an introduction, basic fundamentals, drills and games. The fundamentals are the foundation for skill development, while the drills are designed to reinforce those fundamentals, and are the life-blood of any practice routine. Games are included to help you teach in an effective and motivational manner.

Being aware of the proper fundamentals is a key component of the process. However, we believe learning how to instruct and how to communicate with the player is a critical asset. We have given you our expertise on how you can effectively communicate and instruct the baseball skills necessary for player development. Our goal is to help give you all the tools necessary to help you coach and teach the game of baseball in an encouraging way so all players can enjoy their baseball experience to the fullest. We believe this is the true essence and spirit of baseball. Thank you for participating in our program.

All Pro Baseball Group Staff

A Brief Background of All Pro Baseball Group

All Pro Baseball Group, formerly Get Up and Go Baseball, has been providing player and coaching clinics since the late 1980s. After providing clinics just for Erik Johnson's hometown Little League, San Ramon Valley, All Pro Baseball is now conducting coaching clinics throughout Northern California. Not only has our staff all played Major League Baseball, they have taught the game at almost every level. Ron Wotus is an experienced Major League coach. Erik Johnson is a professional youth league coach, if you will. And Joe Millette is a former college coach and current youth league coach. Through many years of research from player clinics, coaching clinics and private instruction with youth players and coaches, All Pro Baseball has blended their professional experience with Youth League experience and has created a program that is designed specifically to teach those who are involved with players between the ages of 6 through 16 We believe we provide a unique instructional program and hope you enjoy your experience with All Pro Baseball Group.

To purchase Drills and Instruction for Coaching Success, call (925) 296-0628 or order on line at www.allprobaseballgroup.com.

Authors

ERIK JOHNSON

Erik is one of the original founders of All Pro Baseball Group and has been an active member of the organization since the late 1980s. Erik grew up in Northern California and played Little League baseball in the San Ramon Valley area where his teams qualified for the Little League and Senior League World Series. His teams reached the championship game both times. Erik attended De La Salle High School in Concord where he lettered in basketball and baseball. He received an athletic scholarship to UC Santa Barbara and was named to All Pacific Coast Athletic Association baseball team his last three seasons and a preseason All-American his junior and senior years. Erik was an 18th-round pick of the San Francisco Giants in 1987 and played professionally for 10 years, including two seasons with the Giants in 1993-94. In 1995, Erik played in the Triple-A All-Star Game and started at shortstop. Erik was inducted into the UC Santa Barbara Intercollegiate Athletics Hall of Fame in 1998, into the Tri-Valley Hall Of Fame in 2002 and into the De La Salle High School Hall of Fame in 2007. He is currently the President and Director of Baseball Instruction for EJ Sports, LLC. He also the general manager for all of the traveling teams in EJ SPORTS. The Pacific Coast Stars, Titans and the Warriors. His teams play internationally and domestically. Erik resides in the San Francisco Bay Area.

JOE MILLETTE

Joe is one of the original founders of All Pro Baseball Group and has been an active member of the organization since the late 1980s. Joe grew up in Lafayette, Calif., and he played in Lafayette Little League and continued through Pony, Colt and American Legion. He attended Acalanes High School where he played baseball, basketball, soccer and football. Joe attended Diablo Valley College where he was an all-conference player and part of the most successful baseball team in school history. He received an athletic scholarship to St. Mary's College of California, where he finished his collegiate career. He graduated with a degree in Business Administration. After college, Joe signed a free-agent contract with the Philadelphia Phillies in 1988 and played professionally for 10 years. He played shortstop in the major leagues in 1992-93 with the '93 team losing to the Toronto Blue Jays in the World Series. Joe played with four other organizations — the Florida Marlins, Pittsburgh Pirates, Seattle Mariners and Chicago Cubs. He retired in 1998 after shoulder surgery. In 1998-2000, Joe served as an assistant baseball coach at his alma mater. Since 2008 he has coached multiple teams yearly at the youth level. Joe resides in the San Francisco Bay area with his wife Jennifer, daughter Lauren and sons Jack and Will.

RON WOTUS

Ron has been a member of All Pro Baseball Group since the late 1980s. During Ron's 15 years coaching in the Major Leagues he has been involved in the postseason four times and the World Series twice, once in 2002 and again in 2010 with a resulting World Championship. As a bench coach he has served three of the top managers in baseball, Dusty Baker, Felipe Alou and Bruce Bochy. Beginning in 1979, Ron played professionally for 11 years, spending parts of the 1983-85 seasons as an infielder with the Pittsburgh Pirates. After retiring, he became a manager in the San Francisco Giants minor-league system. In seven years, Ron's teams finished 555-411 for a .575 winning percentage. During the 1991-92 seasons, Ron managed at Single-A San Jose, and his 1991 club posted a 92-44 record, the best in all of professional baseball. He was voted California League Manager of the Year and Baseball America's Class-A Manager of the Year. From 1993-95, Ron managed at Double-A Shreveport and led the team to three consecutive playoff berths. The 1995 team won the Texas League championship with an 88-47 record, the best in all of minor-league baseball. In 1996-97, Ron managed the Triple-A Phoenix club, and the team won back-to-back Pacific Coast League Southern Division titles. The 1997 team finished 88-55, the best record in Triple-A baseball, and Ron was voted Best Manager Prospect by his peers. In 1998, Ron was the San Francisco Giants' third-base coach. Ron currently is the bench coach and infield coach for the Giants, a position he has held since 1999. Ron resides in the San Francisco Bay area with his wife Laurie.

All Pro Baseball Group
Drills & Instruction for Coaching Youth Baseball

Table of Contents

COACHING PHILOSOPHY

Enjoying your experience with your players, as well as the players enjoying their experience with you, should be your first goal in coaching. Along with a good rapport, the ultimate goal is to see the players improve their skills in the game and to have their desire to play continue to grow. As a coach, it is a great joy to watch your players perform successfully on the field as they grow in confidence, character and self-esteem. When players are failing on the field — striking out, dropping the baseball and throwing it wildly — you would agree it is much more difficult for them to enjoy that experience and to develop confidence and self-esteem.

Our goal in this section is to help you understand that a quality coach can teach players how to play the game and to develop character, confidence and self-esteem.

In our eyes, helping a player perform while mentoring young men and women is what coaching is all about. But it is not an easy task. It takes a commitment on your behalf to put the player first. It takes an understanding that every player is different and in a different place when it comes to strength, athletic ability, aptitude and desire to improve as a baseball player. If a player has all of these, they have a good chance to develop into a quality player. But not all players are that committed to the sport, or they are lacking in strength or ability at a particular time and place. Remember, all can be developed over time even athletic ability. Although a certain amount is god given the rest can be develop through hard work and dedication.

Expert Advice on Coaching Different Individuals

The best coaches adapt their style to all the different individuals, rather than expecting players to adjust to the coach. The goal doesn't change with what the coach wants to accomplish; what's different is how he handles each player to accomplish that goal. Some players need only guidance and support while others need direction and discipline.

What Is Coaching?

Youth coach? Teacher, mentor, character-builder? What do you want to be? When you take on the position of coaching, whether you realize it or not, whether you want it or not, you will leave an impression on your players. We pose this question because coaching is much more than running the team and its play on the field. It is much more than wins and losses. You will have an opportunity to teach, influence and mentor your players on the diamond, and more importantly, as young men or women. You have a chance, usually reserved for parents, family members and schoolteachers to leave a positive impact on the life of your players. In the big scheme of life, what is important for you to pass along and how would you like to be viewed by your players and their parents? Remember, whether it is a youth coach, high school coach, college coach or professional coach, this game is about the players not the coach.

Three-Time Manager of the Year Dusty Baker on Getting the Most Out of Your Players:
"You have to care about the player. Be honest, firm but fair. Players are looking for love and discipline, but love is discipline."

THE DIFFICULTY OF THE GAME HAS STOPPED MOST OF US FROM ADVANCING.

At some point, the speed at which this game is played has temporarily prevented or has stopped most of us from advancing to the next level of baseball. All three of us authors have been fortunate to play this game at the highest level, the major leagues. But there were hurdles along the way. Whether it was going to the big diamond at the age of 13. Or to high school, where the competition was more dedicated than you to make the team. Possibly it was college, where the athletes were just plain stronger and better than you. And for some the ladder of levels in the minor leagues was too difficult to ascend. The point is, some players can be in that place where the speed of the game where they are asked to hit, field and compete is more than they can handle at that point in time. You need to remember that when the competition is more skilled, faster or stronger than you, it can be a humbling experience for the good player—and discouraging for the average player. So putting the player first and understanding where they are at will help you teach, mentor and build a relationship that will hopefully build confidence and self-esteem in your players.

Now, with an understanding of how important the human element in teaching is, we are ready to tackle the question of how can we help our players improve on the field the most?

HOW CAN WE HELP?

Whether you are a dad, a first-year coach or a veteran coach, learning how to apply your knowledge will enhance your abilities to teach. Everyone's level of baseball knowledge is different. But what we have in common is a desire to help our kids and players. Gaining more knowledge will only help.

As coaches and parents, we try to educate ourselves on the proper fundamentals of hitting, throwing and fielding. In fact, the better a coach understands the fundamentals, the better a coach can be. We emphasis can be. Understanding the fundamentals is an important ingredient of being a coach. But it is just one ingredient.

We believe if you can't communicate knowledge to your players, that knowledge is wasted. So how knowledge is communicated to the player is an important factor in becoming a successful coach.

Two things always take place when coaching the fundamentals is effective. First, the players fully understand what the coach is saying or demonstrating. Second, the players are able to apply their new knowledge into their game. The first part, getting players to understand the point you are making, is the easier of the two but still should not be taken for granted. The second part, helping the players apply their new knowledge into their game can be a challenge, and this ultimately is the deciding factor if we have helped the player become better or not.

For instance, a coach tells a player he is throwing side-armed and instructs him to throw overhand. Or a coach tells a player he isn't getting low enough on ground balls. Even after telling players the correct way to throw or field, they continue to do it incorrectly. Why? We just told them what to do. It all comes back to how we communicate our knowledge to the player. Can we get them to make the adjustment necessary to make the correction or change?

BASEBALL FUNDAMENTALS WILL MAKE A DIFFERENCE IN PERFORMANCE

In essence, proper body positions are proper fundamentals. Getting players into better positions for hitting throwing and fielding gives players a better chance for success. But getting them to do so is not always as easy as it sounds. Once we identify a flaw and decide on how to best communicate our instruction, it is up to the player to make the adjustment.

Coaches cannot control a player's athletic ability and hand-eye coordination. A player's aptitude and desire to improve will also enter into the equation, but improving a player's fundamental position can make a big impact on that player's potential for success. Let's use a golf analogy to clarify this point. On the course, a playing partner notices a fundamental flaw in your swing and gives you a tip. The playing partner is trying to correct your body alignment and/or body position before or during your swing. But once you have been given the instruction, it's up to you to apply the information. It's up to you, your aptitude and your athletic ability and hand-eye coordination to perform and constantly repeat these positions. A coach can't control the outcome, but he can certainly help tremendously in the process. This is why it is very important what information we choose to give the player, how we present it and, most important, how we carry it through.

During this "coaching" process, simple and consistent suggestions will be easier for the player to understand and apply. Even with that being said, it will take more than just words to help your players make adjustments and eventually carry those changes into the games. Some adjustments will take longer than others. Stay patient, consistent and supportive, and over time your teaching will pay off.

Remember, these young men and women are still developing physically and mentally. The human element of coaching should always be in the forefront of everything you do with your player. The fact is, helping them get into better body positions (fundamentally sound positions) to perform each skill will improve their performance. It will take a lot of repetition, support and positive reinforcement along the way.

Expert Advice on Helping Players Make Adjustments

It is very important what information we choose to give a player, how we present it and, most important, how we carry the instruction through.

UTILIZING DRILLS

Drills are the lifeline of developing baseball fundamentals and are used throughout a player's career. When teaching the drills in this book, the coach should conduct the drill or sell his point with enthusiasm and conviction. The organization and attitude of the coach set the stage for the instruction. When explaining the drills and instructing your players, show patience. A misunderstood drill is very difficult to perform. Be sure to emphasize the importance and purpose of the drill so players are aware of that purpose. As a coach you must believe in what you are teaching and get your players to believe in it as well. If the drill's explanation is poor or not set up properly, it will add to the confusion, and will become a waste of time. As drills are learned and repeated at practice, the drill should become more efficient and effective.

EFFECTIVE COMMUNICATION

Below is a teaching progression designed to pass along knowledge of the proper fundamentals so that players will understand instruction. And, most importantly, it will give them the best chance to eventually perform these fundamentals in game action.

> **Expert Advice on Explaining the Proper Fundamentals**
>
> Don't assume players know the correct way to throw, catch, hit or field. Take some time to explain the key fundamentals. But, keep words precise, direct and to a minimum. More importantly, physically demonstrate the fundamental positions.

1. **Explain the Proper Fundamentals of the Area You Are Teaching.**
   Don't assume players know the correct way to throw, catch, hit or field. Take some time to explain the key fundamentals. Psychologists say we only retain about 15 percent of what we hear, and we are talking to young people who have a limited attention span. So keep words precise, direct and to a minimum. Also understand that people interpret things differently. If you explain how to throw a baseball to 10 different people in the same group, you possibly could have 10 different interpretations. Take the time to explain it but keep the words to a minimum. Utilize Step 2 as a staple when coaching a particular fundamental.

2. **Physically Demonstrate the Proper Fundamentals of the Area You Are Teaching.**
   This visual demonstration speaks much louder than words. Now players can physically see the proper position as you explain it. You don't have to wonder if they were listening to you or if their interpretation was different. After verbal instructions and a physical demonstration, the next step is to put the player into the proper fundamentally sound position.

3. **Put Players Into Non-Reaction Drills, Called Dry Drills.**
   Dry drills allow players to perform fundamentals correctly. The athlete is in a position to get a feeling for the fundamental without the bat or ball. Physically help the players into these positions, because players won't always be able to copy the demonstration perfectly. Whether it's the proper batting stance or a ground ball fielding position, help the player get into the position.

   Make adjustments as each player demonstrates the position back to you. This is a step that is too often skipped. We tell players how to do something correctly and we demonstrate how to do it, but then we expect them to do it correctly and they have never or only briefly experienced what it's like to be in the proper position. If a player cannot not feel the position, it is much more difficult to repeat the position. How can we expect them to perform that position not only in a dry drill but also at game speed?

   Dry drills allow players to feel the correct body position. They build muscle memory from performing the fundamental correctly. The more they do it correctly, the more natural the habit will become. After players can perform the correct fundamentals in the dry drill, they are ready to progress to the next stage. But not before they can repeat the dry drills consistently.

Remember this: If we were to explain and demonstrate how to field a ground ball and then put that player on the field and started hitting ground balls at game speed to the player, how often is that player going to get into the proper fielding position? Not very often. Unless that player has already mastered the fielding position in the past.

Here are two reasons why: First, the player has not been in the correct position often enough to expect muscle memory to put them into the new position consistently. Instead, they most often will field the ball with their old habits (old muscle memory). Second, it's much more difficult to change muscle memory at game speed. It is very difficult to think about proper positioning when concentration has to be on reacting to and catching or hitting a moving ball.

4. **Put Players Into Controlled Reaction Drills.**
   This is where coaches should spend the most time. Coaches will end up rolling numerous balls to players and setting up tees and soft-toss for hitting.

   In these drills, players are reacting to the moving ball, but at a distance and speed where they can perform the fundamental correctly. In this environment the game is slowed down just enough for the player to get a feel for what they are doing right or wrong. It also is easier for the coach to see and to suggest a correction if needed. Remember the old saying: Practice makes perfect. It should be: Perfect practice makes perfect. If players are practicing poor fundamental positions that will be the position they take into the games. They will never develop the correct muscle memory. For example, if hitters only work on live batting practice and they are stepping in the bucket and swinging with an uppercut, that's exactly what they'll do in the game. They will not be able to hit correctly. Our point is, we want players to build the muscle memory that is fundamentally correct for fielding, hitting or throwing – all the skills needed on the baseball field. This is why controlled reaction drills are so effective in developing and maintaining players' skills.

   The first key is putting them in drills where they perform the fundamentals properly. The second key is the next step.

5. **Performing Skills Correctly with Many Repetitions is the Quickest Way to Develop Muscle Memory for Success.**
   The more repetitions a player can get, the faster he will develop the muscle memory for that skill. Muscle memory is a result of teaching the muscles how to perform a specific activity and repeating that activity until it can be done freely without methodical thought. This is the ultimate goal in developing correct fundamental positions to hit, field and throw. Players can then compete during a game without clouding concentration by thinking about how to perform the skill.

   Remember there are productive repetitions and unproductive repetitions. This is why the quality of the repetitions is of the utmost importance. We perform these repetitions for proper mechanics, so we want them done correctly. For instance, if a batter who is developing his swing mechanics gets 20 swings against pitches from the mound or 50 swings from soft-toss, which will make his swing mechanics better faster? The more fundamentally sound swing is easier to repeat and coach in soft-toss because the drill is slowed down enough for the player to have success and focus on mechanics. The player isn't worrying about velocity or pitch location as much. Instead, they should be concentrating on the proper fundamentals for a good swing. And they will get 30 more reps in, over the same amount of time.

   Use time efficiently and use controlled reaction drills where players can get in many repetitions of a fundamentally sound baseball skill.

6. **Game-Speed Practice.**
   Even with all the benefits of dry drills and controlled reaction drills, it is still necessary to put players in a game atmosphere. They need to experience the game of baseball at the speed they will be playing. This is true even if players are not yet proficient at all the fundamental positions and drills. As a coach you will need to hit pop-flies, hit ground balls from home plate, throw live batting practice and have players pitch live batting practice. Run scrimmages in which players run bases and have decisions to make on their own.

   Judging the speed and reading the hops on a batted ball, timing a live pitch, recognizing a ball from a strike – players need to be exposed to all these skills. You will find out that your best players will need to practice more at game speed to be challenged.

7. **Mix Game-Speed Practices With Dry and Controlled Reaction Drills.**
   Understanding what your players can perform and what their needs are will help you determine what drills will benefit them the most. For the majority of players there is a balance. For instance, don't spend an entire practice at game speed ignoring the fundamentals. On the other hand, don't spend an entire practice doing drills where players can't experience the game in its proper setting. So, although there is a balance in teaching, developing and perfecting a player's skills, all players are different. You must evaluate and decide what drills and practice plans best fit the development of your players.

Expert Advice on Teaching Progression

Use dry drills to build correct muscle memory and to help change bad habits and body positions. Progress to controlled reaction drills for continued execution of sound mechanics and lots of repetition. Finally, practice at game speed so players can experience the game at the speed at which they must compete.

You will find that once your players are fairly consistent on the fundamental positions, they will need less time performing dry drills. Controlled reaction drills, along with game-speed drills, will benefit them more. Most of the time your better players will also fall into this category.

Early in the season it is safe to say you should spend more time on dry drills and controlled reaction drills so players can understand and get a feel for the fundamentals you are striving to perfect. But as the season progresses and players' skills improve, the majority of players should be able to repeat most of the key positions in dry drills. If this is true they will then need to practice their skills at a faster speed, which could mean a challenging controlled reaction drill or working at game speed.

There will be some players who still need dry drill repetition for different skills, such as throwing, all year long. Individual traits, strengths and weaknesses will need to be developed as well. It will still be very effective to utilize dry drills even late in the season for your better players if you see they are getting away from their good fundamental positions. Dry drills will still be best when a player has a difficult time making an adjustment in a particular skill. Remember, if a player is failing at a skill slow it down to the point the player can have some success and build the proper muscle memory for that skill. Over time the player will develop and improve.

8. **Be Creative. Make Drills and Practice Enjoyable.**
   Drills are the lifeblood of any practice. When drills are done correctly, most of them will invigorate, challenge and encourage. Drills provide an environment that prepares the players and the team for competition. There are many examples of drills and games in the book. It is important to keep the game and practice enjoyable. Some drills will be loads of fun, while some drills have great benefits and should be done regardless of how fun they are.

   Along with selecting the proper drills, time is an important factor. Generally speaking short, snappy drills with quality repetition are more effective than lengthy drawn-out drill sessions.

   Be creative. If a drill is not going the way it is supposed to, find a way to make it a competition between groups of players. When making a drill a competition against groups of players, the coach, or one self, a player's concentration and motivation increases. We are all competitive in nature and a coach should tap into this energy to motivate players.

9. **Do Not Over-Coach During Games.**
   The game should be a time when the players' minds are clear to focus on the competition. Don't fill players' heads with too many fundamental positions that will take their concentration from the game. Practice is the time to work on fundamentals. Limit instruction during the game and encourage players and be supportive when things don't work out.

   Make notes during the game on the items individuals and the team as a whole need to improve upon. Address these notes at the next practice. In the meantime, allow players a chance to compete confidently during the games. Let players know you believe in them, and be there for them when they fail.

Manager Dusty Baker on Connecting with Your Players:
"Try not to ever show up or embarrass a player in front of his peers, unless he chooses that forum in a disrespectful manner."

COMMUNICATION AND COACHING TECHNIQUES

1. **Positive Reinforcement Motivates and Builds Confidence.**
   One of the biggest parts of coaching is correcting faults. Players are constantly hearing what they are doing wrong. Baseball is an interesting sport in that if you fail 7 out of 10 times, you're a success. You're a .300 hitter. Instead of constantly pointing out failures, be supportive and positive to all players. Find something they are doing right and point it out. A positive approach will build players' confidence.

   It is nearly impossible to reach your potential in any arena unless you are confident in your abilities. Given the choice of doing something we are comfortable with and can succeed at or trying something we aren't so proficient at, most of us choose to do things at which we are good. People are much more motivated to perform and succeed as opposed to perform and fail.

Expert Advice on How Players Retain Information and Learn

We Learn by:

- 15% of what we hear
- 50% of what we see and hear
- 70% of what we feel or experience

2. Be Aware of When and How to Correct a Player's Mistakes.

A coach almost always has good intentions when critiquing a player about an error or mistake. But choosing a time when the player is more receptive or feeling confident is important to getting the point across. Coaches should consider how players feel immediately after making an error or mistake, then coming into the dugout after the last out. Chances are, they don't feel their best at that moment. It's magnified when the coach decides to critique the player about the error or mistake and singles him out in front of the team. At this point, the player is not in the state of mind to learn what he did wrong.

A better time will present itself when the coach can discuss the error with the player and help with his fielding. Make a mental note of the play, and wait for that better time. Most players will be more receptive and remember the suggestion if it's done after they have done something well. That's when they are feeling better about themselves and are less defensive.

Just as important as when to approach a player is how to approach him. A coach who begins by criticizing, then telling the player what to do differently has little chance of getting through. Be positive. Players already feel insecure about a bad play. Tell them something positive they can feel good about. Once the player is in a more positive frame of mind, then discuss the mistake. A good way to do this is to find out the player's perspective on the play first, then chime in with the suggestion. Maybe the player already knows what he did wrong and just needs encouragement. End the discussion with a final dose of confidence: Tell the player, "It's OK. It happens, you'll get them next time."

Dusty Baker on Developing Confidence in Your Players:

"Spend time with your players. Spend equal time with your average and poor players as you do with your good players, and put them into a position where they most likely will succeed."

3. Knowing What to Look For.

Have you ever heard a coach yell out to a pitcher after throwing a ball, "Throw strikes!" Have you ever heard a coach yell to a hitter after a swing and miss, "Hit the ball!". What do these coaches think the player is trying to do? Players are trying to throw strikes and trying to hit the ball. This approach does not help the player perform. Instead, it increases anxiety, adds pressure and can destroy confidence.

The key for the coach is to figure out why the pitcher is throwing balls or why the hitter is swinging and missing. To know why, coaches must see what the player is doing wrong. On the other hand, coaches should not get discouraged if they don't know why. It's not always easy to see. And it's especially difficult to see at game speed. But the longer a coach watches, the easier it is to see why something is going wrong.

While watching players practice and play in games, keep this is mind. If there are improper fundamentals on the pitch or swing, there's a high probability that is the problem or part of it. It may not always be, but often it is.

If a coach sees what the player did wrong, he can help. If a coach doesn't see anything incorrect, do not say anything. Don't guess. Remember to keep encouraging and supporting the player's effort. Do not say anything until figuring out the problem.

For example, if a player swings and misses, pulling his head during the swing, there's a good chance that's the problem. Approach the player and give him a specific tip that will help him avoid swinging and missing for that reason. He might still swing and miss, but the swing fundamentals will be improved.

If you are having a difficult time seeing why a player is not being successful, try focusing on a particular area. For example: If you are watching a player hit, there are different areas you can focus on. You could watch the feet or one particular foot. You could focus on the swing path by watching what is happening with just the arms during the swing. Or you could focus on the head throughout the swing. Sometimes watching the whole picture will work, but often we need to focus on a particular area for a number of swings.

Having said that, watching the feet during throwing, fielding, hitting and pitching is always a good place to start if you cannot recognize a flaw from the whole picture. Balance is a key ingredient in everything we do on a baseball field. The feet and legs are crucial for balance. Feet and legs are the foundation for all our movement on the field. Once the bottom half is working correctly, often it will correct flaws in the upper body.

4. Do Not Speak Generally. Give Players Specifics.

As stated above, the player pulled his head during his swing and missed the ball. Some coaches would simply say, "Concentrate." Instead, a coach should give the player a specific tip he can focus on to make the correction, something functional he can attempt to do on the next swing. An example in this case would be, "Keep your head in the hitting zone."

Here is another example: The second baseman misses a ground ball that rolled under his glove and between his legs. A coach could just say, "Stay low." That's true, but what should the player do to stay low? Referring back to "Knowing what to look for," what did the coach see in the fielding position that caused the second baseman to miss the ball? Did he bend over at the waist, not bending his knees? Were his feet too narrow, making it more difficult to bend at the knees and get low? Did he get into a good fielding position but just did not lower the glove enough when the ball approached?

Let's say in this situation the coach saw the player bend with his waist instead of his knees. The coach should demonstrate what he thinks the player did. Bend over at the waist. Then demonstrate the proper fielding technique, bending at the knees. Suggest that the next time a ball comes his way to make sure he "bends at the knees to get low." That is something specific and functional the player can apply the next time a ball heads his way.

Expert Advice on Teaching

Remember to be process oriented not result oriented when teaching, the results will come over time.

5. **Always Try to Put You Players Into a Position to Succeed.** We are often asked if we would allow a player to play first base if the player was not very good. Our first response to that question is, "Is it safe for the player?" We need to think of safety first. Secondly, is it really in that player's best interest to play the position if all they will do is fail and be embarrassed?

   Our philosophy on how to handle players is that we want to give players a chance to play and develop. Whenever possible, we attempt to put players into a position to succeed – not fail. To answer the question posed above, we may give the player a chance to play first during practice and continue to help him develop at the position. But we would not play him in a game until we felt it was safe and the situation was right to give the player a chance. The right situation may be when the team is losing and a mistake at first base would not be as detrimental to him and his teammates.

   You never want to put a player in a position to fail. For instance, you would not send your worst hitter up against the other team's best pitcher. You would not ask your weakest pitcher to pitch the final inning of a tie game. You should not bring in your least experienced and least confident pitcher when the other team's best hitters are coming to the plate. You should not ask a player who shows fear when hitting to bat against the opposing team's hardest-throwing and wildest pitcher.

   There are going to be many situations that are out of our control and these unfortunate match-ups are going to occur, usually because we want to give our players a fair shake with playing time. But, having said that, be aware of these situations. Whenever possible put your players in a situation to succeed so they can build confidence through success and develop self-esteem.

Expert Advice on on Helping Your Players Perform

Unfortunate match-ups are going to occur, but whenever possible put your players in a situation to succeed so they can build confidence through success and develop self-esteem.

THROWING

Throwing is one of baseball's most important skills. If a player cannot throw the ball effectively, the player's possible positions will be limited, as he gets older. Especially at the youth level, many outs are given away by the player's inability to make an accurate throw. Learning to throw correctly should be an important part of any practice routine. It should not just be an activity to get ready for practice.

Proper arm action is extremely important, but do not rely just on the arm when throwing. The arms, legs and body should work together. Being in an athletic position with knees flexed enables players to have balance and leverage. The feet align the body so that the hips can be used most efficiently. After catching a ground ball or fly ball—or when making any routine throw—squaring up to the target, gaining momentum toward the target and keeping the eyes focused on the target are routine fundamentals and should be emphasized.

While the legs and body are important, proper arm action is critical for a player to throw the ball with velocity and accuracy. The arm action should be a continuous fluid motion, starting from the break of hands to the finish of the throw. As players advance in age, there are a couple of positions (catcher, some infield) where the arm action is slightly altered. The arc coming out of the glove is usually shorter in length. Do not expect players to alter their arm action at a young age. Teaching players a fundamentally sound arm action will be a challenge in itself. As players mature and advance in age (13 and above) and strength, they will be able to shorten the arc in their arm action for specific positions such as catcher.

A solid overhand throw is the best arm angle to teach. Outfielders utilize this arm angle because that is where the arm is in its strongest position. Outfielders have to make long, accurate throws. Infielders should develop this arm angle for their routine throws, but they will also need to learn how to throw the ball from different angles with accuracy and velocity.

How much and how often players throw should be monitored at least mentally throughout the season. Practice plans should be designed so the drills do not overtax the arm. But a solid throwing routine, including dry drills, proper warm up, long tossing and accuracy games are important issues that should be a regular part of your practices. All players need to work on throwing drills and their mechanics as this can vastly improve a player's strength and accuracy.

GRIP

Hand size determines whether a player uses a two- or three-finger grip on the baseball. Controlling the ball is more important than a small hand trying to use a two-finger grip. Whether using two or three fingers, always have the finger pads on a seam. If hand size allows the two-finger cross-seam grip, it is the most efficient for the truest ball flight with greater speed and distance. All position players should utilize this grip. **(picture 2-1)**

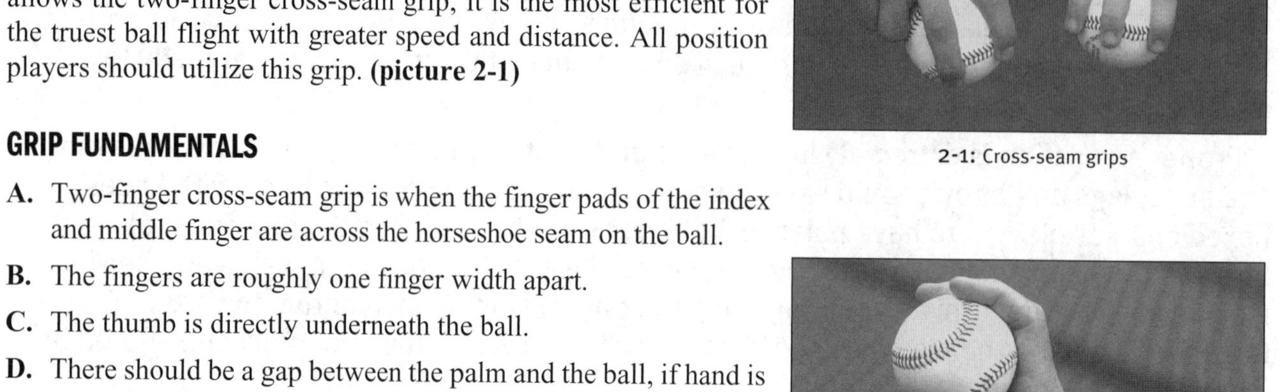

2-1: Cross-seam grips

GRIP FUNDAMENTALS

A. Two-finger cross-seam grip is when the finger pads of the index and middle finger are across the horseshoe seam on the ball.

B. The fingers are roughly one finger width apart.

C. The thumb is directly underneath the ball.

D. There should be a gap between the palm and the ball, if hand is large enough. **(picture 2-2)**

E. The grip is firm but not tight.

2-2

GRIP DRILLS

1. **Check Grip:** Line up players. Physically check hand size to determine how many fingers each player should use to throw.
   Recommended ages 6-12.
2. **Cross-seam Grip:** Toss the ball three feet into the air. Catch it with the throwing hand, rotate the ball to transfer the fingers to the proper seams for the grip quickly as possible. **Encourage players to do this drill at home during idle time or while watching television.**
   Recommended ages 8-12.
3. **Cross-seam Grip Using Glove:** Drill 2 can be done with the glove on. After tossing the ball into the air, bring the throwing hand into a thumb-near-thumb alignment using the glove as a backstop. As the ball comes down, transfer the ball off the glove and into the throwing hand. Rotate the ball to the cross-seam grip as quickly as possible. **This technique should be used all the time while playing catch.**
   Recommended ages 10-16.
4. **Wrist Extension:** Pair up players 10 feet apart. Place them on one knee with the throwing arm in L-shape formation. Place a glove under the throwing-arm elbow for support. Players hold the ball in a cross-seam grip. Players flip the ball to one another with their wrist, emphasizing the proper wrist action. **The arm action should be the same as shooting a basketball. This drill keeps all players active. (pictures 2-3 & 2-4)**
   Recommended ages 12-16.

2-3: Starting Position

2-4: Ending Position

THROWING FUNDAMENTALS

2-5: Throwing position

2-6: Block foot

A. Grip the ball correctly and hold it in the glove centered near the chest with the body in an athletic position. The player is compact and balanced. This is the "throwing position." **(picture 2-5)**

B. Square to target after ball is received to achieve proper alignment. The back foot steps toward the target for momentum and alignment as it is placed almost perpendicular to target (right foot for right-handed throwers and left foot for left-handed throwers). This foot placement will bring the hips and shoulders square when the glove-hand foot steps directly toward target. Shoulders will be squared and in line with target. The player should remain in a balanced athletic position as the legs take the player into the throw. **(picture 2-6)**

B.1 There are numerous ways in which a fielder's legs will get the player squared to the target when throwing. It all depends on where the ball was received and which direction the ball must be thrown. Whether they are using a block step when playing routine catch or shuffling their feet or crow hopping when throwing, the end result is the same. **Get square up and gain momentum toward the target.**

C. From the throwing position, the hands break to start the throw. Throwing hand breaks from glove in a semicircle arc with the palm and thumb facing down (thumb to thigh) reaching back for extension and continuing up at its peak to the "L" position with fingers pointing to the sky. The palm is facing away from the body at this point. **(pictures 2-7 & 2-8)**

2-7: Hands breaking

2-8: Launch position

D. The glove hand breaks thumb down with palm pointing open to target. Arm is slightly flexed and relaxed. Shoulders are level and in line with target.

E. As the hands break, the lead leg steps directly toward the target. Lead foot lands slightly closed and on the ball of foot for balance and control. Weight should remain on the back leg. Once the foot lands and the arm is up at its peak in an "L" formation, with the body balanced and knees flexed, you are in the "launch position." **(picture 2-8)**

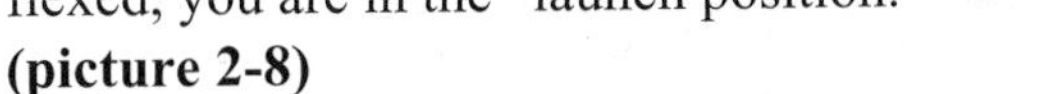

Erik Johnson on the Importance of Good Throwing Skills:
"One of the best things you can do for your players is to develop their arm action and throwing skills. If players use poor arm action for years, it becomes more difficult to change when they are older. If they cannot throw efficiently, it makes it harder to play at the higher levels of baseball and in high school."

F. As the arm continues to accelerate forward, it maintains the "L" position with the elbow at least shoulder height. Back foot rotates from the inside of the big toe to the outside of the shoe. This opens hips to target as weight is transferred to the front side with the arm. Fingers remain on top and behind the ball throughout acceleration forward to release out in front of the body. Glove hand rotates with thumb up and is pulled back near the side or hips as throwing arm comes forward. Head should remain level with eyes focused on the target. **(picture 2-9)**

2-9: Acceleration forward

2-10: Release and follow through

G. Finish the throw by releasing the ball out in front of the body with the arm finishing across the lead leg on the follow-through. All weight should continue to transfer forward with the arm as the whole body and arm work together for velocity in the throw. The head and eyes remain level and focused on target until release. **(picture 2-10)**

H. Note on the arm action. Once the hands initially break to throw, the arm action should be a continuous, fluid motion accelerating arm speed to the release of the ball.

2-11 2-12 2-13

2-14 2-15

DRY DRILL ROUTINE FOR THROWING

1. **Arm Action "Break" Dry Drill:** Place players in 3 straight lines. Coach stands 10 feet in front of players. Players square up and point lead shoulder at coach who is their imaginary target. Players begin in the "throwing position" (athletic position with hands together centered near chest). On verbal command, *break*, players simulate throwing. Throwing hand breaks down, with palm and thumb pointing down past the thigh reaching back and continues up into the "L" position, where fingers point toward sky and palm is facing away from the body. Simultaneously, the lead arm extends out, thumb down pointing towards the target. Lead arm should remain flexed and not be fully extended. Players stop arm action at launch position, as coach checks for proper "L" position and palm facing away. **(pictures 2-16 to 2-18)**

   Drill isolates the proper arm swing from out of the glove and up into the launch position. Also teaches lead arm movement when throwing. This arm action is critical for proper throwing fundamentals. Drill keeps all players active. Can perform numerous repetitions in a short period of time.

   Recommend ages 6-16.

2-16: Throwing position

2-17: Break

2-18: Launch position

2. **Arm Action "Throw" Dry Drill:** This drill follows the arm action "Break" Dry Drill. Players start in the launch position. (Athletic position, spread feet wider than shoulder width, shoulders squared to target, head level, glove pointing at target with thumb down. Throwing arm in strong "L" position.) On coach's verbal command, *throw*, players simulate throwing from the launch position. Players rotate their back foot from the inside of the big toe to the outside of the shoe as their weight transfers from the back side to the front side. Simultaneously, the arm is accelerating forward, extending out front and finishing on the outside of the front leg. The glove hand is rotating thumb up as the elbow pulls in toward the lead hip. Players should maintain balance throughout this throw and at finish. **The drill isolates the rotation and throwing action along with weight transfer when throwing. Works on the players' balance skills and allows them to feel the importance of a strong foundation and proper arm action for the throw. Drill keeps all players active.**

   Recommended ages 6-16.

3. **Catch, Block, Break, Throw, Dry Drill:** Place players in 3 straight lines. Coach stands 10 feet in front of players. Players need to spread out in the lines to leave room to move. Coach positions himself in front where all players can see him. Players start off facing the coach in the receiving position. Coach calls out commands as players perform the key positions of throwing. There should be two seconds between each command. First verbal command is *catch*. Players punch their throwing-hand fist into the glove, which is in front of their chest. Next command is *block*. Players step forward slightly with their throwing-hand foot, placing it almost perpendicular to the coach, who is their imaginary target. Next command is *break*. Players break their hands to throw while stepping with the glove-hand foot directly toward the coach. Players should stop the arm at the launch position, and end up in a balanced athletic position. The final command is *throw*. Players simulate throwing the ball to the coach from the launch position. They rotate their back foot as they transfer the weight to the front side with the throwing arm coming forward in a strong "L" position and the glove-hand arm pulling back by the hip. Coach should check to make sure players are performing positions properly. **Drill covers all key fundamental positions needed to throw the ball properly. Utilize it routinely before players play catch. Drill keeps all players active. (pictures 2-19 to 2-22)**

   Recommended ages 7-12.

Expert Advice on Throwing Dry Drills

After players get a feel for all the key positions, from catching the ball to throwing, the next progression is to make the dry drill more fluid by progressing to these commands: catch, block, throw. Lastly progress to catch then throw. Make sure players are squaring toward their target and gaining momentum toward their target as they throw.

2-19: Catch

2-20: Block

2-21: Break

2-22: Throw

4. **Catch, Shuffle and Throw, Dry Drill:** Follow same set up as previous drill. Players start off facing the coach in the receiving position. Coach calls out the following commands and players perform positions dry. First verbal command is catch. Players punch their throwing-hand fist into the glove, which is in front of their chest. Next command is shuffle and throw. Players square up to target and shuffle feet at the same time by utilizing the block step quickly or shuffling feet and pointing lead shoulder at target. Players also simulate throwing the ball to the coach as they square up and gain momentum towards the coach. **Drill teaches players to always square up and gain momentum towards target when throwing. This drill can replace the previous drill in your dry drill routine after a couple of weeks. This drill is a mainstay at practice and can be done with the ball as well. Drill keeps all players active.**

   Recommended ages 7-12.

THROWING ROUTINE WHICH FOLLOWS DRY DRILLS

5. **Coach Catch Drill:** Block and Throw Drill. This drill is similar to the previous dry drill, except now the ball is used. Distribute your players evenly according to the number of coaches at your practice. Players should be lined up single file, 20 to 50 feet away from each coach depending on the player's age. On coach's verbal command, *go*, the firstplayer runs out to a designated spot and assumes the receiving position. Coach throws a ball to the player. After ball is caught, coach gives verbal command, *block*. Player steps with the throwing-hand foot almost perpendicular to the coach. Player holds that position until next command, which is *throw*, at which point the player throws the ball back to the coach. Player hustles back to the end of the line. Coach should check for proper foot alignment after block. And on *throw* player should have proper squared up alignment when throwing. **Once the drill has been performed a few times properly, take the drill a step further to make it more realistic and to get players' feet moving quickly as they do at game speed. Do everything the same to start, but now throw balls to player in all directions while the player throws ball back quickly as possible. The player must still get squared to target and gain momentum while throwing. This is where a coach can get in a lot of repetition while watching players to make sure they square to their target, get momentum toward their target and maintain good arm action when throwing.**

   Recommended ages 7-16.

6. **Warm-Up Drill:** When players pair off to throw, the coaches should reinforce foot blocking, which is extremely important to get the rest of the body in proper line to throw. Give one line of players the balls. On command, *receiving position*, all receiving players get into the receiving position. The next command is *block and throw*, and all the throwing players block their throwing-hand foot properly, and throw the ball to their partners. Continue using the receiving *position* and *block and throw* commands for the first 5 to 10 throws, then follow into the Long Toss Drill on the next page. As players progress farther back they should utilize the crow hop to throw, as stated in the Long Toss Drill. Whether you have done similar dry drills or not, this drill will set the tone for playing catch correctly. **When players pair up to play catch on their own, often they do not carry the proper footwork into their catch. This drill can be used daily to reinforce the proper foot movement and alignment when throwing. Recommended ages 8-14.**

FAVORITE DRILL

7. **Long Toss:** Pair players by ability and arm strength. Begin playing catch from a close distance, 15 to 30 feet depending on age. After five throws per player, instruct one line of players to move back 5 to 10 feet. As the players get farther back, they should be utilizing a crow hop on their throws. Continue this process until players have reach their maximum throwing distance. All throws should have a slight arc, emphasizing proper throwing fundamentals and a good follow-through. If fundamentals are not maintained, the distance is too far. After reaching maximum distance for a few throws, players should move in and finish by throwing the ball hard on a line at a routine game distance. Moving back in for a few throws will give players a chance to find their release point for a distance they will use a lot in a game. Remember every arm is different and not all players will move back to the same distance. Early in pre-season do not let players go all the way back to their maximum. Gradually build up to that distance over 4 to 5 practices. **By using this process to warm up you will accomplish several goals. First, the arm is warm and ready for any throw in practice or a game. Second, it helps players work on throwing accuracy at long distances, which is seldom practiced. Most importantly, routinely using the arm to its maximum will develop strength and velocity. Long toss should be done before practices and games at least 3 days a week.**
   Recommended ages 8-16.

Expert Advice on Teaching Throwing

There are three keys to successful throwing:

1. Keep teaching proper arm action to your players. They need constant reinforcement on the proper mechanics.
2. Players need to get squared towards their target.
3. Players need to maintain proper foot movement and momentum toward their target.

8. **Quick Toss:** After players have long tossed and moved back in to finish up their throwing they can play quick toss. At a close distance players throw the ball back and forth to their partner. They are working on the glove to hand transfer. When performing this drill all players should receive the ball with their glove in the thumb-near-thumb position. They are trying to catch the ball and throw the ball back to their partner as quickly as possible. Make sure players are still squaring up to their partner on the throw. The feet must be shifted up and down quickly to release the ball quickly. **This is a great drill to work on the exchange from catching to throwing and to teach players how to use their feet quickly and correctly. During the drill remind players to move feet and get squared up on the throw back as they tend to get lazy with their feet. This drill should be utilized often by infielders, especially second basemen and shortstops.**
   Recommended ages 8-16.

ADDITIONAL DRILLS FOR MOMENTUM TOWARD TARGET

9. **Shuffle for Momentum Drill:** Pair up players in two lines 30 feet apart. Give balls to one line of players. The players who will throw first are in an athletic position, squared toward partners with hands together centered near chest. On coach's verbal command, *shuffle*, players shuffle their feet, exchanging their front foot's position with their back foot, throwing the ball to their partner. Coach should observe footwork looking for straight direction toward target and balance throughout the throw. This shuffle is used when the player receives the ball and is already lined up. **Drill isolates proper footwork and teaches importance of getting some momentum when throwing. The drill is useful for younger players who are having trouble blocking to throw or crow hopping to throw. This drill keeps all players active.**

   Recommended ages 6-10.

10. **Crow-hop Drill:** Pair up players in two lines as if to play catch. Give balls to one line of players. The players who will throw first start off gripping the ball with two hands together centered near chest but are facing their partners as if in the receiving position. On coach's verbal command, *lift*, all throwing players lift their throwing-leg foot off the ground, shifting weight to their glove-hand leg. The next command is *crow hop*, and players push forward off their foot toward the target and land on their throwing-hand foot almost perpendicular to their target (blocking the foot). Once they land they continue with the momentum stepping towards their target with their glove-hand foot, throwing the ball to their partners. **This drill teaches players how to transition into a crow hop when they throw. The drill is exaggerated some but will give the players a feel for how to gain momentum and block the foot properly on a crow hop. (pictures 2-23 to 2-25)**

    Recommended ages 8-16.

2-23: Lift throwing hand foot off ground

2-24: Push off leg and block throwing hand foot

2-25: Continue momentum and throw

ADDITIONAL DRILLS FOR PROPER ARM ACTION

11. **One-knee Throwing Drill:** Pair players in two lines 15 to 20 feet apart. Facing their partners, each player takes a knee (right knee for right-handed throwers, left knee for left-handed throwers). Position front foot at a 45-degree angle. Starting with both hands together near chest, players square up shoulders level and in line to target. On coach's verbal command, *throw*, players throw the ball to their partner. The arm action on the throw should be a continuous fluid motion, which includes drawing the arm down and back to extension (thumb to thigh fingers to the sky.) Advance the arm forward in a strong "L" position while extending the arm toward the target, releasing the ball in front of the lead leg. The throwing arm should end up in line with, or on the opposite side of, the front leg for a proper finish and follow-through. Players should concentrate on the proper arm action of both the throwing arm and the glove arm. **This drill isolates the upper-body mechanics and arm action (shoulders squared and level), as well as placing an emphasis on finishing the throw. For players 11 and older, this drill could be used to start the players' throwing routine after they have mastered the dry drills of throwing. This drill keeps all players active. (pictures 2-26 to 2-28)**

    Recommended ages 11-16.

2-26

2-27

2-28

12. **Ball Drag Drill:** Set up players as in the One-knee Throwing Drill. Except the players do not start with their hands together centered near chest. The throwing players grip the ball and place it on the ground just behind their lead foot. Players maintain their fingers on top of the ball as they hold the ball against the ground with their fingertips pointing to their partners. On coach's verbal command, *drag*, players drag the ball back along the ground maintaining the grip and fingertips pointing at their partner. When the ball reaches their back knee the ball is lifted off the ground and up in a semicircle into the "L" position to throw. As the ball is lifted off the ground the fingers remain on top of the ball and the players watch their hand to assure proper arm action as the hand comes up with ball facing away from the body. **NOTE:** As the ball is dragged and brought up into the "L" position to throw, the fingernails should be visible to the player the whole time. Coach then says *throw*, and players throw the ball from the "L" position to their partner. **This drill teaches hand position on the ball as it is taken out of the glove to make a throw.**

    Recommended ages 8-16.

13. **High-elbow Drill:** Start player in the launch position. Coach stands facing the player and points a rolled-up newspaper at the armpit height of the player's throwing-arm shoulder, as shown in picture. Player simulates his throwing action from the launch position attempting not to hit the newspaper. To do so, the player must maintain proper arm action keeping a high elbow. If the elbow drops during the throw the player will hit the paper. **This drill is outstanding to give players a feel on how to maintain the arm in the strong "L" position during the throw.**
(pictures 2-29 to 2-31)
Recommended ages 7-16.

2-29: Set up

2-30: Strong position

2-31: Weak position

14. **Colored Ball Catch:** To ensure that the ball is leaving the hand with the correct rotation, a half-colored ball can be used. Color half of a ball as shown in photo. Grip the ball so the seam of the colored split is between the gripping fingers. When the ball is thrown correctly, it should rotate with the colored hemisphere staying to its original side. The colors will appear solid on both sides without any movement on a good throw. This drill can be done while doing the wrist-extension drill or with regular catch. **This is a great tool to ensure proper rotation and release is taking place. (picture 2-32)**
Recommended ages 10-16.

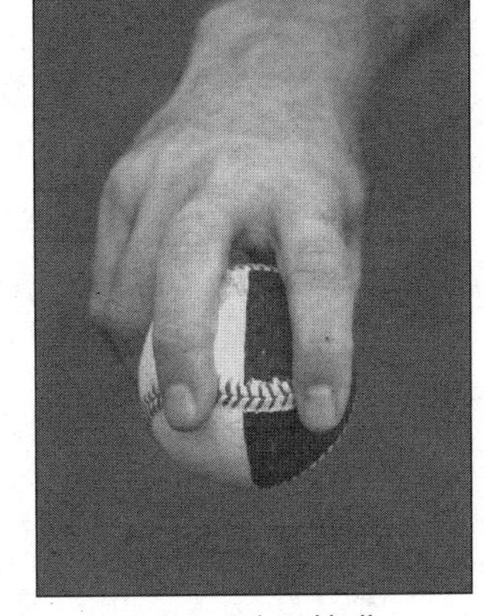
2-32: Colored ball

15. **Hat Drill:** Start player in the throwing position squared up to the target. Wearing a hat, the coach positions himself behind the player's throwing arm. The coach's head should be slightly above player's shoulder height. The coach positions himself where the player can perform his arm swing out of the glove and continue up to the "L" position, flipping off the coach's hat as the hand goes up. Have players perform this drill in slow motion so coach does not get hit in the face. **This fun drill isolates the proper hand position (palm facing away from the player) at the "L" launch position of throwing.**
Recommended ages 6-10.

16. **Slap Five Drill for Extension and Follow-through:** Players start in launch position as in previous drill. Position coach 4 to 6 feet in front of the player. Coach places his hand palm up about waist level to the player. From launch position, players simulate throwing motion, reaching out on follow-through to slap coach's hand. The player can also start from the throwing position and simulate the entire throwing motion. **This is a fun drill that isolates the importance of finishing the throw out in front of the body with a good follow-through. (pictures 2-33 to 2-35)**

    Recommended ages 6-10.

2-33

2-34

2-35

Ron Wotus on How to Make Practice Fun:
"When explaining the games to your players, the coach can really enhance the game by how he or she builds up the competition. Be enthusiastic, and make it a big deal! Always attach a reward to the game and praise the winners."

GAMES

1. **Point Game:** Pair players 30 feet apart. Give balls to one line of players. On coach's verbal command, *throw*, players throw the ball to their partner. The object of the game is to score 10 points. Face area is 2 points. Chest area from waist to neck is 1 point. Receiving player catches the ball and determines if any points are scored. He then throws the ball back trying to score. The two playing catch are playing against one another. Game continues until 10 points are scored. Play a series of best-of-three games. **Winning players do not have to help pick up gear at end of practice. This game helps players focus and work on their throwing accuracy.**
   Recommended ages 10-16.
2. **Accuracy Game:** Pair players 25 feet apart. Give balls to one line of players. On coach's verbal command, *throw*, players throw the ball to their partner. The receiving player acts like a first baseman, maintaining a pivot foot, only being allowed one step to catch a throw. If the receiver has to move more than one step to catch a throw, that team is eliminated. They must turn their hats around backwards and are unable to win the competition, but they continue to play the game for practice. After both players have made one throw, move back one line 5 feet. The coach continues this process until one team is left. **Game works on accuracy from short and long distances. Measure the winning distance at each practice and see how much farther the distance increases during the year.**
   Recommended ages 10-16.
3. **Accuracy Throwing and Receiving Game:** Follow the same rules as above, except the receiver is allowed free movement to catch the ball. If the ball is not caught, that team is eliminated from the competition. If you are coaching 6 or 7 year olds, you can alter the game slightly in following manner for more enjoyment for the players: The receiving players cannot let the throw get by them. It's OK if the throw bounces as long as the ball is stopped and kept in front of them. **This game works on both throwing and receiving skills.**
   Recommended for ages 6-10.
4. **Quick Toss Speed Game:** Follow the Quick Toss drill. After players work on the drill a few minutes, it is time to make it a game. Each pair of throwers is a team. The coach puts a clock on the players for 20 or 30 seconds. The longer you go the more difficult the game will become. The players count out themselves every time the ball is caught. Whichever team catches the most throws in time allotted wins. Play several times to give different players a chance to win. **This game will go fast and works on a quick glove-to-hand transfer for throwing.**
   Recommended ages 9-16.

5. **Four-Corner Game:** Divide the team into as many four-player teams as possible. Each group forms a square 30 feet apart from each player. Give one player on each team a ball. The ball is thrown clockwise around the square. The object of this game is to have the ball thrown around the square as many times as possible without dropping the ball or making a bad throw. The team with the most rotations around the square wins. Give the winning team members a pack of baseball cards. **This game works on throwing and receiving skills, and involves proper footwork to be squared to their target. (picture 2-36)**

   Recommended ages 7-16.

2-36

6. **Four-Corner Speed Game:** Follow same setup as four-corner game. The object of this game is to see which team can get the most rotations around the square in one minute. If the ball is thrown wildly, the receiving player must go get it and continue the game. Keep track of the most rotations in one minute and see if your team can improve upon it throughout the season. **This game emphasizes the importance of a quick glove-to-hand transfer and quick footwork. It also re-creates game anxiety by having a clock on them. It will teach them to stay under control and how to perform under duress.**

   FAVORITE GAME

   Recommended ages 8-16.

7. **Reverse Four-Corner Game and Four-Corner Speed Game:** After working the drills clockwise, have players throw the ball counterclockwise. This will force the players to use different footwork to square up for their next throw. And it will give the left-handed throwers a chance to work in the other direction as well. This direction is more difficult for the footwork of right-handed throwers. There are two different ways a player can square up to his target when the ball is being thrown counter-clockwise. The first is by rotating 90 degrees via the glove side, turning outside. This turn will take one's eyes off the target briefly but helps gain some momentum on the throw. The second is by turning in the opposite direction, turning to the inside, which keeps the eyes focused on the target. Both ways to square up are correct, and where and how the ball is caught should determine which turn is used. When doing the drill in a counter-clockwise direction, teach players to turn and rotate based on how they catch the ball. If the ball takes you to your glove side, turn that way. If the ball is thrown to the other side, turn inside to square up and throw. **Players should work on squaring up both ways so they can get used to the footwork of both.**

   Recommended ages 8-16.

Expert Advice on Four-Corner Speed Game

This game emphasizes the importance of a quick glove-to-hand transfer and quick footwork. It also re-creates game anxiety by having a clock on them. It will teach them to stay under control and how to perform under duress.

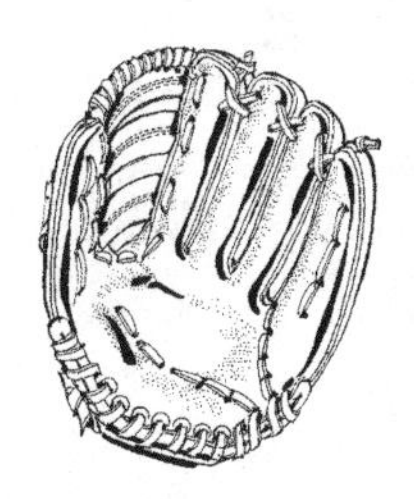

RECEIVING

Catching the baseball is one of the first skills we learn when beginning to play baseball. Whether it's at practice or in a game of catch with dad in the yard, there are some areas we should be aware of to help our players succeed at catching the ball. Having a glove that is the correct size and properly broken in should be the first order of business. At practice, examine each player's glove to make sure it fits properly and that they can control and squeeze it. Follow the instructions on pages 31 and 32 ("The Glove") to ensure that your players are not hindered by their equipment.

Fear of the ball is common for many younger players ages (6 through 9). Indications of fear include: backing up as the ball arrives or turning the head and the glove as the ball approaches the glove. Using softer balls and tennis balls is beneficial when players are first learning to catch and are scared of getting hit with a baseball. Players who show fear are better off receiving the ball with a one-handed catch away from their face area. Utilize the clock drill for helping these players build confidence in improving their catching skills. With time and success through repetition, fear can be eliminated and players will eventually be able to utilize the two-handed catch. At the younger ages, the two-handed catch is helpful at times but not as important as it will be as the players get older and the game speeds up. Getting players to just plain catch the ball and enjoy the experience at these younger ages is what is most important.

Proper receiving technique is a skill that should not be overlooked for players who are beyond fear of the ball. Proper fundamentals will not only enhance each player's catching ability but will allow an efficient transition to throwing. We advocate two-handed catching for both younger and older players who can handle it. While players advance in catching skill as they age, the speed of the game also increases, making the two-handed catch much more valuable.

Another area, which will help your players immensely, is training them to be ready to move there feet to catch the baseball. Players receiving a throw should always expect a bad throw and be ready to move their feet to get into a good receiving position. Doing so will allow them to catch the ball and transition into the throw more efficiently. During your throwing routine, and when they play catch on their own, encourage your players to try to receive throws near the center of their body by moving their feet to get in front of the ball. If the throw is too wide and they have to catch it outside their body the one-handed catch is recommended.

Ron Wotus on Protecting your Players:
"Know which players on your team have a difficult time catching the baseball.
Spend some extra time with them before or after practice,
and never pair them up with players who throw and catch more confidently."

FUNDAMENTALS

A. Start in an athletic position, with the knees flexed and weight on the balls of the feet. The body is balanced and ready to react right or left or forward and backward. **(picture 3-1)**

B. Extend the arms out, slightly flexed in front of the chest. **(picture 3-2)**

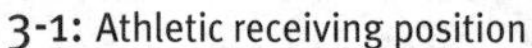

3-1: Athletic receiving position

3-2: Arm position

C. Position the glove at vertical to 1 o'clock, using both hands by lining up the thumb of the throwing hand near the thumb of the glove hand. The glove should be just below eye level, so players can see the ball enter the glove.

D. Expect a bad throw by always being ready to move the feet in order to catch the ball with two hands near the center of the body when possible.

E. Receive the ball in the glove's pocket. As soon as the ball hits the pocket, reach in with the throwing hand, readying the grip and exchange to throwing. **(pictures 3-3 to 3-6)**

3-3: Pocket catch

3-4: Secure ball

3-5: Find grip

3-6: Throwing position

F. Use one-handed catches on throws outside the body. **(picture 3-7)**
Once a one-handed catch is made, the glove and throwing hand should meet centered near the chest to grip the ball and transition into the throw.

3-7: One-handed catch

Expert Advice on Catching a Baseball

A player should anticipate the release of a thrown ball. Their eyes should shift to the release point of the thrower just like a hitter does when hitting off a pitcher. This will allow the player to pick up and judge the throw sooner and help in tracking the throw into their mitt.

G. For throws below the waist, turn the glove over, fingers down and line up both hands in a pinkie-near-pinkie alignment. When catching low throws players should bend at the knees and waist. **(picture 3-8)**

3-8: Low throw position

Expert Advice on Helping Young Players

Fear of the ball is common for many 6 through 9 year olds. Utilize the Clock Drill and use softer balls at first if needed to build there confidence and catching skills. Pass this drill and your knowledge onto their parents and encourage them to play catch at home.

DRILLS

1. **Receiving Position Dry Drill:** Line up all players. On the verbal command, *Target*, players get into the receiving position. On verbal command "low throw" players get into a pinkie-near-pinkie alignment. Check each player's position. Physically make adjustments where needed. **(pictures 3-9 & 3-10)**
   Recommended are ages 6-10.

3-9: Target position

3-10: Low throw position

2. **Glove Position for High and Low Throws:** For more repetitions per player, divide players into as many lines as there are coaches. One at a time start a player in the receiving position. Coaches throw balls above waist, then below waist. Concentrate on proper glove position. **This drill will provide lots of repetitions in a short time.**
   Recommended ages 6-12.
3. **Clock Drill:** Start player in an athletic position with the glove hand slightly raised and open to the coach. Throw balls to the player at the ten, eleven, one, two and three areas of a clock. The player should reach out one handed and catch the throws. This drill will teach the player how to receive throws in all those areas. **This is a great drill to use with players who have fear of the ball or are just learning to catch.**
   Recommended ages 6-10.
4. **Quick Feet:** Follow same set-up as Drill 2. Coaches throw balls slightly to players' right, then left. Concentrate on foot movement to catch the ball in front of the body, with two hands.
   Recommended ages 7-12.

Expert Advice on Utilizing These Drills

Drills 2 through 6.
The coach's distance from player and the speed and difficulty of the throw depends on the age and ability of the player. Remember to challenge the player while still allowing him to have success and perform the fundamental correctly. Having success will build confidence and reinforce the proper fundamental position. Besides, it's just plain more fun to make the catch.

5. **Reaction Drill:** Follow same set-up as Drills 2 and 4. Coaches throw balls in all directions heights and speeds. Encourage players to move their feet to try to get in front of throws and utilize a two-handed catch when possible. Encourage the one-handed catches outside the body when they cannot get in front of the throw. **This is a great drill to use before a game.**

   Recommended ages 8-16.

6. **Football Drill:** Give each player a ball and line them up single file 10 feet from the coach. When the coach yells, *Go!* the first player jogs to the coach, tossing the ball to the coach and continuing to run away. The coach turns and throws the ball in a high arc, similar to a touchdown pass. The player runs under the ball, catches it and returns to the end of the line. Continue with the next player. The distance and difficulty of the throw depends on the age and ability of the player. Build confidence by challenging them while allowing them to have success. Players should work on catching with the glove hand extended and the more difficult across-the-body catch. Instruct the players to run with their arms down in a running position until they need to reach up to make the catch. Two-handed catches are recommended if the player is under the ball and waiting. One-handed catches are encouraged when the player is on the run. **This drill has numerous benefits. It teaches players to keep arms down in running form when chasing a fly ball. It also helps players learn to judge the ball and gives them a chance to work on one-handed running catches. This is a high-activity drill with numerous repetitions in a short time. (picture 3-11)**

   Recommended ages 6-16.

3-11: Football drill

GAMES

1. **Point Game for Quick Feet Drill:** Divide players into 2 groups. Follow Quick Feet Drill. Award 2 points if player catches the ball in center of body with proper two-handed technique. Award 1 point for getting in front of ball but no catch is made. Players do not receive points for a catch made outside the body. Play to 20 points, or after each player goes five times, add up the score to determine a winner. **Winners get 5 extra swings each in live batting practice.**

   Recommended ages 7-12.

2. **Point Game for Glove Position High, Low Drill:** Divide players into 3 groups. Follow Glove Position Drill. Award 10 points for a catch with proper two-handed technique. Award 5 points for glove in proper two-handed position but no catch is made. Players do not receive points for catching the ball with one hand or improper glove position. After each player goes 10 times, add up the scores for first, second and third places. **Set up a rematch for next practice.**

   Recommended ages 7-10.

Expert Advice on Playing Games

Remember the games are a competition. This is the time for players to focus on the goal in mind. It is not the proper time for the coach to instruct or critique on technique. Have fun with it, and enjoy the competition. This is what the players will enjoy most!

3. **Reaction Game:** This game is played as the players versus the coaches. Follow the Reaction Drill set-up. With 5 players in line, throw each player a ball, one at a time. The player must make the catch for a point. Each player goes 5 times. If the players get a total of 22 points, the coach does 5 push-ups. If the players lose, they do 5 push-ups. **This game is great for getting players moving their feet, and catching every type of ball possible.**

   Recommended ages 8-16.

4. **Football Drill Game:** Set up the Football Drill. Have each player go out for a catch five times. Award 10 points for throws that are caught. Award five points if a player gets his glove on the ball even if the ball is not caught. Object of the game is to get more points than the coach has set for the winning amount. Again, remember to make the number challenging but obtainable. If the players have all gone four times, and cannot win even if all players catch their last throw, give them a bonus round by upping the points for a catch to 20. **This is an excellent competitive drill to motivate, build confidence and allow players to be stars because the coach controls the throws. Tailor the throw to the skill of the player and make it a fun activity.**

   Recommended ages 6-16.

5. **Four-corner Game:** This game can be found in the throwing section under "Games." It is an effective drill to work on both receiving and throwing skills.

   Recommended ages 7-16.

6. **Four-corner Speed Game:** This game can be found in the throwing section under "Games." **It is an extremely effective drill to work on both receiving and throwing skills under stress, which simulates game pressure.**

   Recommended ages 7-16.

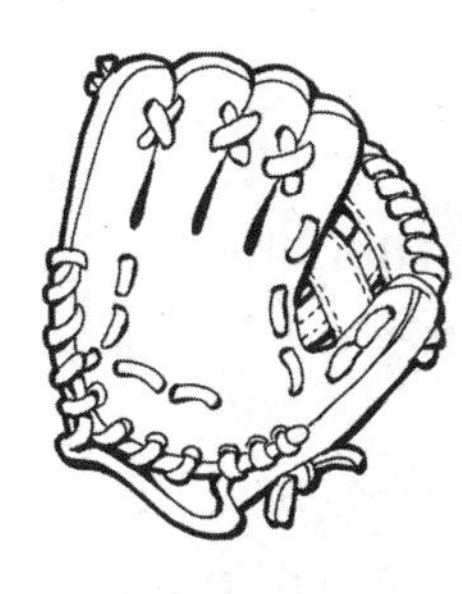

The Glove

Having a proper-sized, broken-in glove that is well taken care of will enhance the player's performance when it comes to fielding and receiving the baseball.

GLOVE SIZE

The glove should be small enough for the player to control and pliable enough for the player to squeeze. Try to avoid purchasing a glove that is too big for the player now believing they will grow into it. It is likely a player will go through 3 to 4 gloves throughout their Youth League days.

INFIELDERS GLOVES vs. OUTFIELDERS GLOVES

Infielder gloves are generally smaller in size, with a shallower pocket for an easier glove-to-hand transfer. Outfielder gloves can be longer in length for added reach, with a deeper pocket that allows the ball to stick into the glove easier. First basemen and catchers have mitts that are specific to their position.

BUYING A GLOVE

When selecting a glove, avoid plastic. They are lightweight, but they are not pliable and the ball will not stick in it, making it difficult to catch. There are inexpensive leather gloves available at most retail and second-hand stores.

BREAKING IN AND MAINTAINING A GLOVE

After purchasing a new glove, start the breaking-in process immediately. Put a ball in the pocket, tie the glove closed with string or twine and place it under a mattress for a night or two. This will start to fold and shape the glove.

Next, the critical process begins – oiling the glove. It's important to use the right kind of oil. Liquid oils will moisturize the glove, but they soak into the leather and gradually increase the weight. This makes the glove more difficult to move and control. Mink oil in grease form will not increase the glove's weight, and it is an excellent moisturizer for the glove's leather.

Oil the glove in key areas to shape the glove correctly. When applying oil, concentrate on lubricating the pocket and the hinged areas that need to bend when squeezing the glove shut. It is not necessary to oil the whole glove routinely. Apply oil to other areas of the glove when the leather appears dry.

Moisturizing the pocket and hinged areas will make the glove more pliable, but that alone will not break it in. The glove will still need repetitive pounding in the pocket and flexing of the gloves hinged portions. This repetitive pounding can be done most effectively with your fist or a bat. Playing catch also helps break in the glove, but will take longer to get the glove game ready. Younger players (ages 6 through 10) especially need help getting the glove ready, mainly because they do not throw hard enough to make a good impact on the leather.

When the glove is pliable enough to squeeze easily, it is ready.

To maintain the glove throughout the year, use saddle soap as needed to remove dirt and grime. Once the glove is clean, use mink oil when the leather appears dry and discolored. To help keep the pocket and shape, put a ball in the pocket when the glove is not being used. This will eliminate those gloves that look like pancakes—the ones with one big folded crease without a wide pocket that helps the ball stick in the glove.

Take the time to get gloves ready before the start of games so players can enjoy the benefits and effectiveness of a broken-in glove.

Expert Advice on Gloves

Moisturizing the pocket and hinged areas will make the glove more pliable, but that alone will not break it in. The glove will still need repetitive pounding in the pocket and flexing of the glove's hinged portions.

INFIELD

The infield positions are very active and critical to the success of your team's defense. This chapter will cover the key elements in becoming a successful infielder.

A good infielder plays with confidence, wants the ball to be hit to him and anticipates that happening before every pitch. This confident attitude can be obtained through preparation, hard work and correct repetition of fundamental skills. An alert infielder is trained to be thinking about where to go and what to do with the ball prior to every pitch. No matter what physical skills the player has, it is the coaches' job to get the most out of that individual's ability. How you prepare, train and instill confidence in your players will go a long way in maximizing their talents.

Teaching an infielder how to track a pitch into the hitting zone and how to get the best jump possible on batted balls should be a staple of your development plan. A quick first step on a hit ball can be improved by anticipation and by utilizing proper pre-pitch movement. No one can get their best jump on a hit ball from a dead-stopped position.

Once you establish a balanced ready position through pre-pitch preparation the proper movement to different balls is important for getting the hop you want. For greater range the fielder should think lateral movement first then forward movement to the ball. When approaching a ground ball, when possible, the infielder should have an angle to the ball that creates a line toward the target to first base. On hard hit balls and some slow rollers this will not be possible. Whether it's a ball hit directly at you, to the glove side, or back hand, reading the hops and using proper footwork is crucial in staying away from in-between hops. An aggressive attitude of attacking the ball while under control and balanced is the correct mindset. Moving the feet to get a good hop means the infielder is playing the ball instead of letting the ball play him. Active feet using shorter choppy steps will help in accelerating or decelerating and will help allow the body and hands to get into a good fielding position. Maintaining balance allows for better control throughout the fielding process and into the throwing motion.

At your levels of competition, getting the infielders into a sound fielding position is going to be a big plus. Common flaws with youth-league players include:

- Not getting the feet wide enough.
- Bending over at the waist instead of the knees to field the ball.
- Not getting the hands out in front of the face.
- Fielding high-to-low instead of low-to-high.

The good news is that you can develop a sound fielding position. As always, focus on developing proper fielding technique through dry drills and controlled reaction drills to start. That way players can understand and feel the proper fielding position. Once this is taking shape, then you can progress to work on different plays and skills your infielders are going to need throughout their baseball careers.

Infielders, like all other players, should use two hands when fielding a routine ball. Not only will the player have a better chance to catch the ball, it will give the player a better transition into the throw. Ball transfer from the glove to the throwing hand will be smoother and quicker. Also, a two-handed approach makes squaring up to the target more efficient.

When an infielder does not have time to get in front of the ball on line-drives and balls that take your momentum away from the throwing target—fielding one-handed is appropriate. A fielder should not try to use two hands when the ball cannot be fielded in front of the body. Whether making a backhand or ranging to the glove side, staying low and watching the ball into the glove are keys to making a one-handed catch.

Bending over at the waist at the last moment to field a ground ball is a common problem for young infielders. Charging the ball is important, but players must allow time to get under control and into the proper fielding position. This allows them a chance to handle all hops tough or routine.

Barehanded and one-handed plays followed by an off-balance throw are difficult to execute for any age player. Infielders should always know the runner's speed and make the play with two hands and a quick shuffle of the feet when time permits. There will be times when the ball is hit slowly or the speed of the runner will make the play "do or die." This is the time to attempt an off-balance, one-handed play. Infielders who are 11 years and above should be shown the proper
footwork technique and practice making the play in order to execute it when needed.

Pre-pitch movement, footwork, glovework and throwing aren't an infielder's only responsibilities, however. Communication on the field will enhance any team's awareness and readiness. The middle infielders, along with the catcher, are the glue to communication on the field. The infielders are your link to the outfield and support to your pitchers. Communicating on cutoffs and relays and holding runners close to second are responsibilities that you will need to teach. Encourage infielders to communicate with each other, the pitchers and with the outfielders to keep everyone alert and mentally in the game.

Gold Glove First Baseman J.T. Snow on Infield Play:
"Expect every ball to be hit to you, so you are ready on every play."

FUNDAMENTALS

4-1: Ready position

A. **Ready Position:** Get into an athletic position with knees flexed and weight distributed evenly on the balls of the feet. The weight should remain inside the knees. The body should be balanced and ready to react in any direction. The hands are off the knees, the arms relaxed hanging somewhere in front of the body, and the eyes are focused on the hitting zone. This is the ready position for players not advanced enough for pre-pitch movement (ages 6-9). It is also the position a player ends up in after pre-pitch movement steps are taken. **(picture 4-1)**

B. **Pre-pitch Movement:** Relax until the pitcher starts his windup. To initiate pre-pitch movement, walk into the ready position with a small, right-left step, and a controlled hop step if right handed. And a left-right step and a controlled hop step if left-handed. The pre-pitch movement should be initiated during the windup and completed as the ball is entering the hitting zone. The feet must be on the ground with the weight on the balls of the feet and inside the knees, when the ball enters the hitting zone. The only forward movement is the first two walking steps; the controlled hop step at the end is a vertical up and down. Continued movement forward will hinder lateral movement. Proper pre-pitch movement, timed correctly, allows for the best reaction to a hit ball. **(pictures 4-2 to 4-4)**

4-2: Relaxed

4-3: Short step

4-4: Ready position

Major League Third Baseman Bill Mueller
on Keys to Making a Good Throw:
"Get a good grip on the ball, then get your feet underneath you so you are balanced. Eye your target and move your feet towards your target on the throw."

C. **Approaching the Ball:** Read the hops, watching the ball all the way, while moving the feet smoothly with rhythm to get the hop you want. Never straighten up completely when going after a ground ball. Stay athletic, balanced and approach the ball under control with the weight on the balls of the feet. Attempt to get in front of the ball and create a line toward the target to first base whenever possible. The last two steps should be right-left for right-handed throwers and left-right for left-handed throwers. The glove is extended out early before the player sets up to field the ball. A quiet open glove is lowered smoothly, opposed to flipping the glove down at the last moment **(refer to picture 4-8)**. The glove continues down to get below the ball as the ball approaches. The ball is centered in the middle of the chest.

4-5: Fielding position

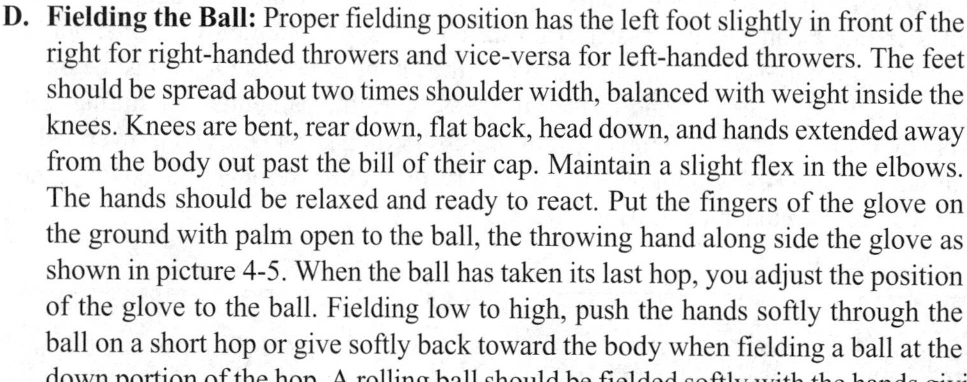

D. **Fielding the Ball:** Proper fielding position has the left foot slightly in front of the right for right-handed throwers and vice-versa for left-handed throwers. The feet should be spread about two times shoulder width, balanced with weight inside the knees. Knees are bent, rear down, flat back, head down, and hands extended away from the body out past the bill of their cap. Maintain a slight flex in the elbows. The hands should be relaxed and ready to react. Put the fingers of the glove on the ground with palm open to the ball, the throwing hand along side the glove as shown in picture 4-5. When the ball has taken its last hop, you adjust the position of the glove to the ball. Fielding low to high, push the hands softly through the ball on a short hop or give softly back toward the body when fielding a ball at the down portion of the hop. A rolling ball should be fielded softly with the hands giving back towards the body as well. Fielding forward through a ball keeps the body in position toward the target. **(picture 4-5)**

4-6: Securing the ball

E. **Secure Ball and Set to Throw:** Keep the head down and watch the ball into the glove. The throwing hand reaches in once the ball makes contact with the glove, to secure the ball and establishes a grip on a seam **(picture 4-6)**. To continue to establish a good grip and keep from rushing the throw the ball should be gathered up past the waist near low chest level, with hands together as feet start their movement towards the target. We call this the "Set Position" **(picture 4-7).** For advanced 10yr old players and older, on routine plays a cross-seam grip should be secured in this set position before the ball is thrown.

4-7: Set position

F. **Set Position and Foot Movement:** After fielding the ball and gathering it past the waist to the chest region, pick up your target as you begin the foot movement to square your body up and gain momentum to target. For right-handers, the right foot replaces the position of the left foot gaining momentum and direction to the target. The feet shuffle forward replacing the front foot with the back accomplishing direction and momentum. Vice-versa for a left-handed thrower. The front shoulder points at the target as the feet move. Infielders should remain in an athletic position during this transition. Do not straighten up completely.

Omar Vizquel on what's most important to learn if you want to be a good infielder:
"I always tell my kids, if you don't move your feet you will not catch the ball, so they should learn how to dance to help develop good feet. When you catch the ball, think of the ball as an egg and bring it softly to your stomach in a circular move so you can develop soft hands."

G. Throwing the Ball: Utilize the legs' momentum to throw the ball. Hands break to throw when the back foot lands as squaring up to target. Two shuffles before throwing are fine if time permits or is needed for the fielder to get balanced and square to target, or if its needed to get a good grip on the ball. Throw the ball hard or firm to the base utilizing the players best overhand arm action while keeping your eye on the target. Refer to arm action in throwing section. **NOTE:** Arm action does not change. A quicker snap-like throw or side arm throw will be used at times on different plays, but a consistant release point and strong throw should be utilized on all routine plays.

Fielding Sequence (pictures 4-8 to 4-13)

4-8: Final approach

4-9: Fielding position

4-10: Secure ball

4-11: Gather ball and set

4-12: Shuffle and square to target

4-13: Throw

Former Philadelphia Phillie Joe Millette on Infielders Footwork and Approach:
"Proper footwork is crucial to an infielder's success. Having an aggressive attitude while still maintaining control and balance of your body is the correct approach. This will allow you to adjust to a tricky hop and transition into making a strong throw."

READY POSITION DRILLS

1. **Ready Position Dry Drill:** Line up all players. On verbal command, *ready*, position players get into the ready position. Check each player's position. Look for a balanced athletic stance with weight inside the knees and on the balls of feet. Hands are carried below the belt and aren't touching the knees. **Physically make corrections where needed.**

   Recommended ages 6-10.

2. **Pre-pitch Movement Dry Drill:** Line up players arm-distance apart and put a coach to act as the pitcher on the mound. Players stand relaxed at their infield position. Pitcher or coach simulates windup, and when the pitcher reaches the release point, all players should start their pre-pitch movement and be in the ready position as the ball enters the hitting zone. One coach should monitor the players performing this drill. Make sure there is not too much momentum going forward, because that will hinder lateral movement. **This drill will show players when to relax and when to be ready to react. The drill keeps all players active.**

   Recommended ages 10-16.

Expert Advice on Ready Positions

Remember, when the infield is playing in on the grass, infielders must start lower with their gloves out and open closer to the ground. If they remain higher with their gloves not ready, a hard smash will be past them before they can lower their gloves to the ball. Third baseman along with First baseman coming off the bag should utilize this position routinely.

Bill Mueller on Getting a Good Jump on the Ball:
"Always anticipate the ball coming to you.
Imagine different scenarios that may occur and how to correctly handle those plays (ie, slow roller, bad hop, backhand play etc.)"

FIELDING POSITION DRY DRILLS

4-14: Triangle position

3. **Triangle Dry Drill:** Line up all players and draw a triangle in front of each one. Size it to the proportion of the player, with the triangle's base closest to them. The base of the triangle should be roughly two times the shoulder width. Have all players step forward and place their feet on the base of their triangle. Then players extend their glove hand in front of their body almost to full extension, keeping a slight flex in the elbow. Their fingertips should be pointed toward the ground. Bending at the knees, players place the tip of their glove on the ground at the point of the triangle. The point of the triangle should be out past the bill of the player's cap.

   This drill helps get the young player into the proper fielding position by using the visual and reference points of the triangle. Players can remember the fielding position better because they remember the triangle position. (Picture 4-14)

   Recommended ages 6-10.

4. **Fielding Dry Drill:** Line up all players. Players start relaxed. On verbal command, *ready position*, players get into their ready position. On verbal command, *triangle position*, players get into their fielding position. Check each player's fielding position. Their feet should be spread about two times shoulder width, with the knees flexed and the rear down. The head is down and the glove should be positioned on the ground out front past their cap. This drill checks proper fielding position. Watch for players bending at waist instead of properly spreading their feet farther apart and bending at knees to lower their hands, body and head.

   Recommended ages 8-16.

Veteran Infielder Bill Mueller on Fielding Position:

"Form a triangle with the feet being the base and the arms and hands being the top of the triangle as you reach to receive the ground ball. Attempt to catch the ball in front of your body."

CONTROLLED REACTION DRILLS

These next four drills (5-8) are perfect for performing one right after the other as a solid routine to set the tone for your fielding practices. Do these before you move to hitting balls and other drills.

5. **Coach or Partner Rolls:** For those 10 years and under, line up players and have coach roll balls. For advanced 10-year-olds and above, pair up and have players roll to each other. Put them in two separate lines, 12 feet apart, and facing each other. Have adequate spacing between groups. Give each pair of players a ball. The receiving player starts in fielding position with the glove on the ground and extended out past the bill of their cap. The player with the ball rolls it underhand directly toward their partner's glove. Then the receiving player rolls it back the same way. As the drill progresses, players should vary the ball speed. We recommend the coach controls when players roll to each other by saying, *roll*. This drill can be taken a step further by working the feet, arm action and proper grip into the throwing position. **This drill works on the players' hands and fielding the ball out in front of their eyes in a sound fielding position. Provides a lot of repetitions in a short time and keeps all players active. (picture 4-15)**
   Recommended ages 8-16.

4-15: Partner rolls and short hop drill

6. **Short-hop Drill:** Set up the same as previous drill. The only difference is the player or coach attempts to give his partner a short hop. The goal is to toss the ball just short of where the player's glove is set up in the triangle position. Then the receiving player tosses it back the same way. The correct way to catch the short hop is to reach and catch it before it becomes an in-between hop by pushing the hands softly through the ball. We recommend the coach controls when players roll to each other. **This drill works on the players' hands and promotes a slight forward action with the glove hand to get those potentially difficult hops. Provides a lot of repetitions in a short time and keeps all players active.**
   Recommended ages 8-16.

7. **Backhand Drill:** Set up the same as previous drill. On coach's verbal command, *roll*, players roll ball to their partner. When first teaching the backhand position, have players get pre-set in the backhand position before the ball is rolled. Check their body and glove positions and make adjustments where needed. Proper body position is shown in picture. Coaches should emphasize that players need to bend their knees to get low to the ground on the backhand. Glove hand is slightly in front of glove-side foot and rotated open to the incoming ball. Once the players are set, roll five or so balls as they stay set in that position. After players understand and feel the proper position, it's time to start players from a ready position. With players in ready position, partners or coach rolls ball underhanded one step to their partner's backhand side. Receiving players start in their ready position and use a crossover step to position themselves for the backhand. The glove should cross over with their glove-hand foot. **Drill works on proper body and glove position on backhand play. The drill keeps all players active. Drill gives lots of repetitions on a play that is common but is not often worked on. (picture 4-16)**
   Recommended ages 8-16.

4-16: Crossover backhand

8. **Glove Side Drill:** Set up the same as in the previous drill. The only difference is that the player or coach throws a ball outside the glove hand. Then the receiving player tosses it back the same way. The correct way to catch the ball outside the body depends how deep it is outside of you. If it is deep, you may give a little more with the glove hand and body to reach the ball. If it is not as deep, you may be able to catch it outside and in front of the lead leg with a forward action. These ball needs to be rolled faster or even throw as a big hop to make the ball outside the body. **This drill works on the players' hands and catching those balls one can't quite get in front of. On balls outside the glove-hand side, carry the glove low and open to the ball. This drill provides a lot of repetitions in a short time and keeps all players active.**
   Recommended ages 8-16.

9. **Crossover Step Drill:** Place all players in a single-file line at shortstop except for the first baseman. The coach positions himself halfway between shortstop and home plate to maximize repetitions. Fielders start in the ready position and the coach rolls balls at medium speed to the player's right. The player breaks for the ball using the crossover step – the right foot pivots open, and the left foot crosses over in front of right foot. A slight angle should be taken to have more time to gain ground on the ball. Player field's ball sets and throws to first. After all players go once, throw balls to the players' left and watch for proper crossover step moving left. Then proceed to throwing balls to both side and watch the reaction. Encourage players to be quick with their feet during this drill. Challenge the players with the throws, extending their range, but make most plays reachable. **Drill works on crossover step and emphasizes quick feet when moving to a ground ball.**
   Recommended ages 8-16.

10. **Partner Ground Balls:** Pair up all players. Put them into two separate lines, 25 to 45 feet apart facing each other. Give each pair of players a ball. Start the balls all in one line. The receiving players assume the ready position. Players throw the ball back and forth as follows: On coach's verbal command, *throw*, players throw grounders at medium speed to their partners. The receiving players work on approaching and fielding the ball correctly. Emphasize the smooth, controlled movement players should have when approaching and fielding a ground ball. Also concentrate on players fielding the ball in the center of the body. This drill can be done to emphasize many different aspects of fielding. Coach can have players roll balls to the backhand side to work on the backhand. Coach can have players roll balls back and forth not emphasizing any particular phase of fielding, but just for lots of repetitions of ground ball practice. Coach can pick focus needed for your players. **This drill keeps all players active. Good drill to use before games to get players ready to play.**
    Recommended ages 6-16.

Expert Advice on Fielding a Ball Hit Hard Right at You

It is much harder to read the speed and hops of a ball hit hard at you. Remember: do not come up and tense up. Try to soften the body and relax the hands, stay low to the ball and catch it first. You will have time to gather and throw after you have made the difficult catch.

11. **Triangle Rotation Drill:** Position players at the three points of a triangle 25 to 60 feet apart, depending on the age group. Point A of the triangle is the roller. Point B of the triangle is the fielder. **(picture 4-17)** Point C of the triangle is the first baseman. The player at Point A starts the drill by rolling a ground ball to the fielder. After the player rolls the ball, he follows the roll and gets in line at the fielders position. The fielder fields the ground ball and throws it to the first baseman, then follows the throw and gets in line with the first baseman. The first baseman catches the ball and immediately throws it back to the roller, then follows his throw, going to the rollers position. Wherever the player throws or rolls the ball, he runs and takes position at that point for his next turn. For players 10 years and younger, don't have the players follow their throw but rather stay put and get back in the same line. After a couple of minutes have the whole groups rotate. Put a base down at each point of the triangle to keep the triangle from shrinking. First base position should work on footwork receiving a throw. The roller position should straddle the base and work on a quick tag when the ball is thrown to him, before he rolls it to the fielder. This drill can be done with a four players at each point with just one coach, but if there are two coaches, break the team into two triangles for more repetitions. **This high-activity drill works on fielding, throwing, first base footwork and tagging. It provides lots of repetitions in a short time.**

   Recommended ages 8-16.

4-17: Triangle rotation drill

GAME SPEED DRILLS

12. **Live Fungo Drill:** Put players at the shortstop position with no more than four players deep. Have a coach hit ground ball to the players and throw the ball to a first baseman. Start off hitting routine, medium-speed balls straight to the players. The key is you want the players to have time to read the hops and get their body in position to catch the ball correctly. Make sure when the players move to the ball they allow time to get under control and catch the ball in the Triangle Position. Then progress to hitting ball to their right where they have to get around the ball to be in a position to throw to first base. Move on to hitting balls to the player's left, making sure they don't overrun the ball. The last two types of ball for the better 10 year olds and above are the backhand play and slow roller. **This drill can be done from any position on the field. Avoid more than four players in one line; there will be much standing and waiting for their turn. The majority of the balls should be hit medium speed so the player can get repetition on routine game-speed balls.**

    Recommended ages 7-16.

13. **Concentrated Ground Balls:** Put as many players at their positions as you have fungo hitters. All fungo hitters hit ground balls to their respective fielders. Fielders toss balls back into coach or throw to coach's catcher. The coach's catcher should stand in front of the coach so that the coach has vision of him at all times. Never have them behind the coach where they can get hit by the coach's back swing. This drill is for fielding practice at game speed. **Good drill when you want a lot of ground balls in a short time and players arms are tired and do not need to throw.**

    Recommended ages 10-16.

14. **Speed Fungo Drill:** Position players at their defensive position no more than four deep. To simulate speed and help players with early glove position hit harder hit balls from a closer distance (approximately half the normal distance) from the infielder. **This drill will force players to get in a fielding position early and help them get their glove out and open on time or they will not make the play.**

    Recommended ages 11-16.

15. **Rapid-fire Infield:** Put players at all four infield positions and have two or three coaches hitting ground balls at the same time. With two coaches, have one on the first-base side of home plate and the other on the third-base side. With three coaches, have one at home plate while the other coaches are 15 feet to the left and right behind the third- and first-base lines in foul territory. Each coach has a catcher to take the return throws from the infield. There are many different possible sequences for where to hit the ball and where to throw. Below are a few examples. Before each sequence, explain who is hitting to whom and where they are throwing the ball. Do it twice to make sure they all understand. Have extra balls to keep the drill moving and pick up missed balls when drill is done.

    a. **First Sequence: Coach 1 (at home plate)** hits to third baseman. Third baseman throws back to a catcher for coach. **Coach 2 (on third-base side)** hits to shortstop. Shortstop throws to first baseman, first baseman throws ball back into catcher for coach. **Coach 3 (on first-base side)** hits to second baseman, who throws back to a catcher near the coach.

    b. **Second Sequence:** Coach 2 hits to first baseman. First baseman throws back to catcher for Coach 2. Coach 3 hits to second baseman, who throws to shortstop covering second base. Shortstop throws ball back to catcher for Coach 3. Coach 1 hits to third baseman who throws to catcher for Coach 1.

       These are just two examples of sequences. There are many more you could do. This drill gets the player a lot of ground balls in a short period of time. Great drill to us before a game.

    Recommended ages 10-16

Bill Mueller Reminds You:
"A good catch and a good throw is an out!"
"A great catch and a bad throw is a double!"
"A great catch and a great throw – they'll invite you back tomorrow!"

FIELDING AND THROWING DRILLS

16. **Relay Drill:** Break the team into two groups with one group at third base and the other group at a relay distance away acting as the relay men. The coach acts as an outfielder beyond the relay man. One player at a time from the relay group pops out and gives a target with hands raised to the coach. The third baseman should be lining up the relay man with the outfielder and third base. The coach varies different types of throws to the relay man. Make perfect throws to start then vary them – low, high, left, right and one-hoppers. The key is for the relay person to move his feet and get his body in position to catch the ball on the glove-hand side. For more advanced players, the relay person should turn sideways and shuffle through as the ball is caught to gain momentum and quickly transfer the ball. The ball is then relayed to third base, where the player makes the tag. Then the ball is thrown back to the relay person, and he relays it back to the coach. Two new players fill their spots, or have the same player stay for several throws in a row. This drill is nice because the coach controls the throw and can challenge the players. On a low throw the relay man cannot reach in time to get momentum moving toward his next throw, the relay man should back up and receive the throw on a big hop. This will give the relay man more momentum on his throw to base. **This drill teaches relay men how to position themselves and the importance of moving their feet to get into position. (pictures 4-18 & 4-19)**

    Recommended ages 8-16.

4-18: Target position

4-19: Receiving the throw

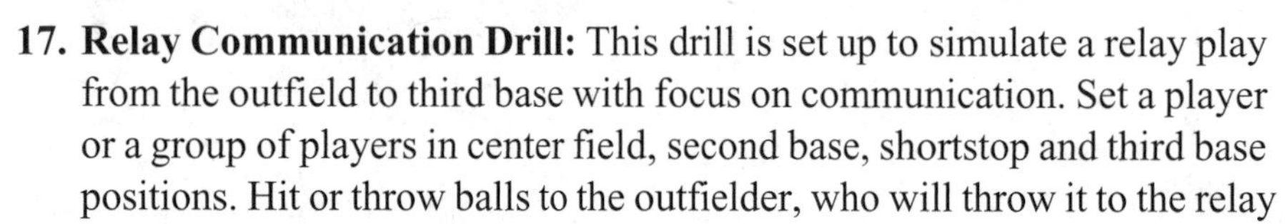

17. **Relay Communication Drill:** This drill is set up to simulate a relay play from the outfield to third base with focus on communication. Set a player or a group of players in center field, second base, shortstop and third base positions. Hit or throw balls to the outfielder, who will throw it to the relay man. Infielders start in regular position and once ball is hit second baseman goes and cover second base. Shortstop lines himself up to third base with third baseman help. Third baseman covers third and his verbal command to help line up the shortstop is *right, left, or good.* Once the throw is made the third baseman's verbal communication to the shortstop is *go, go,* if he doesn't want it cut. If he wants the ball directed to a base, his communication is *two, two* (for second) or *three, three* (for third). If there is no play and he wants the ball cut and held, the command is *cut, cut.* Once each player has gone a few times, have them rotate to the next position. Outfielder goes to second, second to shortstop, shortstop to third and third to the outfield. **This drill helps the players to communicate and to make a decision in a game setting. Getting players to speak up and make a decision can be tough, but the more you do drills like this the better they will be at reading a situation and communicate what needs to be done.**

    Recommended ages 10-16.

Tagging position fundamentals

The best tagging position for all infielders is the straddle position. This allows for the ball to travel the farthest and allows for the fastest tag, the up-and-down tag. The straddle position also gives the runner no place to go to avoid the tag. The infielder should let the ball travel as far as possible to avoid reaching forward for the ball.

Many middle infielders like being in front of the base, which gives the fielder the advantage of blocking the ball when the throw is short or up the line toward first base. When in front the runner has a better chance to avoid the tag. The key is getting to the base early. If the fielder gets to the base early they will have time to react to the throw and move in front of the base on a throw short or up the first base line.

On throws to second base that are low and up the first base line, the infielder should move in front of the base and field and tag the runner from that position or abort the tag and field the ball in front of the runner. Do not let the ball hit the runner. On a throw up the first base line and high, the fielder can move more in a direct line towards first or slide behind the incoming runner and field and tag or abort the tag and cacth the bad throw. The runner will be sliding and the high throw will not hit the runner.

Exceptions: in any first-and-third situation where an attempted double steal is probable, the infielder should position in front of second base to be in a better position to return the throw home. Also, if the catcher is a poor thrower and many throws are short, the shortstop can position in front of the base but must be proficient at letting the ball travel when he tags or dropping his left foot back over the bag to the straddle position on a good throw.

TAG DRILLS

18. **Tag Drill:** Start players at second base and shortstop positions and have player line up behind the second-base cone. The coach should set up between second base and the pitchers mound. Have first player in line break to cover second base on coach's verbal command, *go*. Player hustles to second base and straddles the base and gets down low in a receiving position. Then on coach's command, *tag*, player applies a tag in front of the bag where the incoming runner will slide. Either a two-handed or one-handed tag is applied depending on age and ability. They then run over and line up at shortstop. Rotate all players through this dry drill sequence and make adjustments on player's positioning as needed. Then proceed to doing it live with a baseball. Coach should vary his throws to simulate all types of possible balls: from throws right on the money to short hops, high throws and balls that pull the receiver off the bag. On all these different throws, a tag still needs to be made in the correct position. This drill can be made into a game by awarding five points for getting in the correct receiving position and then another five points if they tag in the correct place. If all players get ten points each then the coach does five push ups. **This is a high-activity drill that teaches the correct tag position. Don't allow players to tag on top of the base and teach them to get down low and to keep their nose in there to make a good tag. (pictures 4-20 & 4-21)**

    Recommended ages 8-16.

4-20: One-hand tag

4-21: Two-handed tag

19. **Four-base Tag Drill:** Position one player at each base, or in a square 45 to 90 feet apart depending on the age group. Players should straddle the base. The player at home starts the drill by throwing the ball to third. As the player receives the ball, he makes a quick tag with the back of the glove. After making the tag, the player quickly crow hops and throws to second base. The procedure is repeated at each base in sequence until the ball has gone around the bases three times. The quickest tag is a one-handed tag, going directly down in front of the base. A key to a quick tag is to let the ball travel to the fielder. Reaching out to catch the throw is not recommended unless the throw is off line. The ball can travel faster than a player's tag. Two-handed tags in a game are good when a player has plenty of time to put the tag down. This will help secure the ball so it will not be kicked out of the glove.

    Recommended ages 10-16.

ADDITIONAL BACK HAND DRILLS

4-22: Reaction backhand

20. **Backhand Reaction Play:** This backhand is used on a sharply hit ball when the defender has no time to backhand the ball with the crossover step. This backhand is initiated by a slight drop step with the throwing hand foot as the body and glove stays low. As the ball is received, it is done so with a giving action towards the outfield. Players throw a one hop ball to backhand side and receive it as stated above. **(picture 4-22)**

    Recommended ages 12-16.

4-23: Slide through backhand

21. **Backhand Slide Through:** This backhand is used when the infielder can't get in front of the ball or when a fast runner is involved. The infielder takes an angle to the ball and sets up for a backhand. The player still has time to move up to the ball so he shuffles forward sideways through the backhand play. The glove starts low with the thumb turned down to open up the glove. The slide forward starts with the glove hand moving forward to catch the ball. The body slides through a split second after the glove and continues into the throwing process. **(picture 4-23)**

    Recommended ages 12-16.

GAMES

1. **Short-hop Game:** Set up the short-hop drill with each coach taking five players. Players do not team up but take turns playing with the coach. Coach throws 10 short hops to each player. The object of game is to see which player can catch the most throws. To keep other players active in the group, have them pair up and play until it is their turn. Another option for this game is as follows: Instead of best of 10, see what player can catch the most throws in a row. Winning player or players lead stretch at next practice. **If playing for most catches in a row, keep track of the winning amount at that day. At next practice, see who can beat last practice's record.**

    Recommended ages 8-16.

2. **Reaction Game:** Set up the same as Game 1. The coach throws every type of ball possible – from all types of ground balls to line drives and balls that require jumping catches – and the player reacts to make the play. **This is great drill for all infielders, especially corner players.**

    Recommended ages 8-16.

3. **Partner Ground Ball Game:** Set up Partner Ground Ball Drill, pairing up partners by ability. The coach doesn't have to control the game like the drill. The partners play against each other. The object of the game is to see which partner misses a ground ball first. Here are the rules: Players must throw the ground balls directly at their partner, and all throws must bounce at least two times. Players can throw ground balls as hard as they want to make the game a challenge. **Have players play a best-of-five series, or a best-of-seven World Series. This will give them a chance to lose a game but still possibly win the series.**

    Recommended ages 8-16.

4. **Relay Game:** Divide the team into three groups of four to six players each. Each group forms a straight line with 25 to 50 feet of space between each player, depending on the age group. Have players at the same points throughout each line. Give a ball to each player at the beginning of each line. The object of the game is to throw the ball to each player in his line. Once the ball reaches the last player in the line, they return the ball back down the line until it reaches the player who started the game. The players at the ends of the line rotate to the middle after each game. If a player is overthrown, the ball must be returned to that player before the ball can continue down the line. Every player in the line must handle the ball. The first group to throw the ball up and back three times is the winner. Winning players get to decide what drill or game to perform next. **The game is designed to work on the proper fundamentals of an infielder being a relay man. Each infielder should face the player throwing to him with his arms raised high in the air, giving the thrower, the outfielder, a target. As the ball is in flight, the infielder should move to the ball, positioning his body to receive the throw on the glove-hand side. Once the ball is caught, the player crow hops directly toward his target, the next player in line. This game is great for teaching players the quickest way to relay a throw and keeps all players active.**
   Recommended ages 8-16.

5. **Concentrated Ground Ball Game:** Set up drill as stated in drill section. Play the line of players versus the coach. Set a total number of catches that must be made consecutively for a player's victory. If any player bobbles or misses a ball before reaching that total number, the coach wins. **Be sure to put a reward for the winners or a task to be performe by the losers to add to the build-up and competition of the game. Example, if players lose they must carry the coaches' gear to the car.**
   Recommended ages 8-16.

6. **Create Your Own:** Almost every drill can be made into a game. Be creative. After utilizing a drill for a while, see if you can make it a competition or a game. **The Triangle Rotation Drill and the Four-corner Tag Drill are perfect for making up your own game.**

Playing First Base

Developing a good first baseman is crucial to the success of a strong defensive team. Time should be spent on specific first-base fundamentals before, during or after practice. Most players want to play first base—or their parents want them to. But be aware that not all players have the ability to play this position. Remember to think of safety first. If a player has trouble catching a ball and can't get out of the way of a hard throw, then they shouldn't be playing first base. All infielders can benefit from learning how to receive a throw like a first baseman does. They will use this footwork on force outs at their respective bases.

FIRST BASE FUNDAMENTALS

A. **Setting Up on Base:** Once the ball is hit, the first baseman should get to the base as quickly as possible. There are two ways a first baseman can set up his feet. The easier position is to place the ball of the throwing-hand foot in contact with the middle of the bag. The glove-hand foot is wider than shoulder width, and both knees are flexed. The first baseman faces the infielder making the play. It is important the first baseman is in a balanced athletic position so he can adjust to a bad throw. The second and more advanced foot position on receiving throws allows the first baseman more mobility around the bag, but there is more footwork involved. When the first baseman gets to the bag using this method, he straddles the bag with his heels in contact with the base. From there, the technique is the same. **(picture 4-24)**

4-24: Straddle set up

B. **Receiving the Throw:** From the athletic position and facing the infielder making the play, the first baseman waits to see the flight of the ball. After seeing the throw direction, he steps with the glove-hand foot directly toward the throw. From the more advanced straddle position, the fielder has to adjust his throwing-hand foot in contact with the base as he steps toward the throw. This technique allows for movement on the base. On very wide throws, a first baseman can shift his feet to one side of the bag and then stretch for the ball. This is where mobility around the base is gained. It's important on low throws that the first baseman bends his back knee to maintain his foot on the base. Once the ball is caught players, should pull their foot off the base to limit getting stepped on and look for the next play if other men are on base. **(picture 4-25)**

4-25: Step to ball

C. **Holding Runners on Base:** Whether right- or left-handed, the basic body position is about the same. The right foot is parallel and against first base on the home plate side. The left foot is in line with pitcher. Knees are bent low and the target is given with the glove hand extended toward the pitcher. Left-handers have their left foot more open in line with the first-base line. Once pitcher commits to home, first baseman shuffles off base and gets into ready position. **(pictures 4-26 & 4-27)**

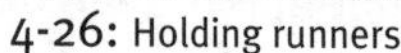
4-26: Holding runners

4-27: Ready position

FIRST BASE DRILLS

1. **Receiving Throws:** Start player at regular first baseman's position. Coach sets up 40 to 60 feet away with a bucket of balls. On coach's command, *go*, player breaks to the base, gets under control and sets up on the bag correctly with either set up. The first baseman then faces toward coach's location and waits to see where the ball is thrown. After reading the ball direction the first baseman steps to meet the throw with the glove-hand foot, or shifts both feet if using the straddle technique. Once catch and out is made, pull foot off bag and look for another play. Have another bucket placed near first to drop the balls into. The coach should vary the location and height of throws. When working with younger players who have limited first-base experience, set up much closer—about 20 feet away.
   Recommended ages 8-16.
2. **Receiving Bad Throws:** Set up the same as Drill 1, but the coach throws balls that can just barely be caught maintaining the base and throws where the player must come off the base to catch. **This teaches the first baseman his stretching limit and that it's acceptable to come off the base and save an errant throw.**
   Recommended ages 8-16.
3. **Tagging Runners:** Set up the same as Drill 1. Coach throws balls that are up the line (toward home) that the player must leave the base to catch. The first baseman catches the ball in fair territory. Once making the catch, keep the glove low in case the runner slides to avoid a tag. The tag should be made lightly, letting the runner's momentum force the tag. A tag with a giving action will help prevent injury by softening the contact. A coach can simulate a runner to make this more realistic. **(pictures 4-28 & 4-29)**
   Recommended ages 10-16.

4-28: Start low

4-29: Give with runner

4-30: Picking low throws

4. **Picking Low Throws:** Coach starts 10 to 20 feet away from first base with a bucket of balls. Player starts in the stretch position with glove out front and low with the knee flexed in an L position to maintain contact with the base. The coach throws short hops and the player works on picking the throw and maintaining the bag. Have the player work on backhanded short hops as well. After a few throws from this distance, the coach should back up 40 to 60 feet away and the first baseman starts on the base in his regular receiving position. Now working on stretching out and picking the ball at the same time. The only time a first baseman shouldn't step to the ball on a low throw is when the throw is very short and the ball can't be picked on a short hop. The player stays back to catch the big hop. **(picture 4-30)**

   Recommended ages 10-16.

5. **Just React:** Combine all of the above and have the player just react to all the possible throws a first baseman may receive. For older players, a coach may use a fungo and hit balls as if thrown to a first baseman to save the arm and put more velocity on the ball.

   Recommended ages 8-16.

GAMES

1. **Picking Low Throws:** After performing the drill for a while, end with a little competition. From 40 to 60 feet, put three players at first base. The players are playing against each other. Have players alternate taking throws. Players keep going in succession until they miss two throws. When they miss two they are out. Keep going until a winner is crowned. **Winning player gets to decide what fielding game the team plays at the next practice.**

   Recommended ages 10-16.

Infield Play

The infield is a unit that must be totally in synch to perform its best, and therefore requires a lot of teamwork. To excel as a unit, the infielders must be able to observe, communicate, and have the instincts to adapt to given situations. Below are some areas that all infielders should make part of their game.

Gold Glover J.T. Snow on Infield Play:
"Always ask yourself before every play, what do I do if the ball is hit to me?
And, what do I do if the ball is not hit to me?
Because every player on the field has a place to be on every play."

FUNDAMENTALS OF INFIELD PLAY

A. **Infield Movement:** The infield should move together as a unit. This will ensure proper spacing and help the team defend as much of the field as possible. Each infielder should be aware of where their teammates are and talk to them to ensure proper coverage. The coaches should constantly be observing their team's defensive positioning and making adjustments when needed.

B. **Communication:** Communication between infielders can help prevent many mistakes. For example, the shortstop and second baseman must know who is covering second on a steal attempt before every hitter (and before every pitch for older players.) With a man on first base and less than two outs, the pitcher and middle infielders must communicate before every batter so the pitcher knows who is covering second base on a ball hit back to him. Normally the shortstop is the leader of the infield and makes these decisions unless otherwise stated by the coach. These are just a couple examples of situations players should be talking about. But the more we can get our players communicating about any aspect of the game, the better prepared they will be.

Expert Advice on Communication

The shortstop and second baseman must know who is covering second on a steal attempt before every hitter and before every pitch for older players.

C. **Positioning:** There is no set way to play a right-handed hitter or a left-handed hitter. Knowledge and observation will determine how infielders should position themselves. There are many criteria to review before a high-percentage decision can be derived. Every hitter is an individual, and time will tell each one's tendencies. Infielders should observe hitter's swings to determine if they swing late or pull the ball. They should adjust to the swings when tendencies are shown. If players cannot determine any sure tendencies in the swings they are reading, they should maintain normal straightaway positioning. Observe, and don't forget to take into account tangibles such as the speed of the pitcher, pitch location, the pitch (offspeed or fastball), and the count. A pitcher's velocity will influence whether the swing is early or late. Observation and time will be the judge of where to play hitters. Make an effort to learn the tendencies of hitters you play against, and know your pitcher's strengths and weaknesses. The number of outs, the score, the count, the inning, the pitch and field conditions all factor into defensive positioning. Evaluate each situation and play accordingly.

D. **Adjusting to the Pitch:** It's the middle infielders' job to watch the catcher's signs to see what kind of pitch is being thrown and where it's supposed to be located, so the infielder can play the percentages. In general hitters ahead in the count usually become more aggressive and are more likely to pull the ball. The same is true of an offspeed pitch where hitters have a greater chance of being out in front and pulling the ball. The opposite is true of hitters behind in the count or if a good fastball is thrown. The tendency is to be late and hit the ball up the middle or the other way. The infielder must understand when a hitter is ahead or behind in the count, know what the pitch is and adjust accordingly. The defender can move with the count much more easily than with the pitch. As the count changes, infielders can position themselves before the pitch is made. It's a little trickier moving with the pitch, because there isn't much time for adjustment and a good hitter will observe the movement if done too early. Normally this movement takes place while the pitcher is releasing the ball, and it's no more than a short step. Possibly no movement will take place, but the infielder will just anticipate the ball being hit a certain direction .

E. **Corners Play Off the Line:** Generally speaking, the first and third basemen should play off the lines. More balls will go through the holes of shortstop and second base than down the lines. Sacrifice one or two balls down the line for the many heading for the holes between infielders. The only exceptions are when a player proves he is dead-pull hitter or to guard the line in the late innings of a close game to stop a possible double down the line.

Major League Third Baseman Bill Mueller on In Between Hops at Third Base:
"If you are getting a lot of in-between hops, you may try changing your depth by moving forward or backward. When you get an in-between hop, blocking the ball is most important. When blocking, make sure to keep the ball in front of you to help you finish the play quickly."

F. **Regular Depth:** Corners are off the line and positioned behind the base. Depth will be determined by age and arm strength. The middle infielders split the distance between second base and their respective corner. The middle infielders should be as deep as their arm allows them to make a little better than a routine play. Some players that don't quite have the arm strength will have to play tighter. All infielders should shorten up in depth when a speedy runner is at the plate. Remember, all infielders depths will vary with the speed of the runner and the arm strength of the player.

G. **Double-play Depth:** The corners move toward home a few steps, while the middle infielders move in and closer toward second base. This allows them time to get to the ball or base soon enough to complete the double play. A little ground must be given up in order to be in the proper position to turn the double play.

H. **Covering Second Base:** When covering second on a steal attempt, the middle infielder should break straight in when the runner takes off and then over to the base once the ball passes through the hitting zone. This will allow the infielder to maintain good range in both directions while cutting down the distance to second. If your league doesn't allow stealing until the ball crosses home plate, then the infielder can just break straight to the base.

FUNDAMENTALS OF THE DOUBLE-PLAY FEED

The feed from third to second should be smooth and firm. The third baseman should get rid of the ball as quick as possible while still making a controlled throw. A firm, accurate throw to second will hopefully allow the second baseman time to turn the double play. An ideal throw is chest level; a low throw is the most difficult to handle.

Shortstop: On a ball hit directly to the shortstop or to his right, the shortstop should field the ball with the left foot dropped back a little more than normal **(picture 4-31).** This gives the hips a head start to clear for the throwing motion. Older players can throw from this position; younger players should shuffle step. The pivot is quicker, but balance and body control must be maintained. If not, the shuffle step is fine.

4-31: SS feed position

The shortstop should stay low to maintain control and use a shorter snap-type throw, making the feed as quick as possible. On a ball hit to the shortstop's left, if there is momentum toward second base, the shortstop can turn the double play himself (if close enough) or flip the ball underhand to the second baseman. If the shortstop makes the play himself, he should yell, *I got it*, to alert the second baseman to clear away from the base. For a flip, the ball should be cleared away from the glove so the second baseman can pick up the ball as soon as possible. The shortstop should follow through on the flip a couple of steps for a firm, accurate toss. By following the flip, all the momentum travels in the same direction as the ball. Too many times a bad flip occurs because the flipping action is cut off short or momentum is shifted away from the target. **(pictures 4-32 to 4-34)**

The most important thing is to at least get one out.

4-32: Field

4-33: Clear

4-34: Underhand flip

Second Base: On a ball hit at the second baseman or to the left, field the ball and either pivot on the balls of the feet or jump-step to square the body to throw. The pivot is done by rotating on the balls of the feet to allow the hips and shoulders to square up to second. This movement requires a good deal of coordination, balance and strength, but is smooth and fast once mastered. The second baseman sets up to field the ball in a normal fielding position, but the right foot is dropped back a bit to help make the pivot easier. The second baseman should stay low and rotate his knees downward, with the left knee almost touching the ground **(pictures 4-35 & 4-36).** The jump-step is preferred for most young players. All the player must do is jump and turn to square the hips and shoulders in order to make an accurate throw to second **(picture 4-37)**. This allows the player to focus on fielding and then getting balance to throw to second. Players will be more consistent fielding with this method.

Regardless of which position is used, throwing action is the same. First, clear the ball from the glove and bring it to a strong throwing position – where the arm is nearly in the L position. Next, make a firm, quick, accurate snap throw.

Another type of feed the second baseman makes is on a ball hit far to the left when they can't quite get in front of the ball. In this instance, field the ball by reaching outside the body, then rotate 180 degrees toward the outfield to square up to second base. Rotating this way is quicker and easier than rotating toward home plate. **(pictures 4-38& 4-39)**

On a ball to the second baseman's right, he should flip the ball underhand to the shortstop in the same manner as described in the shortstop section.

4-35: Field

4-36: 2B pivot feed

4-37: Jump turn feed

4-38: 2B outside body catch

4-39: Outside body throwing position

First Base: Whether right-handed or left-handed, the first baseman's responsibility is the same. He must catch the ball and square up to second base to make the throw. It is easier for a left-handed player to square up, which is another advantage to having a left-handed first baseman.

If the runner is in line between the shortstop and first baseman, the first baseman should take a step to his throwing-hand side to avoid hitting the runner with the throw and so the shortstop has a clear view of the ball's path. This also holds true when a runner is picked off first and is directly between the first baseman and shortstop.

Once the throw is made, the first baseman must hurry back to the base and find the bag to be in position to catch the return throw. Again, the lead out is the most important, so the first baseman should not rush the throw or his body to retreat for the return throw.

Sometimes the pitcher will cover first base on balls that pull the first baseman too far from the base. If the first baseman has time to retreat to first and can make the play easily, the first baseman should call off the pitcher.

FUNDAMENTALS OF THE DOUBLE-PLAY PIVOT

Shortstop: Get to the base as quickly as possible with the body under control. This makes it easier to adjust to an errant throw. Either put the right foot on the back of the base or set up just behind the base. At this point the shortstop should be in a balanced athletic position ready to react. **(pictures 4-40 & 4-41)**

4-40: SS right foot on base

4-41: SS drag foot behind base

Give the fielder a target at chest level with hands extended outward and step to meet the ball with the left foot. If set up behind the base, drag the right foot against the back corner of the bag and square the body to first base to be in position to make the throw. If the foot was already on the base, just shuffle both feet to square the body to throw.

After releasing the ball, if the runner is closing in and sliding, jump to clear the runner's feet to help prevent injury.

The easiest way to turn the double play on a throw directly over the bag is as follows: Instead of crossing the bag to meet the ball, let it come to you. Receive the ball and take a jab step with the front (left foot) back off the base while stepping toward first base to complete the throw. It is very important that the left foot shoelaces are facing toward first base on the throw to avoid injury. Also, keep your momentum heading towards first base on the jab step as opposed to stepping too far back. You don't want your momentum heading back toward right center field, which would take your direction and arm strength away.

Second Base: Get to the base as quickly as possible with the body under control, making it easier to adjust to an errant throw. The left foot should start on the back of the base. At this point the second baseman should be in a balanced athletic position ready to react. **(picture 4-42)**

Give the fielder a target at chest level with hands extended outward and step to meet the ball with the right foot **(picture 4-43)**. The right foot then plants to allow the body to square up and make the throw to first **(picture 4-44)**. The easiest way to turn the double play on a throw directly over the bag is as follows: Instead of crossing the bag to meet the ball, let it come to you. Receive the ball and take a jab step with the front (left foot) back off the base while stepping toward first base to complete the throw. It is very important that the left foot shoelaces are facing toward first base on the throw to avoid injury. Also, keep your momentum heading towards first base on the jab step as opposed to stepping too far back. You don't want your momentum heading back toward right center field, which would take your direction and arm strength away.

After releasing the ball, if the runner is closing in and sliding, jump to clear the runner's feet to help prevent injury.

4-42: 2B pivot starting position

4-43: Step to ball

4-44: Throw

Giants Infield Coach Ron Wotus on Turning the Double Play:
"Work on the glove to hand transfer daily when playing catch
and do not try to be to quick on the turn.
Smooth is quick enough, and quickness comes form repetitions of executing the play."

DRILLS

Expert Advice on Shortstop Feeds and Second Baseman Pivots

By moving closer to the infielders the players can get in more repetitions and the coach can control the drill better. The more a player practices and gets familiar with different feeds and pivots, the more natural they will become.

1. **Shortstop Feeds, Second Baseman Pivots:** Set up shortstops and second basemen at double-play depth. This drill can be done with one at each position but works best with multiple players at each position. The coach sets up on the infield next to the mound in line with home plate and the shortstop. The coach can either roll or lightly hit balls under control to the shortstop. Concentrate on one area at a time so players can get familiar with that particular play, and progress through different location and types of feeds. The three main plays to work on: Ball to the shortstop's left, ball right at the shortstop and ball to the shortstop's right. Once the ball is in play, the second baseman breaks to the base and gets under control to receive the throw. The pivot is turned, and a throw is made to first or a shorter distance to save the second baseman's arm. If no other help is available, the second baseman can go through the footwork and just drop the ball to the side or flip it back to the coach. This drill can also be done with the coach acting as the shortstop if the desired result is for second basemen to work on their pivot. **By moving closer to the infielders the players can get in more repetitions and the coach can control the drill better. The more a player practices and gets familiar with different feeds and pivots, the more natural they will become.**

   Recommended ages 8-16.

2. **Second Baseman Feeds, Shortstop Pivots:** This drill is identical to the one above, except the coach sets up on the other side of the mound, in line with home plate and the second baseman. This time, the coach rolls or hits balls to the second baseman, and the shortstop covers the base. Just like above, vary the balls to the second baseman, to his left, at him and to his right. **This drill's benefits and variations are identical to Drill 1, except the emphasis is now on the second baseman's feed and the shortstop's pivot.**

   Recommended ages 8-16.

3. **Double Play:** Set up the middle infielders at double-play depth. The coach sets up between the mound and home or at home plate. Coach randomly hits ball to the second baseman or shortstop, and players react to the given ball and turn a double play. **This drill may also be done with the third and first basemen involved. This drill simulates game action and teaches the players where to go and what to do in a double-play situation.**

   Recommended ages 8-16.

4. **Second Baseman Tagging Runner Double Play:** Set up second basemen at double-play depth and a baserunner at first. This runner may be a player or a coach. Slower ground balls are rolled or hit to the second baseman. He comes in, fields the ball and tags the runner if he is close and still between first base and the second baseman. After the tag is made, he throws to first to complete the double play. If the runner is not close and in line to be tagged, the second baseman feeds the ball to the shortstop for the double play. **This drill simulates the unassisted tag double play and recreates game-like decision making. It teaches the player this option if the proper situation arises.**

   Recommended ages 8-16.

5. **Third Base Unassisted Double Play:** This play occurs when runners are on first and second and a ball is hit toward the third base bag. Set up the third basemen at double-play depth and roll or hit balls to their right side. Players will field the ball and then tag third base if they are close enough to do so. They then complete the double play by throwing the ball to first. If they are not close enough, another decision must be made: Is there still enough time to throw to second, or just throw to first to get the out? After the third basemen have worked on this, roll or hit balls in different locations. The third basemen will get familiar with their options. The location of the ground ball will usually determine where to get the out or throw the ball. **This drill recreates game-like decision-making and teaches third basemen when to get the lead out or the out at first, and their double play options.**

   Recommended ages 10-16.

6. **First Base Double Plays:** This double play is the hardest to turn, and at the lower levels the safe play is just to get the out at first. Set up the first basemen at double-play depth. The coach is at home plate or at a closer distance rolling or hitting ground balls. Start by rolling or hitting balls directly at the first basemen. They field the ball and make the throw to second. After the throw is made, the first basemen retreat to cover the base for the return throw. Second, work them with balls hit or rolled to their right, where the pitcher will attempt to cover the base. The last play to work on is balls close to the bag where they field the ball, tag the base and complete the double play by throwing the ball to second base. After making the throw, the first baseman should yell, *tag*, to let the shortstop know there is no force out and a tag needs to be applied on the runner. **On all double plays, the most important out is the first one. This is especially true when the ball is hit to the first baseman. This drill gives first basemen a chance to work on throwing to second base and their footwork when retreating to get a return throw from second.**

   Recommended ages 10-16.

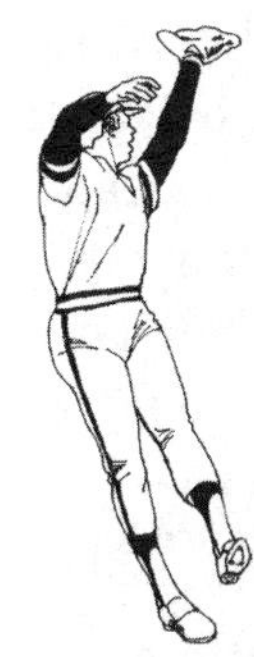

OUTFIELD

Outfielders should anticipate every pitch being hit to them and think about where they should throw the ball before it is hit. All outfielders should be in the ready position, utilizing pre-pitch movement as the ball approaches the hitting zone. Pre-pitch movement will help players focus on the hitter, the game and improve their jump on the ball. Players can relax between pitches but should return to the ready position as the pitcher is ready to deliver the ball.

Encourage communication among outfielders. They should remind each other the number of outs after each play to keep them alert. Runs can be saved by teaching outfielders how to back up bases and their teammates correctly. Charging ground balls, fielding them properly and getting them back to the infield quickly are valuable skills that also save runs.

The most obvious aspect of playing the outfield is catching fly balls. Sometimes outfielders have a difficult time, because their judgment skills are not fully developed. Judgment can be developed through practice—repetition of thrown or batted balls. Take time to teach the fundamentals below to enhance your team's outfield play.

5-1: Ready position

FUNDAMENTALS

A. **Ready Position:** It's an athletic position, with the knees flexed and weight on the balls of the feet. The body is balanced and ready to react. Hands are off the knees and eyes are focused on the hitting zone. **(picture 5-1)**

B. **Pre-pitch Movement:** Relax between pitches until the pitcher starts his wind-up. To initiate pre-pitch movement, walk into the ready position with a small, controlled right-left step if right-handed or a left-right step if left-handed. The pre-pitch movement should be initiated during the wind-up and completed slightly before the ball is in the hitting zone. This allows the best reaction to a hit ball.

C. **Initial Step**: Balls hit to the right or left utilize a crossover step. Balls hit directly overhead utilize a drop-step. When a line drive is hit directly at the outfielder, the player should drop-step to 90 degrees with either foot getting in position to go forward or backward. The player holds this initial step until determining whether to charge or back up on the ball. **(pictures 5-2 & 5-3).**

5-2: Drop step on ball hit over left shoulder

5-3: Drop step on ball hit over right shoulder

Defensive Star Calvin Murray on Getting a Good Jump on the Ball:
"In order to get a good jump on a batted ball you have to be in a good athletic position when the ball is in the hitting area. Most importantly you must believe every pitch will be hit to you."

D. **Tracking a Hit Ball:** With eyes focused on the hitting zone, anticipate a swing and the ball being hit. After contact, run quickly to where you expect the ball will land buy keeping your eyes focused on the ball and extending the arm up in time to make the catch. As players improve there judgment skills they should learn to run to a spot by taking there eyes off the ball during there tracking phase. This is done by reading the ball at contact, then taking the eyes off the ball, running fast towards the location of the batted ball, and then picking up the ball again as you sense it is time to retract the ball and make the catch. This technique takes time to develop but is the fastest way to cover ground in the outfield.

E. **Catching Fly Balls:** Attempt to get under the baseball whenever possible with glove position at vertical to 1 o'clock. Use two hands by lining up the thumb of the throwing hand with the thumb of the glove hand. The ball is best received slightly to the glove hands side of the face area. This is best for vision, staying balanced through out the catch and transitioning into the throw. If the player cannot get under the ball, one-handed catches are the most efficient. Using two hands is awkward and can throw off a players balance when attempting to catch the ball on the run. Players who are 10 years old and above should begin to learn to catch the ball with the proper foot work needed to catch and throw to a base. For a quicker transition into a throw the glove hand foot should be placed in front with knees flexed and body balanced. This allows an easy transition into the crow hop to throw. **(picture 5-4***)*

5-4: Two-handed catch

F. **Charging Ground Balls:** Getting to the ball quickly is important, whether there are baserunners or not. It's important to learn how to judge the speed of the ball off the bat. When the ball is hit slow, immediately charge hard. Regardless of the ball's speed, when approaching it, slow down and get under control using short, choppy steps to get into the proper fielding position. Slowing down to gain body control prepares the fielder for bad hops and gives him a better chance to field the ball. The fielder will also be in a better throwing position. Bending over at the waist at the last moment leads to poor body balance and gives the fielder little chance to make adjustments on a bad hop.

G. **Fielding Ground Balls:** With no one on base, field the ball like an infielder or drop to one knee so ball does not get past. If runners are on base, field the ball with two hands in order to return the ball quickly to the infield. In this instance, do not drop to one knee. If baserunners are trying to advance, field the ball one-handed using glove-hand, glove-foot technique. The glove position is slightly in front and to the side of the glove-side foot. Field forward and through the ball, coming up to the throwing position. **(pictures 5-5 to 5-7)**

5-5: No one on base

5-6: Man on base

5-7: Throwing out a runner

H. Getting the Ball to the Infielder: Never hold the ball and not know what to do with it. Always anticipate the play before it happens. After fielding the ball, pick up the infield target as soon as possible. Square up for proper alignment, and crow hop for momentum to make a strong throw to the proper base or cut-off man. When throwing to a base, make a throw an infielder can handle. Know when to throw the ball all the way in the air or when to make an accurate one-hop bounce to the base. When throwing to a relay or cut-off man, hit him chest high if possible. **(pictures 5-8 to 5-10)**

I. Outfielders Throw: When there is no immediate play, outfielders should get into the habit of setting their feet and throwing the ball firmly to a base or cut off man. When attempting to throw out or stop a runner from advancing, the throw should always be made hard and on a line.

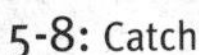

5-8: Catch

5-9: Crow hop

5-10: Throw

DRILLS

1. **Ready Position Dry Drill:** Put players in a single-file line with space to move between them. On verbal command, *ready*, players get into the ready position. Check each player's position. Look for a balanced stance with weight on the balls of the feet and hands carried high and off the knees. **Physically help players get into proper position if needed.**
   Recommended ages 8-16.
2. **Pre-pitch Movement Dry Drill:** Place four players at each outfield position and a coach or player on the mound. Players stand relaxed at their outfield position. Pitcher simulates wind-up. When the pitcher reaches his release point, all players should have utilized the proper pre-pitch movement sequence as explained in the fundamentals section. One coach should monitor the players performing this drill. **This drill will show players when to relax and when they need to be ready to react, and it keeps all players active.**
   Recommended ages 8-16.

3. **Pop-up Drill/Game:** Give everyone in your group of 4 to 6 players a ball. Spread them out with plenty of room to move between each other. On your command each player underhand tosses their ball into the air. Each player then catches their own ball utilizing the two-handed thumb near thumb above head catching position. (Fundamental E) As players' skills improve, players toss the ball higher and higher. **This drill keeps all players active and is a great way to achieve proper technique for above-head catches, with lots of repetition. This drill is easily made into a game by seeing how many catches can be made in a row on high tosses.**

   Recommended ages 6-10.

FAVORITE DRILL

Drills - Initial Steps

4. **Drop-step Dry Drill:** Line up all players 5 feet apart. Start them in the ready position. A coach stands 15 feet in front of the players where all the players can see him. When the coach points up and to his left (players' right), players drop-step with their right foot to 90 degrees simulating a ball hit over their right side, and hold that position. When the coach points up and to his right (players' left), players drop-step with their left foot to 90 degrees, simulating a ball hit over their left side, and hold that position. Establishing the drop-step to 90 degrees allows a player to run in a straight line to any ball. A drop-step to 90 degrees does not have to occur on every ball hit to the side. The drop-step depth will vary depending on the angle needed to run directly to the ball. **(pictures 5-11 & 5-12) This drill teaches the correct first step for a more efficient route and angle to the ball over their heads, and it keeps all players active.**

   Recommended ages 8-16.

5-11: Drop step dry drill

5-12: Drop step dry drill

5. **Drop-step Drill:** Follow the same set-up as for the drop-step dry drill. One player at a time, the coach throws a ball over the player's right or left shoulder. The throw should have a high arc and be made catchable. After catching the ball, the player throws it back to the coach and hustles back to their position in line. The coach continues down the line, monitoring for proper drop-step. If a player does not drop-step correctly, repeat with that player. To take this drill a step further, throw balls straight over the player's head. Here, the correct technique is to drop-step with the glove-hand foot so the ball can be caught without reaching across the body. **This drill teaches the correct first step to a ball over their heads and practices making running catches.**

   Recommended ages 8-16.

6a. **Crossover Step Dry Drill:** Players line up single-file and the coach stands 15 feet away, facing the first player in line. The coach points to each player's right and left, letting the player focus on proper technique. Monitor the drill to ensure the first step is not with the near-side foot. The near-side foot should pivot open and the far-side foot should cross over the near-side foot as the player runs for the ball. **This drill teaches the correct first step to a ball hit to the side.**

   Recommended ages 8-16.

6b. Crossover Step Drill: Follow the same set-up as for the crossover step dry drill. Give all players a ball. The first player in line throws the ball to the coach, who rolls the ball back to the player 15 to 20 feet to their right or left. The player breaks with proper crossover step and fields the ball. The player keeps the ball and hustles to the back of the line. **This drill should be utilized for all players since all infielders use this technique frequently. It is fast moving, and will give players many repetitions in a short period of time. This drill keeps all players active.**

Recommended ages 8-16.

7. Reaction Drill Incorporating Drop and Cross Over Steps: Pair up players and place them in two separate lines 20 feet apart so that each player is facing his partner. Keep plenty of space between players in the same line so they can move freely. Give each player in one line a baseball. The coach stands behind the line of players without the baseballs. The receiving players start in the ready position. The coach controls the drill by pointing in which direction he wants the ball thrown. Point down and to the right for ground balls to the right side. Point up and to the right for fly balls over the right shoulder. Do the same thing for the left side. The coach monitors the receiving players and makes corrections when needed. After 5 to 10 repetitions, make the receiving players the throwers. The coach switches sides and repeats. **This drill is the next step after players have mastered the crossover step and drop-step drills. This drill can be utilized for all players, and it is a high-repetition drill that will keep all players active when coaching alone or with limited help.**

Recommended ages 8-16.

Drills - Fielding Ground Balls

8. Situation Ground Balls: Line up all outfielders in center field in a single file. Put the third baseman at his position and the shortstop as the relay man lined up to third. Put second baseman at second base. With a bucket of balls, the coach takes position between the mound and second base and yells out one of two situations, *No one on base* or *Man on first base*. Hit ground balls at various speeds and directions – either right at or to the side of the center fielders. Outfielders work on charging ground balls hard from initial steps, slowing down and getting under control to field the ball in proper position. If coach yells, *No one on base*, the player fields the ball as an infielder or goes down to one knee, then quickly squares up to second base, crow hops and makes a strong throw. If coach yells, *Man on first base*, the player charges hard, gets under control and fields ball like an infielder. Then he quickly squares up to third, crow hops and makes a strong throw chest high to the shortstop, who will cut it off if necessary. **This drill covers the key skills needed to field ground balls and throwing to the correct base or the relay man. It also allows the relay man to make decisions about relaying the ball to third base or cutting off the ball if proper communication skills are used between the third baseman and shortstop. This drill also teaches players to make decisions based on the game situation.**

Recommended ages 8-16.

Olympic Team Member Calvin Murray on Outfielder's Throws:

"When making a throw to the infield make sure you know where you will be throwing the ball before the ball is hit. When throwing to the infield or relay man your only job is to throw the ball through the chest of the relay man. Remember a shorter throw is better here because you still have a chance, your infielder can pick the throw and still make a play."

9. **Backing Up Drill:** Divide outfielders into two groups. Place one group in left-center field and the other in right-center field. The coach takes position between the mound and second base. Hit ground balls at various speeds into center field between the two outfield groups. Starting from the ready position, one outfielder from each group breaks for the ball. The outfielder who gets there first fields the ball with the other outfielder peeling off to back up the other outfielder once he realizes he cannot get to the ball first. Players backing up should be 20 to 30 feet behind the player fielding the ball. **This drill simulates game situations and gives the players a chance to work on their judgment skills. It also teaches players not to get too close to teammate when backing up a play.**
   Recommended ages 8-16.

Drills - Catching Fly Balls

10. **Live Fungo Drill:** Simply place all the outfielders at an outfield position. Utilize one player as a relay man or have the players throw to a base. The coach hits all types of fly balls to the players. After catching the ball the outfielders finishes the play by throwing the ball into the base or relay man. **There are many drills in this book that allow outfielders to get lots of repetition on catching fly balls. Most of these drills accomplish this by the coach throwing the ball, so players can work on their coordination of running and catching with out chasing poorly hit balls all over the field. This drill should be done often as players need to see live balls hit off a bat so they can develop skills for reading the swing and judging a hit ball.**
    Recommended ages 8-16

11. **Communication Drill:** Divide players into two separate lines. Lines should be 30 to 60 feet apart, depending on age level. Older players should be farther apart. The coach centers himself between the two lines, 30 to 60 feet in front of each. The coach then tosses high pop flies between and in front of the two lines. Starting from the ready position, the first player from each line breaks for the pop-up. The player who gets there first calls for the ball loudly at least two times. The player can call, *Ball, ball!* or *I got it, I got it!* The other player backs off to allow for the catch. **NOTE:** If both players calling for the ball becomes a problem, designate one line the center fielder's line and the other line the left fielder's line. The center fielder has priority over the left fielder, so if both players call for the ball, the center fielder stays with the catch. **This drill teaches players how to take charge and call for a ball. It also simulates a game situation that is seldom taught at practice.**
    Recommended ages 8-16

12. **Line Drive Drill:** Players stand 100 feet away from the coach. The coach throws or hits line drives directly at, in front of, or over the player's head. Players should remember to drop-step and freeze until they determine whether to come in, stay put or go back. Vary different types of balls without the player knowing so he can react and make the correct decision. **This drill assists players to make reads on difficult balls.**
    Recommended ages 9-16.

Former San Francisco Giant Calvin Murray on Line Drives Right at You:
"The most important thing to do on a line drive is to get side ways so you can go forward or backwards. Never commit until you know where the ball is going. If you have to stand still for a second or two that is fine. You should remain sideways until you get a clear idea on where the ball is going."

13. **Fly ball Correction Drill:** Have players line up and, one at a time, they break in the direction the coach points. The coach then throws the ball to the opposite side, and the player must make the adjustment. When the initial break and drop-step is to the wrong side, the proper adjustment is done by rotating the head and turning the body via the outfield direction. This means a player must take his eyes off the ball for a split second, but the change of direction is made much more quickly and easily. **This drill teaches outfielders proper adjustment when in pursuit of a fly ball.**

    Recommended ages 12-16

GAMES

1. **Glove Position:** Divide the team into two groups. Each group has a coach to toss balls and record the score of his team. The object of the game is to award points for players catching pop flies with the correct glove position (glove at 1 o'clock, two hands, thumb-to-thumb alignment). Award 10 points for a ball caught above the head with the correct glove position. Award five points for players getting glove in correct position but did not make the catch. Award one point for balls caught one-handed or basket style. Have each player in the group go five times. On the fifth round make it a bonus round. Award 15, 10 and five points respectively. Add up the points to see which team won. **Winners hit first at batting practice.**

   Recommended ages 7-16.
2. **Barrel Game:** Place all players in left, center or right field. The coach takes position between the mound and second base. The object of the game is to have the players throw the ball into the bucket on the fly or on one or two hops. Award 100 points for balls thrown into the bucket. Award 50 points for balls hitting the bucket. The coach can throw fly balls or roll ground balls to simulate a game situation. Have all players make three throws at the bucket. The player plays against the coaches. The coach picks the number of points the team must get in order to win the game. Make it a challenging but obtainable number for the team. **Play for five push-ups, or the losing group picks up the balls. Players love to beat the coaches.**

   Recommended ages 8-16.
3. **Football Drill Game:** The details of this drill can be read on page 29 in the Receiving chapter.

RECREATING GAME FLY BALLS AND GROUND BALLS

There is a balance in practicing. Remember the dry drills and the controlled reaction drills are excellent to work on technique and fundamentals and should be utilized often. Players also need some exposure to balls being hit at game speed and game distance. Spend time hitting fly balls and ground balls identical to what they might see in game conditions. It's just as important to place outfielders at their positions during live batting practice. This is, perhaps, a more accurate indicator of the balls players at that age level will see during game conditions.

Center fielder Calvin Murray on Defending Hitters:
"You have to watch how the hitter is attacking the pitcher to read swings. Pay close attention to foul balls pulled or hitters being late with their swings. After you have seen a hitter once, trust what you see and play accordingly. Of course if you have a dominant pitcher that throws really hard then you have to play hitters to be a little tardy on their swings."

Calvin Murray on Judging Fly Balls:
"You have to work really hard in batting practice. You must get used to seeing the ball in front of you. Always get behind the ball because it is easier to come in than it is to go back. Practicing during BP will give you a look at different heights and you will have different guys with different strengths hitting the ball. This will give you repetition and more knowledge on reading fly balls and will also help you with your jumps."

HITTING

Everybody's favorite activity in baseball is hitting. Players can't wait to hit in practice. You will hear more than once, "When are we going to hit?" The highlight of the game usually revolves around an at-bat and often players are judged by parents, coaches and themselves based on how they performed at the plate.

Many ingredients go into being a successful hitter. Some players are naturals, but most are a work in progress. Hitting takes dedication, hard work, confidence, proper swing mechanics, rhythm and timing.

Remember, hitting a pitched baseball is one of the hardest single feats to do in sports. It can be a painstaking skill to develop. As stated in the coaching philosophy section, "More success is obtained through praise than by criticism." That really rings true when developing hitters. If you can help the hitter create a good mental picture of themselves at the plate, it will go long way in helping them hit successfully.

Be patient, understanding and instill confidence in each hitter. Be positive with your hitters at all times. Negative thoughts can destroy a player's psyche and confidence. It takes years and years for players to fulfill their talents as hitters.

Proper swing fundamentals are something all hitters constantly strive to perfect. Once a swing can be repeated without much thought, a player can maintain all concentration on the pitched ball. Solid swing mechanics can be developed through a number of drills. Practicing correctly – whether that means dry swings, tee work, short toss or live hitting – is crucial. Quality repetitions are essential because muscle memory is being developed with every swing. In order to help players perform the correct fundamental swing, you should encourage them to hone their swing outside of team practices. Let them know what they need to improve on and give players drills they can work on at home.

Teaching hitting will be easier with a good understanding of swing fundamentals. Good swing fundamentals start and end with balance. Balance is a key to athletics and all skills on the baseball field. A hitter should maintain balance in the swing from start to finish to be most effective.

STANCE AND STRIDE POSITION

Players actually hit from their stride position, not their stance. The stride's purpose is to create separation between the upper body (including hands) from the lower body. This puts the hitter in the strongest position to strike the ball. We call this completed stride position the "Launch Position." Begin by getting your players into a comfortable, balanced athletic stance. Starting a hitter in a sound stance can make his transition into the launch position simpler and easier. This is why a proper stance is so important. Professional hitters have many different styles and stances, but they all transition into strong launch position no matter how they begin their stance. In reality all Major League hitters are unique in how the stand at the plate and begin their stride, but historically they all look very similar as the stride foot touches down and get to the Launch Position. Professional players have the athleticism and unique ability to get to the launch position from stance alignments that are not always simple. Encourage your players to develop a stance that will help them get the most out of their ability.

TIMING THE PITCH

This is really the first phase in hitting, the hitters trigger and stride, the second phase being the swing. Getting from the stance to the launch position—with rhythm and timed properly to the pitch—often is the difference between a good hitter and average one. Hitting is rhythm and timing, and if you do not have rhythm it will be more difficult to have good timing. Hitting involves a load (or trigger) which initiates the stride. A load is simply a move away from the pitcher before the hitter makes his move forward to swing. How effectively a hitter loads, strides and times his swings is unique to each individual. But, in general, the stride foot needs to be down before the ball is halfway to the plate. When a player triggers his stride depends upon his stride lift height and length. Good-hitters start their stride an instant before release. Starting earlier can give the hitter the time needed to get the front foot down so he can transfer into a firm front side on the swing. This is why teaching young players how to load and stride can be more difficult than teaching proper swing mechanics.

WEIGHT TRANSFER

From the launch position, the hitter makes his move toward the ball to swing. The first movement is a linear move toward the ball. Make sure you understand the "Transferring into the Ball" fundamental H. Often we see hitters spinning to hit by first pivoting on the back foot without returning their weight to center before they pivot and begin their swing rotation. By doing so, the bat is in and out of the hitting zone very quickly without the benefits of the weight transfer into the ball. The pivot can be a very helpful part of a young hitter's swing, but the accompanying weight transfer into the ball is often incorrect for optimal performance. Another common flaw seen with proper weight transfer into the ball is the opposite of spinning, which is lunging to hit. This is when hitters push off their back foot and their weight transfers forward too much onto the front side. Golfers should understand this delicate first move to the ball and weight transfer, because the golf swing starts forward with a very similar linear transfer. There is a fine line when transferring weight into the ball and, if done correctly it, can enhance the player's hitting ability.

SEEING THE BALL

No matter how good the swing fundamentals are, a player will not hit if he does not see the ball well. Teach your hitters about a pitcher's release point and tracking the ball to contact with the bat. It will be useful to teach them the technique of soft focus and fine focus, which will show them how to use their eyes to effectively recognize and track pitches. Keeping the head in position throughout the swing will be critical to making contact. As most of us have seen, pulling the head on a swing is a common problem with hitting. During at-bats, players should not think about mechanics. You cannot concentrate fully on a moving ball while also thinking about your stride, pivot or swing. Once the pitcher has taken the rubber to throw the pitch, all concentration and focus should be on seeing the ball. As players mature, their ability to recognize different pitches and velocity will improve. Helping your players use the eyes correctly and keeping their head on the ball will improve contact, even with some flaws in their swing fundamentals.

Expert Advice on Making Better Contact

The batter's head should be looking down at the ball and behind the barrel of the bat at contact. Remind your players to keep their head in this position at contact. Regardless of their swing, if they do not watch the ball to contact, there will be more swings and misses.

SWING THE BAT

Most good hitters have "aggressive patience," which means they are aggressive in their hitting zone but are able to lay off pitches out of their zone. Aggressive hitters anticipate every ball coming down the middle of the plate and they are ready to hit every pitch. A player's pitch recognition and plate discipline take time to develop and will improve with years of experience. Teach players to be aggressive when hitting; there has not been one great hitter who has developed by looking for a walk.

When you are at hitting, you are on offense. You should not be on the defensive. It's more difficult to hit if you posses a timid approach. The important point is for hitters to attack the ball and not let the ball attack them. Make contact out front and on the sweet spot of the bat.

BAT SELECTION

Monitor the bats your players use. The bat should be relative to the hitter's size and strength. If the bat is too long or heavy it can hinder performance. When choosing bats, players should find one they can swing comfortably. Bat speed produces power in a swing, not bat size. The bat should be a size the player can handle and control easily. This will promote better contact and bat speed. Often bats are purchased too big for the player with the thought they will be able to use it for a few years. If a bat is too long, encourage the player to choke up.

PRESSURE WHEN HITTING

Coaches and parents should keep in mind that many players experience anxiety during games, especially while at the plate. Anxiety can hinder focus and concentration, so it's a coach's job to decrease anxiety by finding a way to help players relax. Many times it is as simple as downplaying the expectation and alleviating the pressure to succeed. Fear of failure is a common reason many hitters experience anxiety. Players need to learn how to relax when on-deck and bring that relaxed, confident mentality into the batter's box. Taking a deap breath before stepping into the batters box can help control anxiety. It is much more difficult to hit when tense.

All-Star Rich Aurilia on Becoming a Good Hitter:
"The first, and probably the most important thing, is to be open to learning new things. Not all theories are going to work for each player. Each individual should take what he thinks can help him and work with that. It may not happen right away. That is why this game is so hard. Secondly, there is the area of balance. In our everyday lives we need good balance to function correctly. The same goes for hitting. Balance is the key."

FUNDAMENTALS

6-1: Grip

A. **Grip:** The bat is gripped in the calloused part of the hand, not in the palms. The grip is relaxed but firm. Grip the bat as if holding a bird. (If you squeeze too tight, you hurt the bird. If too loose, the bird will fly away.) The middle digits of the fingers are lined up, or the knuckles can be lined up as shown in the picture. Notice how the top hand's small knuckles are lined up between the bottom hand's big knuckles and small knuckles. This promotes better hand action. If the grip is within these areas, it is a sound grip. If it is not, it can hinder a player's bat speed and bat path to the ball. **(picture 6-1)**

B. **Stance and Set-up: Balance, Balance, Balance.** A simple set up with the body relaxed, comfortable and balanced is what you want to start with. Weight should be distributed evenly between the legs and on the balls of the feet with the feet at least shoulders' width apart. The knees are flexed and best positioned inside the feet. The weight is strong on the inside of the back leg. The feet and shoulders are squared to the pitcher, with the hips and shoulders relatively level. The hands are relaxed and start in a comfortable position somewhere near the back-ear helmet flap. The arms are flexed with the lead elbow never fully extended. The elbows are down, which must happen before the bat can have a proper path to the ball on the swing. The head is level and turned toward the pitcher with both eyes focused on the pitcher. The waist is slightly bent forward in a balanced athletic position. We call this the "Stance Position." A player should not stand frozen in the batter's box waiting for the pitcher to deliver the ball. Players who can find some rhythm in the legs and in their stance will benefit when starting their load and stride in hitting. **(pictures 6-2 & 6-3)**

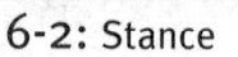
6-2: Stance

6-3: Stance (side view)

C. **Bat Position:** The bat should start somewhere around the back shoulder, in line with the back leg with the hands placed even with or slightly above the shoulder. The arms are relaxed and tension free with the elbows down. An easy reference point: Grip the bat correctly and rest it on the back shoulder. Lift the hands straight up and back to the back shoulder near ear height. **(pictures 6-4 & 6-5)**

6-4: Rest bat on shoulder

6-5: Lift hands up and back

D. **Loading (getting ready to hit):** A load is quite simply a slight movement away from the pitcher before the stride and the swing. The player is shifting some weight onto the back side settling inside and against the back leg. The hands pull back ever so slightly, getting the hands into a strong position to strike the ball. The load and stride work together. You may have heard the term separation, which is referring to separating the upper body from the lower body. In essence this is what we are doing to get into a strong launch position. Most hitters move instinctively as the ball is being pitched, but are not moving properly to enhance their swing. As the pitcher goes into the wind-up, a hitter must prepare to swing. All good hitters have some type of trigger or load which initiates the stride. This loading ideally should be a smooth movement that will bring rhythm into the swing. The body, weight and hands works together to set into your load and the stride. Subtle and controlled is better than mechanical and big movements. Successful hitters have rhythm and can time their load and stride to the pitcher. The load begins, by timing the arm of the pitcher sometime when the pitchers breaks his hands to throw and starts forward with his arm. Depending on the velocity of the pitcher, the load is started between these movements.
(pictures 6-6 & 6-7)

6-6: Stance

6-7: Load

E. The stride: There are a few different ways a hitter can stride. The most conventional stride is with a controlled short step forward. Distributing the weight properly while striding forward is important. If the player just steps straight out, often too much of his weight will follow—especially with young players. To avoid this we recommend the player adjust their stride. Instead of stepping out, pick up the foot slightly while tucking the knee in and back toward the back leg. The foot should not come high of the ground. That would make timing the stride and pitch more difficult. Keep the stride foot low to the ground on the movement. The stride foot is placed right back down a few inches forward from where it started, or in the same location. The hitter strides to balance. The distance will vary with the individual. The step is for balance, and to create separation of the hands and upper body from the lower body. The majority of the hitter's weight remains back as the hitter completes his stride. The weight that comes with the leg is minimal and distributed on the inside of the stride foot. The stride foot must be down before the hitter transfers the weight and hands forward to swing. Timing this properly is extremely important. The foot needs to be down before the ball is halfway to the hittter. The stride direction is straight forward at the pitcher and consistent on all pitches. The stride foot lands as squarely as it started. Remember, the stride foot must land before the swing starts forward so the hitter has something to hit against.

Expert Advice on Understanding a Load and Stride

One of the more difficult areas to teach is an effectively timed load and stride, which sets up the body into a strong launch position. Hitters who are termed "natural" usually posses a rhythmic type of load and can time their stride effectively, which means shifting their weight and hands back as the front leg strides forward.

E1. No-Stride Option: There are coaches teaching a no-stride hitting approach to promote more contact. This is effective but if taught without rhythm, load or separation, the result is going to be limiting and will not help the hitter develop to his potential. The no-stride approach recommended here can accomplish every aspect of a sound hitting approach, while simplifying the conventional load and stride. It also can be used throughout the player's baseball career, as many Major League players utilize this hitting technique.

6-8: Stance

Place the player in their stance, spreading their feet slightly farther apart to account for a no-stride approach **(picture 6-8)**. This is not extreme; just make sure the feet are wide enough to create leverage. In place of the load and stride, the player is going to push back and up onto the front leg's big toe. The hitter must push the front knee in and back as well **(pictures 6-9).** On this movement the hitter should not raise up. This movement pushes some weight back onto the back leg and initiates the upper body's movement for loading as well. The weight that is pushed back should never cause the back knee to travel past the back foot. Keep the weight toward the inside of the back leg like any normal load and stride. The front foot never leaves contact with the ground, and is pushed back into the ground as the player addresses the pitch to start their swing. This same thing happens on a check swing. Example: The hitter's weight returns to center, when the front foot is pushed back down and the hitter makes their move toward the ball to swing, but then stops because it is a bad pitch. **(picture 6-10)**

6-9: Push back and up on toe

6-10: Foot returns to ground on address of ball

Major league Hitting Coach Joe Lefebvre on When to Start Your Stride:
"In general, hitters get started as the pitcher cocks his arm up toward release. The hitter anticipating the ball to follow starts his hands back as he lifts his front foot up to stride, separating the hands from the front foot. When the front foot lands, the bat is back and ready to fire forward upon the planting of the front foot."

F. **Launch position:** Hitters hit from their launch position, not their stance. This is a position with absolute rules if you want your players hitting from their strongest position. The hitter's stride foot is down, as the stride has been completed. Hands are loaded at least as far back as the back foot when the pitcher's foot has landed and the pitch is being delivered. The hands are within shoulders' height or just above. The arms remained flexed, never fully extending the lead elbow. The hitter's hands should not drop and the bat should not be wrapped around the hitters' head pointing towards the pitcher. The weight that has moved back on the load should never cause the back knee to travel past the back foot. The weight is settled toward the inside of the back leg with the back hip inside the back foot. The hitter has remained balanced with eyes level and head still. This hitter is fully loaded and ready to explode forward, creating force into the baseball. **(picture 6-11)**

6-11: Launch position

G. **Addressing the Pitch:** Every hitter should learn to address each pitch as if it is coming down the middle. From the "Launch Position" the hitter addresses the pitch by starting their linear move toward the ball as if they are going to swing. During this movement the hitter's weight returns to the center of their body by transferring into and against the inside of the stride leg. Basically, it is practicing a check swing. The ball has been addressed consistently every time, with the hitter expecting to swing the bat. If players are taking pitches from the launch position, they are not expecting to swing at that pitch.
(pictures 6-12 & 6-13)

6-12: Loading to launch position

6-13: Addressing the pitch

6-14: Transfer into the ball and swing rotation

H. Transfer Into the Ball and Swing Rotation: The start of the swing is the hitter's weight from the back side transferring forward up against the inside of the lead leg. This returns the weight to center as he makes a move toward the ball to swing. This is the same as "Addressing the Pitch." The hands bring the weight but do not fire at the ball until the hitter has committed to swing. The back knee drives forward, initiating this linear move toward the ball. After the initial move forward to the ball, the hitter's transferring weight firms up against the front leg and begins the rotation of the hips and back foot. This happens fast. The hands, wrist and forearms control the action of the bat. The hands continue forward toward the ball as the hitter is into rotation, firing the hips and shoulder open as the hands continue forward to contact. During this rotation the hips should rotate in a level plane, with the back hip pushing the front hip open. The shoulders do the same with the back shoulder forcing the front shoulder to open. The back foot is pivoted forward on the ball of the foot and finishes pointing toward the pitcher to complete rotation. This rotation helps the speed of the swing and needs to be timed properly with the weight transfer into the ball. If done prematurely, the hitter opens too soon. If done late, the hitter is jammed. The pivot and the forward-and-down action of the hands should be explosive movements. This creates better bat speed. Once into the swing rotation there is no head movement. This all occurs with the player maintaining his balance. **(picture 6-14)**

6-15: Hands continue toward the ball

I. Bat path: The bat should move forward and down, from the launch position to the leveling-off area in the contact zone. This is the quickest and most direct line to the ball. Envision a straight line from the bat head to the ball. The bat head and the hands should not drop between launch position and swing rotation. Keep the hands above the path off the ball. The hands' path is not down and forward or out and forward but forward and down to level. If the hands move out first this is referred to as casting the bat and it will slow down the swing and be weaker at contact. Swinging out first leaves players vulnerable to the fast inside pitch. Dropping of the hands is common as well, and breaks our first rule of keeping the hands above the path of the ball. These swings result in upper-cuts or players only being able to handle the low pitches because the barrel is dropped into the flight of the pitch. To fix these common flaws, keep the hands' path forward inside the line of the ball, as is explained in the drill "Hands Inside the Ball.'' **(picture 6-15)**

Silver Slugger Award Recipient Rich Aurilia on Swing Plane:
"One of the keys to a good swing is to keep the bat in the hitting zone for as long as possible. In other words, try to have a nice, level swing. Not all players are built to hit home runs. A whole bunch of line drives with a level swing will do just fine."

J. **Contact point:** The hands, wrist and forearms control the action of the bat. The head should be down and behind the barrel of the bat during contact, with the head still and eyes focused on the ball. Head position in reference to the body is in the middle of the back leg. This ensures that weight has not shifted forward too much. Often, the head position is not in a sound position at contact. Often, the head is turned prematurely with the swing or early rotation of the hips. As contact is being made, the back foot should be into its rotational pivot position. At contact, the hands are near a palm-up and palm-down position, with arms slightly bent. The ball should be struck somewhere in line to with or in front of the stride leg depending on the location of the pitch. The ball is caught out front more on an inside pitch, and is hit deeper toward the body on an outside pitch. **(picture 6-16)**

6-16: Contact point

K. **Finish:** Once the ball is struck, the bat head continues forward through the ball. This allows the hitter to properly extend. The wrists are rolled after full extension, as the bat head comes up to the follow-through position. The top hand rotates or folds over the bottom hand after contact. The head remains still and the eyes stay focused on the hitting area until the ball leaves the bat. Maintain two hands on the bat to ensure hitting through the ball. The bat should continue through the ball in the direction the ball is intended to go. The back foot has completed its pivot rotation with the toe facing the pitcher on most pitch locations. Hitters should maintain balance and control from the beginning of the swing to the completion. If players start balanced remain on the balls of their feet as they execute the swing they should end with balance. In general, if this is accomplished, many proper fundamentals are being touched throughout the swing. **(pictures 6-17 & 6-18)**

6-17: Hands are released

6-18: Finish with balance

HITTING SEQUENCE

Stance

Load and stride

Address the pitch

Swing rotation at contact point

Hitting through the ball

Finish with balance

HITTING PLAN FOR SUCCESS

Know Your Hitting Zone

As players develop their swing over the years, they will eventually know where they hit the ball the best. They may be a low-ball hitter or a high-ball hitter. They may best hit the ball in the middle-to-away portion of the plate. Or maybe they are best at hitting the ball when it is in the middle-to-inside portion of the plate. The best approach is to expect the ball down the middle of the plate. Any pitch that is in the center or two-thirds middle of the plate is a pitch you want to swing at. The hitter's hands and timing have easy adjustments from this approach if the ball is slightly inside or slightly outside. These are the easiest pitches to hit consistently. This will also give the hitter an aggressive mentality. The worst thing you can do as a hitter is take three strikes without lifting the bat off your shoulder. That gives you no chance for a hit. The second worst thing you can do is take strikes that are in the middle of the plate, leaving yourself one swing to hit a pitcher's pitch. You hear coaches talking about zoning a pitch. That means swinging if the pitch is in a specific location. That takes time to develop because young hitters are still developing their pitch recognition. Well, youth league hitters who are trying to develop their zone, down the middle should be their zone. Any pitch that is on the corners should be a more difficult pitch to hit. So those are the pitches that are out of your "zone." Your "hitting zone" is the middle two-thirds of the plate.

Expert Advice on Your Hitting Approach

The worst thing you can do as a hitter is go to home plate and take three strikes without lifting the bat off your shoulder. Attempt to hit the ball back up the middle with a line drive or a hard ground ball.

Hitting The Ball Back Up The Middle

What is your hitting approach? Even at a young age, hitters should have a plan for where they want to hit the ball. Ideally, we want to hit the ball where it is thrown on the plate. Inside pitch, we pull. A ball down the middle, we hit back up the middle. An outside pitch, we hit to the opposite field. This is a well known fact but not an easy feat to accomplish, especially for most hitters under 12 years of age. Hitting the ball where it's pitched takes years for hitters to accomplish, and very few hitters perfect this approach. But, there is one approach that all hitters should strive to perfect before they are ready or able to hit the ball consistently where it is pitched. That approach is to hit the ball back up the middle. Doing so will help the hitter's alignments, balance and swing path to the ball. It goes hand in hand with where we want the baseball. In general, hitters who constantly pull are very susceptible to the pitch away, and hitters who only hit the ball to the opposite field are susceptible to the inside pitch.

As well as trying to hit the ball back up the middle, all hitters should attempt to hit line drives and hard ground balls. It is well documented that line drives give you the best chance for a hit, followed by hard ground balls and then fly balls.

Batter's Thought Process

A hitter's mentality should be hit, hit, hit not take, take, take. Anticipate every pitch to be a strike and be prepared to swing at every pitch. Learn to stop on pitches outside the strike zone. That way, a hitter is always prepared to swing the bat. Expect to hit that first pitch in your zone. Taking a strike in your zone just to do so will only put the hitter in the hole. Prepare to swing, and address the pitched ball. If it's a bad pitch, take it. A good hitter should maintain an aggressive approach, especially when ahead in the count 2-0 or 3-1. This is the time the hitter has an advantage because the pitcher needs to throw a strike. Expect to hit those pitches in your zone and don't look for a walk.

Major League Hitting Coach Joe Lefebvre on Better Strike Zone Discipline:
"Go to your zone up until two strikes. Not the strike zone, your zone, which is where you make the most consistently hard contact. No matter where you see the ball in space go to your zone first then react off of it."
The best hitters "hit to take." They start their swing mentally by anticipating their pitch in their zone on every pitch while addressing the ball physically with their weight shift and their hands stopping their swing on balls."

Watch The Opposing Pitcher

This is where players first prepare to hit. They need to watch the opposing pitcher as much as possible. Watch him warm up before the game in the bullpen. Watch his warm-up pitches before each inning. Ideally, hitters should attempt to watch every pitch in the game. At the very least, the on-deck batter should be observing the pitcher's release point. Also recognizing the pitchers speed, control and what types of pitchers are being thrown. Figure out what pitches are being thrown for strikes and decide on a plan against that particular pitcher.

On-Deck Preparation

This is where a hitter gets prepared both mentally and physically. Once on deck, focused concentration begins. The player must believe he can hit the pitcher and look forward to getting into the batter's box. Make sure the muscles are warm and ready to swing the bat. Take some swings on deck as if they were actually facing the pitcher. After the hitter feels ready physically, players should concentrate on timing the pitcher's fastball. Work on timing the load and stride to the delivery of the pitch. Find your rhythm versus that pitcher to create timing. If there is not an on-deck circle, the same preparation can be done without a bat near the dugout. Leave the on-deck circle confident, relaxed and be prepared to hit the first pitch.

San Francisco Giant Rich Aurilia on Mental Preparation:
"The moment right before I get into the batter's box is a very important time for me. I try to envision the situation I will be in and try to come up with a way to either get on base, move a runner over, drive in a run from third, and a number of other things. This is the time to prepare for your at bat. I also try to remember how the pitcher on the mound pitched me in the previous at bats. Odds are if a pitcher has had a certain way with you, he will continue that way until you beat him."

At The Plate

Before stepping into the box, most hitters develop some type of routine that mentally finalizes their preparation. Taking a deep breath can help relax the muscles and help decrease anxiety, which can hinder concentration and focus. Anxiety is something many players feel while hitting, especially players who have a difficult time hitting, and may stem from fear of failure. So, at this point, do not yell instruction to your hitters. Encouragement and praise will help them more and also let them concentrate on the ball during their at-bat.

Grip the bat correctly, take a deep breath and step into to box. Plant your back foot in a level area of the batter's box. The back foot is the foundation of your legs while hitting. After the back foot is positioned firmly, step in with the lead leg in proper alignment. Do not go into your stance position too soon because this will cause you to stand for a long period and the arms and body will get tense. The muscles will not fire as quickly when you are tense. Stay loose and stand relaxed, with feet planted. If the pitcher is not ready to throw, keep some movement with the hands and bat or body and legs until the pitcher begins the windup or takes his sign reading to come into the set position. Then get into your stance unrushed and in time to load, stride and time the pitch. Hitters have many routines from this point on. Do I step out of box after every pitch or do I stay in the box? Once that back foot has its toehold, we recommend keeping it there after a pitched ball, even if that means turning for a sign by moving the lead leg out of the box. This will help you maintain your eye for the strike zone and stay focused on tracking the baseball. A good time to step out of the box is when you need to regroup. That might be after a poor swing or when you feel you need to take a deep breath and start over again.

Tracking The Ball

Once a hitter is in the batter's box, all thoughts about fundamental positions should take a back seat to focus and concentration on the baseball. The longer a hitter watches the ball, the better chance he has to hit it. A hitter should focus on the pitcher's release point to pick up the pitch. The release point is where the ball leaves the pitcher's hand. Do not take this for granted. Release points can vary. Some pitchers throw from over the top, others three-quarters while others throw side-armed. While the pitcher is in the stretch or starting his delivery, the hitter should start with a soft focus (looking in a general area) of the pitcher's chest area. When the pitcher breaks his hands to throw, the eyes shift to a fine focus (looking at a specific point) of the release point to pick up the ball. Make sure the players understand what a release point is and when and how to focus on it. From there, track the ball all the way while maintaining concentration on the ball until contact is made.

Joe Lefebvre on Using the Eyes Correctly:

"Visually, as the pitcher is getting ready to start his delivery, the hitter has a resting spot for his eyes on the pitcher's upper body, close to release point. As the pitcher cocks his arm upward toward release, the hitter anticipating the ball switches from the resting spot on the pitcher's body to his release point to view the incoming pitch."

As Hall of Famer Ted Williams wrote in his landmark book, "The Science of Hitting":

1. "Hit only strikes."
2. "Never swing at a ball you're fooled on or have trouble hitting."
3. "After 2 strikes, concede the long ball to the pitcher."

Adjusting In The Batter's Box

The distance from the plate and the depth within the box should be consistent per at-bat. Adjustments should be made at times depending on the speed and type of the pitcher. The hitter's initial stance should be close enough to home plate to allow total plate coverage when the hitter strides. Many young hitters do not address the plate close enough to cover the outside corner properly. Sometimes, it is a fear issue and sometimes they are just a little more comfortable away from the plate. How deep a hitter stands in the box can be determined by the pitcher. A normal depth position is where the front foot is in line with the front to middle of the plate. When a pitcher is throwing extremely hard, and the hitter is late on his swing from the normal depth position, he should move to the back of the box to allow more reaction time. Other adjustments a hitter can make versus a hard-thrower is to choke up on the bat or to start their load and stride earlier. When a pitcher isn't throwing hard and the hitter is having a difficult time waiting on the pitch, he should move up in the batter's box. **(pictures 6-19 to 6-21)**

6-19: Normal depth

6-20: Hard thrower

6-21: Soft thrower

Choking Up On The Bat

Choking up on the bat will make the bat head easier to control and lighten the bat on the swing. It can improve the bat speed as well. Choking up allows the hitter to wait longer before committing to the swing, which means he can watch the flight of the ball longer. Choking up is commonly used by players at all levels when hitters want to shorten their swings and put the ball in play. This is used most often when hitters get two strikes on them, and is referred to as a two-strike approach. When players swing and miss often, have them choke up and see if the results improve.

6-22

Even players who have purchased their own bat may need to choke up. Often, new bats are purchased with the thought the player will have the bat for a few years. Sometimes the bat is actually too long or heavy for the player when it is new. With this in mind, check the bats being used to help determine if the bat size is contributing to the player's lack of bat speed or success. **(picture 6-22)**

Two-Strike Approach

The two-strike approach is a philosophy and an adjustment the hitter makes when he gets two strikes on him. Whether it's 0-2 or 2-2, the hitter's swing zone now moves from "his hitting zone" to the total strike zone, along with not letting the umpire decide the at-bat with a called strike three. So the first adjustment made by the hitter is to swing at any pitch that may be called a strike. The second recommendation is to choke up for more bat control. The last slight adjustment is to move slightly closer to the plate because choking up might limit bat coverage on the outside corner of the plate.

DRY HITTING DRILLS

The dry drills can be done together as a team, in smaller groups or with an individual. They can be utilized for specific areas your players need corrections with. Perform these drills in sequence for an overall proper mental picture and understanding of the swing. These drills will allow the player to feel the proper positions needed for a successful hitter. While performing the dry drills, players can put their fielding gloves down to represent home plate. The drills are recommended for ages 6-16, but ages 6-12 will need them more.

1. **Stance:** With hands on hips, hitters get into their stance displaying the correct "Stance Position." Go around and lightly push players to see if they are balanced and have the weight distributed properly on the insides of the legs and on the balls of the feet. They should have a sturdy foundation and should not fall off balance on your push. Once stances are corrected, coach says *relax* and players relax. On verbal command, *stance position,* players repeat this position. **Repeat 5 times or until all players stances look good. (picture 6-23)**

6-23: Stance position

2. **Stride:** With hands on hips, on coach's verbal command, *stride*, players stride straight forward to a balanced position. The distance is unique to each individual. The stride foot lands closed as it started. Minimal weight transfers with the step and is distributed on the inside of the stride leg. The majority of the weight is back with the back hip inside the back foot. The head should be steady and still. Players hold stride position for coach's critique. **Repeat 5 times or until players are performing stride correctly. This drill can be performed with the "No-Stride Option" as well. (picture 6-24)**

6-24: Stride

3. **Pivot:** Players begin this drill in the post-stride position with their hands on their hips. On coach's verbal command, *pivot*, players transfer their weight forward up against their lead leg while pivoting on the ball of their back foot. In essence, you want players to drive their back hip forward and open their belly button to the pitcher. The back foot's toe should be facing the pitcher while head and shoulders remain behind the lead knee. Players hold pivot position for coach's critique. **Repeat 5 times or until players are performing pivot correctly. (picture 6-25)**

6-25: Pivot

4. **Stride and Pivot:** Players begin in their stance position with their hands on their hips. Now combine the two above drills. On coach's verbal command, *stride*, players stride. Once the stride foot is down, coach yells, *pivot*, and players fire their hips forward and open while pivoting the back foot correctly. The pivot should be explosive with players maintaining balance on the balls of the feet, as coach checks for proper positions. **Repeat 5 times or until players are performing stride and pivot correctly.**
5. **Load and Stride:** Once the players understand how the legs and feet work, it is time to bring in the load. Starting in their batting stance, on coach's verbal command, *load and stride*, players make their slight movement back, shifting some weight onto the back side and getting the hands into a strong position to strike the ball as they stride straight to a balanced position. Players hold stride position for coach's critique. **Repeat 5 times or until players are performing the load and stride correctly. (picture 6-24)**
6. **Forward and Down to Level:** Start players in their batting stance. On coach's verbal command, *swing*, players go through their load, stride, swing and pivot. Coach watches for correct swing path of hands moving forward and down then finishing all the way around near their back shoulder. Encourage players to keep two hands on the bat to completion of the swing. **Repeat 5 times or until players are performing the swing path correctly and hands are completing their finish. (pictures 6-26 to 6-28)**

6-26: Stance

6-27: Forward and down to level

6-28: Finish with balance

7. **Shoulder to shoulder:** Start players in their batting stance. Focus on a proper head position with two eyes on the pitcher with head and eyes level. Player takes a full swing, keeping the head still and focused on the contact area as the shoulders rotate around the head until the back shoulder is near the chin. This drill focuses on keeping your head in position when hitting. **Too often players' heads move around their body with their swings, taking their eyes off the ball.**
8. **Balance:** We finish up the dry drills with the coach simulating a pitcher throwing an imaginary pitch to the hitters. With the coach out in front, all hitters start in their stance, aligning as if the coach is the pitcher. The coach goes through a windup and simulates the throw. Players begin their load and stride as the pitcher cocks the arm back. Once the coach's arm extends forward to release the imaginary ball, each hitter's stride foot is down and the hitter takes a full swing to completion at game speed. Once the swing is completed, the player is to hold their finish position for 5 seconds. You can also go around and push them lightly to see if they can hold their balance against you. If players are not balanced, that means they aren't using their feet correctly and need to stay on the balls of their feet. Players should be able to hold and maintain their balance after they complete their swing in this drill. **Repeat until players can maintain their balance for 5 seconds.**

THE BATTING TEE

The batting tee is not just a tool for T-ball players. It is a very effective non-reaction drill for swing mechanics. Because the ball is stationary, it gives the player a better chance to repeat a good swing consistently. It will allow players an opportunity to work on hitting by themselves and should be utilized at home as well as during practice. For advanced players, it's a good place to work on hitting different pitch locations, as you can easily adjust to the tee to make a pitch an inside or outside location. Not only will it help the player, it is an easier place for a coach to analyze a swing. To improve your hitting stations at practice, ask your players to bring their batting tees to practice. Now you can have more players active at once.

Use the tee to work to improve any fundamental position. Have the player swing and focus on correcting one fundamental at a time. In our progression of teaching, dry drills are the easiest to perform correctly, followed by hitting off a tee, soft toss, then live batting practice. Use the tee to give players more repetitions of a fundamentally sound swing so they can build the muscle memory for sound swing mechanics.

A. **Basic Tee Position. Position the hitter in his stance.** The tee's stem height should be between the hitter's mid-thigh and waist. The hitter is positioned behind the tee where the lead foot is just behind the stem of the tee. The ball is placed on the stem out in front of the body. To determine how close a player should stand to the tee, simulate a swing stopping at contact point. Remember, the hands are not fully extended at contact, and the ball should be struck on the sweet spot of the barrel. This will determine the correct distance from the hitting tee. Position the tee accordingly **(pictures 6-29 & 6-30). After each swing allow time for players to get their feet and stance set in the correct position.**

6-29: Tee out

6-30: Simulate a swing

DRILLS

1. **Line Drive Drill:** Position the batter to the tee so the ball simulates a pitch down the middle. Player attempts to hit balls directly forward into the net at the same height as the tee stem. Player repeats swings to see how many line drives he can hit in a row. This drill will develop a swing for a line drive right back up the middle.

   Recommended for ages 6-16.

2. **Forward and Down to Level:** Place two tees together in a straight line roughly 12 to 18 inches apart. Have both stems at the same height. Place the ball on the forward tee stem. The hitter attempts to strike the ball without hitting the back tee. If the player hits the back tee, the swing plane has a slight uppercut, which is very common. This drill can be done another way if two tees are not available. Place a bucket behind the tee stem with a small construction cone on top of the bucket. Place the tee stem in front at the same height as the cone. Place the ball on the tee in front of the bucket approximately 12 to 18 inches away from the top of the cone. **This drill will promote a forward and down swing, which is the quickest and most direct line to the ball. (pictures 6-30 & 6-31)**

   Recommended for ages 6-16.

6-30

6-31

3. **Inside Pitch:** Place the hitter at the tee as if the ball is coming down the middle **(picture 6-32)**. Now have the player move the tee to the inside corner by placing the tee more toward the pitcher and putting it in line with the inside corner **(picture 6-33).** The size of the player will determine how far in front they move the batting tee. Moving the ball farther out front simulates where an inside pitch must be struck. The player works on hitting the ball by striding the same as if the pitch was down the middle. The swing path to the ball must now bring the hands in closer along the body more to get the sweet spot of the bat on the ball. **The adjustment to hit the inside pitch is made by the hands and by hitting the ball out in front of the hitting zone more than on a pitch down the middle.**

   Recommended ages 11-16.

6-32: Down the middle

6-33: Inside pitch

4. **Outside Pitch:** Place the hitter at the tee as if the ball is coming down the middle. Now have the player move the tee to the outside corner by placing the tee back on home plate more and in line with the outside corner **(picture 6-34)**. The size of the player will determine how far back they place the tee. But remember the ball is still struck off the front leg, not behind it. By moving the batting tee deeper back, this will position the ball as if it is an outside pitch. The player works on hitting the ball with the same stride as if the pitch was down the middle. But now the ball is deeper in the hitting zone and that is where the outside pitch is hit. The hitter should finish with this weight more over the plate opposed to falling off away from the plate. As he is attempting to drive through the ball in the direction he is hitting it. **The adjustment to hit the outside pitch is made by waiting longer on the pitch and hitting the ball deeper in the zone, the opposite of hitting the inside pitch.**

   Recommended ages 11-16.

6-34: Outside pitch

Rich Aurilia on Practicing Off the Tee and Taking Soft Toss:
"Being at the Major League level now, I still think some of the most important work I do takes place hitting off a tee or taking some soft toss. I like these drills because they slow things down. You don't have to worry about the pitch coming toward you at a decent speed. You can just work at your own pace and break your swing down step by step."

SOFT TOSS

Soft toss is one of the best drills available to players at any level, from Little League to the Major Leagues. This controlled reaction drill has numerous benefits. It allows players to work on swing mechanics but also brings in timing and tracking a moving baseball. It has all the elements of live batting practice but in an environment where a player should be able to repeat their swing much easier. Similar to the batting tee, soft toss is an easier place for a coach to analyze a player's swing. Players will have an easier time making adjustments in their swing in a soft-toss drill than they will during live batting practice. This is a great drill to use daily and should serve as a substitute when live batting practice is not available. Not much space is needed to set up the drill and hitters will be able to get many repetitions in a short period of time. When a hitting net is not available, use wiffle balls to hit into a fence or into the open field. Be careful when working with young players or any player who does not control the bat effectively. In those cases, we recommend you toss from behind a screen.

Two concepts that should be explained to the hitter during soft toss are "loading" and "tracking the ball to contact." As stated below in "setting up soft toss," the coach should show the player the ball, then start the toss with a deliberate arm movement back and then forward to release of the ball. This is when a player should focus to track the ball and time the arm movement to start loading accordingly. Loading, which initiates a hitter's stride, is done before the ball is released. This is identical to how players should time a pitcher in batting practice and in a game. Soft toss is an excellent drill to work on load and stride development. Soft toss can also be used to work on any fundamental position a player needs to improve upon. Remember to work on only one area for improvement at a time.

Hitting Coach Joe Lefebvre on Grip:
"A proper grip drops both elbows down while setting the bat between the head and back shoulder, with the barrel up. The shoulders are more relaxed allowing the batter to be more tension free."

Setting Up Soft Toss

A. The player positions himself 7 to 8 feet from the hitting net and at a 45-degree angle from the coach tossing ball.

B. The coach takes a knee or sits on a bucket and tosses the ball one-handed at the player's belt buckle for a pitch down the middle. The coach tosses the ball at the player's front hip for an inside pitch and the back leg for an outside pitch. **(Caution: Do not work on the outside pitch with a hard ball unless the tosser is behind a net because the ball could be hit near him.)**

C. **The toss should be made as follows**: Show the hitter the ball, then in a deliberate manner start the arm back and then forward to the release. The ball should be tossed smoothly on a straight plane, where the hitter has time to react. This is a standard toss. **(pictures 6-35 & 6-36)**

6-35: Show ball then move arm back

6-36: Arm comes forward

DRILLS

1. **Line Drive Drill:** Toss balls at the player's belt buckle to simulate a pitch down the middle. Player attempts to hit the ball on a line into the middle of the net. See how many pitches the batter can hit on a line. Keep the tosses standard and consistent. This drill will develop a swing for a line drive back up the middle. **This drill should be used the majority of the time until players can repeat a fundamentally sound swing consistently.**

   Recommended ages 8-16.

2. **Fake Toss Drill:** While performing the Line Drive Drill fake a toss every third or fifth pitch. The hitter should maintain balance with the majority of the weight back. If the hitter's weight transfers more than against the lead leg and onto the front leg, he is shifting too much weight forward and is most likely geared for one speed pitch, the fastball. The hitter should load and stride but read the pitch, swing or take the pitch against his front side. This lunging to hit happens frequently with live batting practice or in games when a slower pitch is thrown and the hitter can not keep weight back and ends up on the front side. **This drill will teach players to read the pitch before committing to the ball and how to take a pitch properly.**

   Recommended ages 10-16.

FAVORITE DRILL

Expert Advice on the Line Drive Game

This drill will develop a swing for a line drive back up the middle. Work on this drill every day when soft tossing. This drill should be used the majority of the time until players can repeat a fundamentally sound swing consistently.

3. **Change of Speed Drill:** After players have been able to understand and perform correctly the Fake Toss Drill, this drill will help batters hit pitches of different speeds. While performing the Line Drive Drill, change the toss speed at times. Every three or four tosses, mix in a slower toss. Mix in back-to-back slower tosses. Do not use faster tosses while in close proximity to the hitter because they will not have time to react. Keep the majority of tosses at the standard speed. The desired result for the hitter is to load properly and stride to hit but also be able to wait on the speed of the pitch before committing the hands and going into swing rotation. **This is what hitters need to do when hitting a changeup or a curveball. This drill will help hitters learn how to hit off-speed pitches.**
   Recommended ages 10-16.
4. **Location Drill:** In this drill, start off by throwing 5 pitches down the middle. Then toss 5 pitches on the outside corner and remind players to wait and watch the ball longer on the outside pitch. Lastly, toss 5 pitches on the inside and remind players to get their hand through the hitting zone quicker and hit the ball out in front of them more. On the inside pitch, the hitter should also fire his hips open with a good quick pivot when recognizing the ball coming to the inside part of the hitting zone. The next step to this drill should only be done when players can hit the pitch where it's pitched after being told first. The next step is toss balls to different locations at random without letting the hitter know. Remember, the coach needs to have a screen in front of him when tossing to the outside part of the hitting zone. **This drill reinforces the proper approach to hitting inside and outside pitches. It gives the hitters a chance to work on it with a moving ball. It is very difficult to accomplish this during live batting practice.**
   Recommended ages 10-16.

FAVORITE DRILL

Expert Advice on the Stride for Different Pitch Locations

A hitter's stride lands in the same spot.
The hands adjust to the pitch inside and outside, not the stride. Hitters should go to their zone where they like and want the ball. Recognize the pitch location and time it accordingly.
The hands will adjust.

SHORT TOSS

This drill can only be done with a screen, which the coach throws behind. It is very similar to Soft Toss, except the toss comes from directly in front of the hitter, just as a live pitch does. The protective screen is moved in about two-thirds of the way to the plate. The coach can continue to toss underhand on a line the same as in Soft Toss, or he can use an overhand toss for older players. More room is needed to run this drill because the balls are hit into a field and not into a net or fence. Both hard balls and wiffle balls can be used. This drill is very productive because the tosses are coming in at the same angle as a real pitch and the pitcher can control and locate his pitches easier. The pitcher will be able to throw more pitches before fatigue sets in, and the hitters will get more quality repetitions. **Recommended ages 6-16.**

SHORT TOSS FOR SPEED

This drill is set up the same as Short Toss above but, it is carried out differently for a different purpose. The protective screen is about two-thirds of the way to the plate from the mound. Hard baseballs are thrown at a very fast speed to the hitter. The drill's purpose is to show players they must start their load and get their stride foot down early or the will have no chance of hitting the ball out front. **Executing this drill will help players time fast pitchers properly and help players feel the importance of getting ready to hit and getting the foot down before you swing the bat. Recommended ages 10-16.**

DRILLS

Short Toss Drills: All the same drills should be used as Soft Toss. Just like Soft Toss, the Line Drive Drill should be utilized the majority of the time until players can repeat a fundamentally sound swing consistently.

PITCHING MACHINE HITTING

When using pitching machines in practice or in games, remember these points. It is much more difficult to time the machine's pitch because there is no arm action from which the hitter can time their load and stride. To help the player time the pitch, hold the ball up for the player to see then insert the ball into the machine with a consistent tempo. Also, place a four-seam grip into the machine; how the seams hit the machine can affect the pitches movement and consistency.

BATTING PRACTICE FROM COACH

Regardless of the player's skill level and mechanics, every player needs to participate in batting practice thrown by the coach. This is when players need to focus on seeing the ball, timing the pitch, learning the strike zone and being aggressive in the strike zone. It is much more difficult and confusing for the player to work on both mechanics and timing issues during live hitting. Do not teach too much about mechanics at this time; there are plenty of other drills for that. Live batting practice allows the players to track the ball and time the pitch. No matter how good a player's mechanics are, if he doesn't train his eyes to watch the baseball and learn the strike zone, he will not make consistent contact. **(picture 6-37)**

6-37

Former San Francisco Giants Hitting Coach Joe Lefebvre on Batting Practice:
"The purpose of batting practice is about developing your hitting stroke and seeing how many balls you can hit on the barrel on a line with out lifting it. Focus on a gap-to-gap approach and hitting hard ground balls and line drives at the infield/outfield dirt line. If you miss, miss down not up. Remember home run derby at batting practice speed most of the time becomes a foul ball, pop up, or a swing and a miss at game speed."

BATTING PRACTICE AGAINST LIVE PITCHERS

One of a young hitter's biggest fears can be getting hit by a pitch. At the same time, young pitchers also fear hitting the batter. This is why it is a good idea to let hitters face live pitching in pre-season practices and at times throughout the season. It helps both the batter and pitcher get more comfortable with game action. In addition, it helps hitters learn the strike zone and gives them more experience competing against their peers. This should definitely be done at least a couple of times before the first game.

Major League Veteran Rich Aurilia on Taking Batting Practice:
"When taking batting practice, I try to work on things that I feel I am not doing too well at that particular time. The important thing is to take your practice seriously. If you take a careless batting practice, you most likely carry it over into the game."

ADDITIONAL HITTING DRILLS

1. **Grip Drill:** Grab the bat loosely in both hands. Lift the bat directly in front of the body and slightly over the head. With fingers relaxed but firm, hold onto the bat and throw bat and arms straight down in front of the body. Do not let the bat hit the ground. Where the bat ends up in the hands is a proper grip on the bat when hitting. **This drill shows players where the bat is gripped in the hands.**

   Recommended ages 8-16.

2. **Stride and Pivot Drill:** The player gets into a solid stance position with a bat behind his back as shown in the photo **(picture 6-38)**. The player works on striding and pivoting while the bat is in this position. **This drill is very effective in getting players to feel the proper use of the legs during the stride and pivot, by isolating the lower body. Remind players to fire the back hip through while pivoting on the ball of the back foot. (picture 6-39)**

   Recommended ages 8-16.

6-38: Set up

6-39: Stride and pivot

3. **Shadow Swinging with Eyes Closed:** Get the player into his stance with a bat in his hands facing the coach (acting as the pitcher). On coach's verbal command, *eyes*, player shuts his eyes. On command, *swing*, player takes a full swing with his eyes closed. At the completion of the swing the hitter should hold his finish position for 3 seconds. **Excellent drill to teach the hitter balance throughout the swing. The hitter will have to use his feet properly to maintain balance.**
   Recommended ages 10-16.
4. **Top-Hand Swing:** This drill can be done off a batting tee or in soft toss. Our preference is to utilize the drill during soft toss. Give the player an extremely small bat for his size. The hitter chokes up on the bat so he can easily control the bat with one arm. Player starts in his normal stance with two hands on the bat. Remove the bottom hand and let it hang naturally down to the side. Soft toss balls to the hitter. Hitter attempts to hit line drives and ground balls with the top hand only. To do this well, the hitter should time the pitch and go back with his hand some before he swings forward. Basically loading with one hand. This will give the hitter some momentum to help swing the bat. It will be very difficult to swing from a dead stop. **This drill teaches players to time the pitch with a load with the hands, and helps the player feel the proper path for the top hand. (pictures 6-40 to 6-43)**
   Recommended ages 10-16.

6-40: Stance

6-41: Load and stride

6-42: Swing

6-43: Finish

5. **Bottom-Hand Swing:** Follow the same set up and procedure for the Top-Hand Swing. **This drill has the same benefits as the previous drill except now they are for the bottom hand. (pictures 6-44 to 6-47)**
   Recommended ages 10-16.

6-44: Stance

6-45: Load and stride

6-46: Swing

6-47: Finish

6. **Hands Inside The Ball Drill:** Position a hitter in his stance, facing a fence or net. Player places the knob of his bat to his belly button and the end of the bat so it is just touching the fence. Player then gets into his hitting stance at this distance away from the fence. Still facing the fence, the hitter picks a spot on the fence at waist level and even with his front leg. This spot is the hitter's imaginary reference point for a pitched ball. The player swings at the spot on the fence without hitting the fence. To swing properly, the hitter's hands must go forward and down, keeping the hands and bat head inside the fence. A poor swing is made when the player hits the fence on the swing. **This drill forces the player to use the proper swing path to the ball. (pictures 6-48 to 6-50)**

   Recommended ages 12-16.

6-48: Setup

6-49: Hands inside and forward

6-50: Hands outside the line

HITTING GAMES

1. **Line Drive Game:** This game can be played during Soft Toss or Batting Practice. The player is told to hit line drives and ground balls or he will lose his turn at bat. The player hits until he hits a fly ball, pop up or swings and misses. When he does, the next hitter takes his turn. Set a limit for the maximum number of swings in one round so your good hitters do not stay at bat all day. This drill forces the hitter to concentrate on hitting the ball on a line, which is a swing plane all hitters should develop. **It is a good drill for players who uppercut and hit a lot of fly balls.**

   Recommended ages 8-16.

2. **Contact Game:** During batting practice the hitter is told he can stay at bat as long as he does not swing and miss or foul a ball off. You may want to set a maximum number of swings per round to make sure everyone gets a turn at bat. This is a fun game to help players concentrate on seeing the ball. **The game adds the same pressure hitters feel when they have 2 strikes on them, but makes it even tougher since they cannot even foul a ball off.**

   Recommended ages 8-16.

Expert Advice on the Line Drive Game

The Line Drive Game will help players to stay on top of the baseball. This is a fun and effective way to help develop the hitters' proper swing plane.

3. **Situation Hitting Game:** During batting practice the coach calls out four different situations for the hitter to execute. The hitter gets an added free swing for every situation he executes correctly. The four situations are: sacrifice bunt (batter must get the bunt down on that pitch), Hit-and-Run play (player must hit a ground ball on that pitch), move the runner to third (player is to hit a ground ball to the right side of second base) and man on third with the infield in and less than 2 outs (the hitter must hit a fly ball to the outfield.) **This game teaches players how to execute when these situations arise in the game. Also, it's a very good routine to use for players during their second round of batting practice.**

   Recommended ages 12-16.

4. **Base-Hit Game:** During batting practice, make the hitter's last swing in each round a base-hit swing. This means the hitter gets to stay up at bat for another swing if he gets a base hit. The coach throwing BP is the judge. If it is ruled a hit, the player gets another base-hit swing and keeps hitting until he does not hit a ball ruled to be a hit. **This is a fun drill for players to compete with one another to see who can stay up the longest.**

   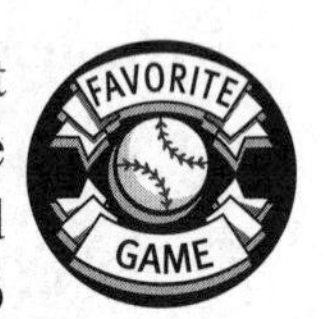

   Recommended ages 10-16.

5. **Focus Game:** Coach stands in front of players in a position where all players can see him. The coach extends his left arm palm-up straight out in front of his body. He then extends his right arm palm-down out to his right side. The object of the game is for the players to watch the coach's right arm and hand, and clap when it passes over the top of the left hand's palm. The coach is to do anything he wants to try and get the players to clap when he doesn't cross the bottom hand. Examples: He can move his right hand fast. He can start his right hand and stop it before he crosses the left palm. He can go fast back and forth. If the players clap when the coach did not cross the left hand with the right they sit down and are out of the competition. Coach continues to play until he has a winner. **This is a fun drill that teaches players to concentrate and focus their eyes on a target.**

   Recommended ages 8-12.

BATTING PRACTICE ROUTINES

There are many ways to run your batting practice. Utilize several different routines throughout the season. Keep in mind early in the year that you want to utilize dry drills, the batting tee and soft toss often so that you can build player's swing fundamentals. As the season progresses you can shift to more live hitting off coaches and players because your hitters need to stay sharp at the speed they are competing against. That does not imply you quit attempting to correct swing fundamental flaws using the tee, soft toss and dry repetitions. While you are focusing on hitting during BP, part of the value in batting practice is having your shaggers on defense playing the balls live off the bat of the hitters. It is a great time to have runners on the bases working on reads and breaks when you can incorporate it. Whichever routine you choose, get as many swings in as possible and limit the standing and waiting.

KEYS TO EFFICIENT BATTING PRACTICE ROUTINE

- Much of the dead time is prevented by good organization. Get all hitting equipment out and ready, coach your players to jog from station to station and keep a sharp clock on each rotation.
- Count swings instead of balls put in play and cut out "one more" when the station time is up.
- Biggest time waster: not enough balls at the live station. Keeping a minimum of thirty six balls will help keep things moving. More balls could end up behind the batter with the younger 7-9 year olds and could also be affected by the accuracy of the coach pitching.

Four Station Hitting (40 minutes)

Split your team into 4 groups of 3 (tees, soft toss, live on field and a shag group) and conduct 9-minute stations with 1 minute to rotate. Rotation starts at batting tees then moves to soft toss, then to live hitting off a coach then to the field for shagging.

Group 1 is hitting live, one player at bat, one ready on deck, and one or two players on the bases. After the hitter completes his first round of swings, he heads to first base to run. Let players take two reads on batted balls at each base, then move up to the next base. After reacting at third, they wait their turn to hit. Rotate the groups after the live hitting group has finished three rounds of swings or after nine minutes. **(Being efficient in this station can keep you on schedule and if not your hitting portion of the practice will drag on.)**

Group 2 is on tees hitting wiffle balls into fence or open field with extra players retrieving balls and a coach setting the fundamental to focus on.

Group 3 has a coach soft tossing with hard balls into a net or cage. If there is another coach, get two players soft tossing.

Group 4 is spread out in the outfield field shagging with a bucket in center where all the batted balls are thrown.

Need three coaches for this routine. Routine is more efficient with a minimum of two batting tees. First round for live is two bunts and 6 swings. Second round is 5 swings. Third round is 4 swings.

Recommended ages 9-15.

Two Man Group Hitting (42 minutes)

Split your team into 6 two-man teams. Each group has six minutes in each rotation. A total hitting time of 36 minutes for the team plus 2 minutes to have each group get to its next station.

Position players in left, center and right field with a bucket in center to gather the balls. When the first hitter has completed his swings, he runs out to right field to shag, right fielder to center, center to left and left fielder comes in to hit. Call in the left fielder to hit early before the previous hitter has completed all his swings.

Group 1 is hitting on the field. Player 1 takes live batting practice from coach for one minute straight. Player 2 is hitting soft toss off to the side next to the plate in a safe area from another coach. After one minute these players switch. They continue to do this for 6 minutes, alternating after each minute.

Group 2 is hitting off the tee down the left field line with wiffle balls or hard balls into a hitting net. You are trying to get 25 tee swings each in 6 minutes during this station. One coach should be here to monitor swings.

Group 3 is bunting down the right field line. The players are 30 feet apart. One player is pitching to the other. Put down cones to mark where you want the players to bunt the ball. Each player bunts 6 balls then they switch turns.

Group 4 is on the buckets in the field. Each player has an empty bucket for shagging batted balls from the live hitting group. One player is in deep right center field deep and the other is in deep left center field. These players are putting balls into bucket after each hit. The fielders in the infield and outfield throw the ball along the ground to bucket guys.

Group 5 is in in outfield working on defense. One player is in left field and one is in right field shagging balls live off the bat. Remember they also have to get batted balls when hit to center field so you might want to pinch the outfield gaps when they are shagging the balls.

Group 6 players are in the infield at shortstop and second base. Playing balls live off hitters' bats just like it's the game. They field balls and throw them out to the bucket guys (group 4).

Minimum three coaches for this routine. This batting practice allows players to work on the fundamentals of: Bunting, Tee, Soft toss, outfield defense and infield defense. And there's no waiting for your turn.

Recommended ages 10-16.

Three Station Hitting with Defense (30 minutes)

Split players into 3 groups of four players. Nine minute hitting groups with one minute for each group to rotate to next station. Recommend two batting tees for the station and wiffle balls to hit into fence.

Group 1 is hitting live and also soft tossing off to the side with another coach. Hitters bunt one ball each round, and 6 swings per round until time expires.

Group 2 is hitting off batting tees with a coach down left field line using wiffle balls. Focus on a coupe of basic fundamentals when working off of the tee.

Group 3 is shagging balls live. Spread out your four defensive players evenly in outfield and have them shag balls as if it's a game situation. Make it a competition to see who can catch the most pop flies in each group. Players will be more engaged when doing this activity.

Minimum two coaches, three is recommended. Two to four tees work best.

Recommended ages 7-12.

GUIDELINE WHEN TEACHING HITTING

Many coaches and parents have asked us over the years, "Where do I begin when teaching the fundamentals of hitting?" So, here are some thoughts to keep in mind when helping players learn to hit. Remember, there are no absolutes on what to teach first or last, but below is a general order or checklist to follow.

1. Before making changes with a hitter, make sure you have seen him hit enough. Do not make evaluations on a few swings. Once you are sure of the consistent flaws, it is usually best to start from the ground up.
2. Start off by checking the bat. Make sure it is a size and weight the player can control and handle.
3. Check the player's grip.
4. Get the player into a fundamentally sound stance, with the hitter comfortable and balanced. Everyone needs a sturdy foundation, so make sure the legs and feet are correct in the stance.
5. Check to make sure the hitter is using his feet properly by focusing on the stride and pivot. Many problems can be corrected by fixing the feet. The feet control the stride, the pivot and the balance throughout the swing.
6. Check the hitter's head position. Make sure the head is staying in the hitting zone during the swing and, most importantly, in a good position at contact.
7. One of the more difficult areas to correct can be the swing itself. Look to fix the swing path to the ball. Keep in mind most player's ages 6-8 will drop the bat head and hands some due to lack of strength. Many players drop their hands and hit underneath the ball or the hands start out instead of starting forward. These are issues that are common throughout player's careers.
8. Loading and getting the stride foot down early so the player can time his swing to the ball properly is an area you will be constantly monitoring throughout a players career.
9. Number 8 is very important and really stands alone no matter what swing fundamentals a player has.

BAT SIZE

There is no specific bat weight or bat length for a particular age group. The player should be using a bat they can control. If you are unsure what size bat a player should use, it is usually better to go lighter and smaller as opposed to bigger and heavier. If only bigger bats are available, make sure the hitter chokes up on the bat.

GUIDELINE FOR BAT LENGTH TO BAT WEIGHT

Ages 6-8	26 inch - 16oz 27 inch - 17oz
Ages 8-10	28 inch - 15.5oz 29 inch - 16.5oz or 17oz
Ages 10-11	29 inch - 16.5oz or 17oz 30 inch - 17.5oz or 18oz
Ages 12-13	30 inch - 17.5oz or 18oz 31 inch - 18.5oz or 19oz
Ages 13-14	31 inch - 23oz to 26oz 32 inch - 24oz to 27oz
Ages 15-16	32 inch - 29oz 33 inch - 30oz

Batting Order

Knowing the team's make-up is important when making a batting order. Which players can run? Which players hit consistently? Who can handle pressure? Who can cope with failure? Who likes to hit? Who doesn't like to hit? For coaches teaching 6-to-12-year-olds, letting players hit in different spots in the batting order is healthy for team morale. This gives all players a chance to feel good about themselves and understand what it is like to hit in different spots in the order. Also, this is a way to let players know that one player is not bigger than the team.

Characteristics of batting order positions:

1. **Leadoff hitter:** Fast, good contact hitter, gets on base frequently, runs bases aggressively without hesitation. Will take a walk and is not afraid to steal at any time.
2. **Second hitter:** Good contact hitter, above-average speed, good hitter, gets on base frequently, can bunt and steal.
3. **Third hitter:** Best hitter on the team, can hit for average. Clutch hitter who can drive in runs.
4. **Fourth hitter:** Good hitter who can drive in runs, hit for power and be a run producer.
5. **Fifth hitter:** Your second-best hitter. Can hit for average. Same characteristics as third hitter but may lack one characteristic. Good RBI man.
6. **Sixth hitter:** Good hitter, picks up the RBIs that are missed by the heart of the order. Surprise clutch hitter.
7. **Seventh hitter:** Least efficient hitter, patient hitter who uses whatever skills they have.
8. **Eighth hitter:** Your second clean-up hitter who can surprise the other team. Not a consistent hitter, but someone who is streaky.
9. **Ninth hitter:** Second-best leadoff hitter, similar characteristics as the leadoff hitter. Has to be a good hitter who can keep an inning alive. Fast, bunts, aggressive player, a good clutch hitter, two-out hitter.

BUNTING

Bunting is an area that often is overlooked by Youth League coaches because run manufacturing via the bunt doesn't come into play as often until higher levels of competition. However, proper time should be spent on this aspect of the game early in a player's baseball development. Teach all players the proper fundamentals of bunting regardless of where they bat in the batting order.

Teaching the concept of bunting early in a player's development will also help improve hand-eye coordination, demonstrate the concept of tracking the ball and bolster self-confidence. Bunting forces a player to track the ball all the way to the bat. Simply by concentrating on the incoming ball, the player enhances hand-eye coordination and gains confidence by making contact. For these reasons, in addition to developing bunting skills, a player should bunt the first few pitches of every batting practice before swinging away.

To ensure more success, have the player square around early enough to get into proper bunting position. Whether sacrificing to advance a runner or attempting to bunt for a base hit, it is necessary to have enough time to get into the proper bunting position. This preparation, along with ball placement after contact, are two keys to being a good bunter.

FUNDAMENTALS

Sacrifice Bunt:

This bunt is used to advance a runner to second base, or multiple runners to second and third base. The purpose is to move the runners into scoring position for the following batters to drive in. It's most commonly done with no outs and in a close game. Although there are numerous approaches for the sac bunt, the pivot method is best and safest for our targeted ages. Once the batter receives the bunt sign, he should move closer to the plate for better coverage, and move forward in the batter's box to improve the percentage of a fair bunt. The pivot action generally begins when the pitcher breaks his hands to start his throwing motion.

A. **Pivot method:** Set up closer to the plate than your normal hitting stance to assure plate coverage when pivoting to bunt. This method is nothing more than rotating the back foot as if a swing has already occurred. This rotation allows for the hips and shoulders to face the pitcher and still maintain balance throughout the body. **(picture 7-1)**

7-1: Pivoting to bunt

B. **Balance and Weight Distribution:** Feet should be wider than shoulder width for a solid foundation, and knees are bent as in photo 7-3. The legs are very important in bunting. Adjust to the height of the pitch by bending the knees. This way, the bunter keeps body control, proper bat position and form while adjusting to different pitches.

C. **Grip**: Keep the bottom hand on the bat choked up slightly, and slide the top hand up the barrel just past halfway. The top hand must pinch the bat at this point. To do this, the player should make a fist with the thumb extended and pinch the bat between the thumb and index finger. Make sure no fingers are exposed to the bunting surface. **(picture 7-2)**

7-2: Grip

D. **Arms:** The arms should be extended in front of the body, and the bat should cover home plate, at least to the outside black. The elbows should be pointing in with a slight bend to maintain proper athletic positioning. Very seldom is an athlete in a good reaction position when a joint is fully extended.

E. **Barrel Above the Knob (top of strike zone):** The bat should be angled slightly upward, keeping the barrel above the knob. This will allow for the bunted ball to travel downward – and hopefully fair. The bat starts at the top of the strike zone where the bunter has vision of both the bat and the incoming ball. The eyes should be almost on the same plane as bat, focusing on the pitch. To maintain proper bat position and vision, the bunter must bend at the knees to adjust to lower strikes. This will allow the eyes and the bat to stay at the same level and the barrel to stay above the knob.

F. **Bat Angle:** Pre-setting the bat angle toward first or third base will eliminate unnecessary bat movement when the pitch is in flight. Ideally, bunt toward first base with a runner only on first; bunt toward third base with runners on first and second. **(picture 7-3)**

7-3: Sacrificing bunt to 1B

Tony Womack on the Sacrifice Bunt:

"First of all, the player should know the strike zone.
Remember guys, you're not bunting for a base hit.
That means, you need to square around and give yourself up early.
The bat should be at eye level, going eye level down not up.
You should choke up to insure better bat control.
In the end, letting the ball hit the bat without poking at it,
will give you the best chance of being successful."

Bunting for a Base Hit

The fundamentals don't change much between a sacrifice bunt and bunting for a base hit. A batter wants to use the element of surprise, however proper time still must be allowed to get into bunting position. Good placement of the ball is just as important as the element of surprise.

A. **Right-handed Drag:** Take a short jab step back with the right leg. Drop the knob of the bat toward the left hip while bringing the barrel over the top of the strike zone and in front of the plate. In this process, create a bat angle toward the third-base line. Try to keep the ball just fair, and if it goes foul, the only harm is a strike. **(pictures 7-4 to 7-6)**

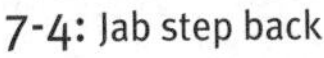

7-4: Jab step back

7-5: Barrel over the top

7-6: Contact position

B. **Right-handed Push:** A stride is taken just as if swinging, but the bat is brought around with the hands in bunting position. Bunt the ball with both hands pushing the bat toward the second baseman. The object is to just get the ball past the pitcher and have the first baseman commit to the ball. Don't bunt it too hard, allowing the second baseman a chance to make the play. This is attempted more frequently with left-handed pitchers since their follow-through takes them towards third base. **(picture 7-7)**

C. **Left-handed Push:** First, take a short jab step toward home plate with the left foot. This creates balance and a better direction line to bunt. Bunt the ball down the third-base line. **(picture 7-8)**

7-7: Right-handed push bunt

7-8: Left-handed push bunt

D. Left-handed drag: The bat leads the way with the hands in bunting position and aim between the first and the second baseman. Bunt the ball while bringing the left leg up into a crossover step, initiating the run to first base. **This is a good offensive weapon against left-handed pitchers since their follow-through takes them toward third base. (pictures 7-9 & 7-10)**

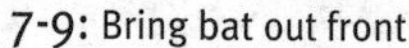

7-9: Bring bat out front

7-10: Crossover step to bunt

Tony Womack on Left Hand Hitters Bunting for a Hit:
"Once again one should know the strike zone.
Once it's established the bat angle is the next step.
The bat should be angled out in front of the plate to insure that you are in the hitting zone.
You should bunt the ball before running, but that doesn't mean
you shouldn't have any momentum getting out of the box.
Momentum should come in the form of either a jab step or
a crossover step towards the pitcher.
Last but not least, know which direction your bunting the ball and let the ball hit the bat.
Never poke at the ball."

Squeeze Bunt: The element of surprise makes the squeeze bunt an effective tool. If executed properly, the defense will not have enough time to tag the runner at home plate. As the pitcher releases the ball, the batter turns to bunt and the runner on third base breaks toward home. The ball is bunted anywhere on the field. Most importantly, the batter must do whatever it takes to at least make contact with the ball, otherwise the runner will be an easy out.

Slash: A slash is when a batter fakes as if he's going to bunt, then pulls the bat back and takes a compact swing. The batter is attempting to hit a ground ball and is not worried about power. This is done when defenders are charging hard or to create movement in the defense. **This play will typically open holes in the defense because players should react to the bunt.**

BUNTING DRY DRILLS

These dry drills can be done with or without a bat. Allow plenty of space between players if bats are used. Repeat all drills 5 times or until all players can perform correctly.

1. **Stance to Turning to Bunt:** Players line up and face the coach. On the command, *Hitting stance*, players get into their batting stance. On the command, *Pivot* or *Square* (depending on the method being taught), players turn to bunt. Make sure players are in the proper bunting position as spelled out in the fundamentals. Physically make adjustments where needed.
2. **Low Pitch and High Pitch:** From the squared or pivot position, the next commands are, *Low pitch* or *Take a high pitch*. On *Low pitch*, the players bend their knees to lower the bat. On *Take a high pitch*, players remove the bat from the strike zone. The coach should vary the commands to get the players familiar with the fundamentals of bunting and to make the necessary adjustments.
3. **When to Turn:** Finally, the coach should simulate a pitcher throwing from the stretch (or a full wind-up) and tell the players to turn to bunt when he breaks his hands to start his throwing motion.

DRILLS

1. **Bunting to Targets:** Place bats as targets about one-third of the way down each baseline. With the coach pitching from a close distance, have players (one at a time) bunt toward the bats. Each player bunts three times down each foul line. The rest of the players fan out to pick up the bunted balls and wait their turn. This drill is for a sacrifice bunt, and players should turn to bunt when the coach breaks hands to start the pitch. The coach should throw mostly strikes, but mix in a ball or two to see if the player pulls the bat back correctly.

   Recommended ages 8-16.

2. **Fair or Foul:** Place a bat parallel to the third-base line about three feet into fair territory. The goal is to bunt balls between the bat and baseline. Emphasize if the player misses the mark, it should be into foul territory and not to the right of the bat, because that's an easy play for the pitcher in a real game. This drill emphasizes the importance of placing the bunted ball very close to the foul line when bunting for a base hit toward third base. Since batters are trying to reach base safely, they should turn to bunt later than a sacrifice, but still soon enough to get into proper position.

   Recommended ages 8-16.

Expert Advice on Bunting to Targets

The "Bunting to Targets" drill is for a sacrifice bunt, and players should turn to bunt when the coach breaks hands to start the pitch.

3. **Bunt Hit Between Pitcher and First Base:** Place a bat in no man's land between first and second base on the infield grass. Have right-handed hitters work on their push bunt and lefties on their drag. Again, batters are trying to reach base safely, so they should turn to bunt later than a sacrifice, but still soon enough to get into proper position.
   Recommended ages 8-16.
4. **Squeeze Bunt:** Incorporate the squeeze bunt into Drill 1. At any time during the bunting drill, the coach will call out *Squeeze bunt*. On that pitch, the player should turn to bunt later than they would for a sacrifice and can bunt the ball anywhere on the field. When working on the squeeze, the coach should vary pitch locations to simulate what can happen in a game. The player must still bunt a bad pitch.
   Recommended ages 13-16.

GAMES

1. **Hats as Target.** Have players fan out from the pitching mound to the foul lines. Set three hats upside down with brims facing home plate as targets. Place them one-third of the way down each foul line. Each player gets six bunts, three in each direction. Award 10 points for a ball that rolls up the brim and stays in the hat, five for contact with the hat and one for a near miss. Have the players rotate around two times each and see who gets the most points. **(pictures 7-11 & 7-12)**

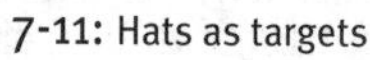
7-11: Hats as targets

7-12: 10 points

FAVORITE GAME

2. **Bats as Targets.** Follow the same set up in Game 1, but use one bat near each foul line. Pick two captains to choose teams. Each player on each team gets four bunts. Award 100 points for every bunt that hits a bat. Award 25 points for balls that bounce over the bats. The winning team's players get five extra swings during batting practice. Or play the best-of-five bunting world series by continuing the game at the next four practices. Whichever team wins three bunting competitions first is the world champion of "Bats as Targets."
3. **Bunt for Swings**. During batting practice, have players bunt the first three pitches they see. For every quality bunt the player gets down, an additional swing will be given. This will help them concentrate on bunting by giving them a reward for a bunt successfully executed.

PITCHING

If you are coaching at any level and you want your team to be successful, then you need to learn more about pitching. It's plain and simple. Your pitchers are going to influence the game more than any other players on the field. As you have seen on television or in you own leagues, there are many different styles of pitchers: hard-throwers and soft-throwers, breaking-ball pitchers and fastball pitchers, command-and-location pitchers and power pitchers. So do not let a preconceived notion determine whether a player can pitch or not. At least give them a chance in practice—they just might surprise you. And be aware, most of your players are going to want to pitch.

How do I choose my pitchers? And what do I do to get them better? Find out in your first practice or two who wants to pitch. Once you determine that, give them a chance to pitch and develop in practice. Whether you hold separate pitching practice or you keep all the pitchers for the last half-hour and let them throw to a catcher, you need to begin to determine who your pitchers will be right away.

Develop at least four to six pitchers on your team. You will need them throughout the season. Plus, if you are in Little League, there is a pitch count total that will not allow you to pitch the same players over and over again.

Once you have established your potential pitchers, individual time should be spent with them to teach them the aspects of pitching. It is not always easy to work individually with your pitchers at practice, especially if you have limited help coaching. If you do not have enough coaches to work this into your practice before games start, then set time aside before or after practice to work with pitchers. There are at least three different pitching activities you should focus on in practices:

1. Performing dry drills to benefit the pitching delivery.
2. Throwing bullpens (to a catcher) at least once a week.
3. Throwing to live hitters, either for a scrimmage or for batting practice.

If it is for batting practice, remember this is really pitching practice and the hitters will not benefit as much. Good pitching makes the game a lot more enjoyable for all participants.

SELECTING YOUR PITCHERS AND BUILDING CONFIDENCE

In a perfect world, we want our pitchers to have good arm strength, an accurate arm and the ability to locate the baseball within the strike zone. We want our pitchers to handle the spotlight and pressure that goes with being on that mound. Ideally, we also want a good, sound delivery to keep the arm healthy. This will allow pitchers to get the most out of their arm and will also help with locating the baseball. But we are not playing in a perfect world and that's where your coaching can have an impact. If your players show decent arm strength or the ability to throw strikes, you have something to work with. So help polish the pitchers' delivery mechanics, give them a simple philosophy to guide them, and build confidence and self-esteem by encouraging them. Show them you believe in their ability to pitch.

DEVELOP THE FASTBALL

Encourage pitchers to develop the fastball and strive to command it on both sides of the plate. Many young pitchers are throwing too many off-speed and trick pitches in an attempt to get hitters out. They may be effective at times in getting young hitters out, but it is not helping the pitcher develop his fastball, which he will definitely need as he progresses and competes at higher levels of baseball. The only way to develop the fastball is to use the fastball. Long toss and improving the delivery will also help enhance a pitcher's arm strength. But if the pitcher is not utilizing the fastball, he is unlikely to develop his arm to his maximum potential.

LOCATE THE FASTBALL

Not all good pitchers are blessed with a dominating arm. There are many Major League pitchers who dominate a game by locating their fastball. Greg Maddux is a classic example of how good a pitcher can be by using and locating the fastball. Do not let pitchers get preoccupied with velocity, although velocity is something we strive to develop over time through improving the delivery and using the fastball.

The best pitch a pitcher has is Strike One. Getting ahead of the hitter will enhance your pitcher's success. Every year studies show a hitter hits for a lower average when he is behind in the count. Commanding the baseball, especially the fastball is something all pitchers and coaches should strive to achieve. Locating the fastball to the inside corner and outside corner, as well as up in the zone and down in the zone, should be a focus throughout the season.

CHANGING SPEEDS

Changing speeds is next on the progression. Of all the off-speed pitches a pitcher can throw, the change-up is our choice for young pitchers. The change is thrown just like the fastball but gripped differently. It is less stressful on the arm and easier to repeat with the fastball than a curveball or slider. Although the curveball and slider are safe pitches to throw for older players, the potential for injury increases with these pitches for a few reasons.

1. Most of the players' deliveries are not sound and consistent at the younger ages.
2. Breaking balls often are not taught correctly, resulting in a player turning and twisting the arm incorrectly. This is where an injury is more likely.
3. Breaking balls are not as easy to repeat for strikes, which are always at a premium for the youth league pitcher.

The change-up is an overlooked pitch by many because it is not as glamorous as the breaking balls. But it is a pitch that will disrupt a hitter's timing that is safe and easier to repeat. The pitcher will use it his whole pitching career.

MOUND PRESENCE AND BODY LANGUAGE

Even pitchers with great command and stuff sometimes have bad days. A pitcher's body language, whether good or bad, will be read by opposing hitters. Successful pitchers learn how to stay composed during the bad times. Staying poised and composed is easier said then done when a player is in the moment of competing. This is where the coach can help remind the player to keep cool and stay focused on making your pitches. You never want to let the other team know they have you on the ropes. How we handle adversity when competing will ultimately have an effect on what kind of player we will be. The importance of mound presence and good body language are lessons a coach needs to take advantage of.

When pitchers are getting hit, they often try to throw harder and begin to lose focus on what is important. Pitchers need to take a deep breath, try to relax and remember to stay under control and focus on the next pitch. This is where a pitcher should get back to focusing on his delivery mechanics, concentrating on throwing the ball to the catcher's glove and not worrying about who the batter is.

THE DELIVERY

Whatever qualities a pitcher possesses, teaching the player a fundamentally sound delivery is something coaches and players should attempt to develop. A pitcher's velocity can improve as the delivery is improved. Pitchers who can consistently repeat their deliveries locate their pitches better. A sound delivery will help decrease the amount of stress placed on the arm and will help keep the arm strong and healthy. The style of the delivery may look different from player to player, but there are certain absolutes that take place in all good deliveries.

The pitching delivery is nothing more than balance and direction. Whether in hitting or in fielding or pitching, balance and controlling the body are keys to success. Balance starts with the feet and legs and that is a good place for you to begin. A pitcher's legs and feet must be used correctly to maintain balance and control and to create a good direction line to home plate. You can think of the pitcher's backside as the "power side" and the front side as the "direction side." In general, a pitcher's weight should remain on the back leg until the hands separate and the stride forward begins. If a pitcher's weight gets ahead of his arm, he will be only throwing with his arm, which is a common fault in pitching at any level. This occurrence causes the pitcher to loose a lot of potential velocity and adds more stress to the arm. To get everything going toward the hitter with maximum weight transfer, the arm and weight transfer have to work together.

Expert Advice on the Delivery

The pitching delivery is nothing more than balance and direction. Think of the back side as the power side, and the front side as the direction side.

The front side (direction side) is important for the player to get all their momentum going straight home. Common flaws include striding open too much or striding and landing closed. That second problem, not getting open enough to home plate, causes the pitcher to throw across his body.

Keying on the position of a pitcher's head is a simple way to help a pitcher have correct balance and direction to home plate. If the head can be maintained over the power leg until "balance point," the pitcher will have his weight in the correct location, and the delivery will be under control up to this point. Once the acceleration forward begins, the pitcher should keep his front shoulder and head moving straight toward home plate. This will help ensure their direction line will be on target. Remember, wherever the head goes, the body will follow. An effective phrase to help keep the pitcher's direction line straight towards home plate is "put your face in the catcher's glove."

Another important point in the delivery is the pitcher's effort behind the throw and finishing of the pitch. We see many pitchers who do not complete this phase of the delivery properly, thus losing velocity and location. Work on getting your pitcher's momentum and direction straight home as the ball is released out in front of their body. If a good effort is being put into the pitch, the transferred weight should finish on and over the knee of the front leg. The term finish the pitch is used to remind players to do just this. From there, the back leg will be released off the rubber from this good effort and a pitcher should end up near a fielding position.

RHYTHM, TEMPO AND PACE OF GAME

Delivery rhythm and tempo are unique to each individual. Set a tempo that is comfortable to the player as long as the player is balanced and under control throughout the delivery. A smooth rhythmic cadence is ideal. Remember, there is no reason to hurry the delivery; going to fast usually will lead to other problems. If you are a golfer, you know what we are talking about.

The pitcher will set the pace of the game more than any other player on the field. Pitchers who toe the rubber always ready to throw the next pitch are a pleasure to play defense behind because they keep the game moving and everyone alert. Have your pitchers take the offensive. Get the ball back from the catcher, get onto the rubber and challenge the hitter with the next pitch.

Expert Advice on Pitchers Controlling the Pace of the Game

The pitcher will set the pace of the game more than any other player on the field. Pitchers who toe the rubber always ready to throw the next pitch are a pleasure to play defense behind because they keep the game moving and everyone alert.

THE IMPORTANCE OF DRY DRILLS

Dry drills are a great starting point to teach a pitcher about the delivery and should be utilized throughout the season. Dry drills give both the coach and player key reference points throughout the delivery, and will give the coach and player a chance to isolate and work on different phases of the delivery. Understanding these positions make it easier to identify flaws and make the necessary adjustments. Obviously, a pitcher does not stop in mid-delivery during a game, but for teaching purposes we need to identify and distinguish between the key fundamental positions.

With a ball, the pitcher will have a much more difficult time feeling and understanding what the body is doing. Over time, with an understanding of what the body is supposed to do in the delivery, and many repetitions of getting the body into the correct position, muscle memory will take over and the pitcher's delivery will be performed without much thought.

These drills will allow pitchers to work on skills without over-using the arm. Pitchers especially need more repetition if they want to develop their skills. The arm action and balance through out the delivery are areas that can be worked on often with these drills. A dry-drill routine before throwing a bullpen session or pitching in a game can also be successful at setting the tempo for success.

TEACHING THE STRETCH POSITION FIRST

When teaching pitching, it is easier for a pitcher to execute the stretch delivery than to execute the wind-up delivery. The wind-up delivery must hit all the key positions of the stretch delivery—and then some. If a pitcher is not fundamentally sound out of the stretch, it will be difficult to be fundamentally sound out of the wind-up. Extra body movement does not result in more velocity or accuracy. A more efficient delivery will result in more velocity and accuracy. Have pitchers master the stretch delivery first and progress to the wind-up.

Many leagues have their pitchers pitch from the stretch the first year and then teach them both deliveries the following year. Keep in mind that every individual is different. Some may be better out of the wind-up and struggle with the stretch. Ultimately, you be the judge about whether the player is better off. Remember, a lot of players may have been imitating their favorite Major League pitcher or practicing with dad in the backyard for a while on the wind-up delivery and they are just more comfortable and advanced with it.

FUNDAMENTALS OF THE WIND-UP DELIVERY

8-1: Address rubber

8-2

A. Wind-up Starting Position:

1. Start power foot over the front of the rubber and at a 45-degree angle.
2. Direction foot rests alongside comfortably where the pitcher is balanced.
3. Left-handers start power foot in middle to third base side of rubber.
4. Right-handers start power foot in middle to first base side of rubber.
5. Body is upright in a relaxed and comfortable position.
6. Head and eyes are level looking in for signs and location.
7. Grip the ball and hold it in the glove, centered in front of the body.
8. Focus on target. **(pictures 8-1 & 8-2)**

8-3: Small step back

8-4

B. Preliminary Motion:

1. Eyes remain focused on target
2. Take a small step back with the stride foot, and perform #3 at the same time.
3. Lift hands to the bill of the cap or keep them at the chest if less movement is preferred. **(pictures 8-3 & 8-4)**

8-5: Block foot

C. Block Foot:

1. Power foot is placed in front of and parallel to the rubber before the body begins moving forward. **(picture 8-5)**

D. Balance and Gather Position:

1. The weight is then transferred onto the power leg as the pitcher lifts the lead leg to a position where the thigh is at least parallel with the ground. Hips and shoulders are rotated closed off together with the lifting motion from the front leg. Shoulders are level to ground and in line to home plate. Hands move down, settling in front of chest, if hands were raised during preliminary motion. This full movement should be smooth and controlled as the pitcher comes up to the important balance and gather position. **(pictures 8-6 & 8-7)**

8-6: Balance point

8-7: Side view

2. At this balance point, the power foot weight is on the inside ball of the foot, never on the heel, and the balance leg should be slightly flexed at the knee. There should be no arching of the back or leaning back at this balance position. Head is level and over power leg, eyes focused on the target.
3. At this position pitchers should be able to maintain their balance comfortably.

E. Separation and Stride:

8-8: Down then out

1. With palms facing together, hands separate out of glove near the sternum and stomach.
2. Simultaneously, with the hands out of the glove, the stride foot begins to slide down. The stride foot continues down, then out, as the weight is transferring forward towards target. The stride foot continues directly at the target landing on the ball of the foot, not the heel. **(picture 8-8)**
3. When landing, the toes point to home plate with the knee slightly flexed. The foot turns open to home at the very last moment before foot hits the ground—any earlier and the front hip is opening to soon. Stride length is unique to each individual but is dictated by a proper landing.
4. Head remains level and lead shoulder remains pointing at target.

F. Arm Action and Launch Position:

1. While striding home, the glove hand reaches directly home with the thumb pointing down, opening the glove. The elbow and shoulder are staying in line directly to the target.
2. The throwing hand comes out smoothly in a downward separation. The thumb is turning down at the ground, (thumb-to-thigh) and continues up in a "C" arc into the "L" position with fingers pointing to sky.
3. Arm action is the same as described in the throwing section, with the fingers remaining on top of the baseball throughout the "thumb to thigh, fingers to sky" rout of the arm.
4. Once the stride foot has landed, the arm already should be at its peak and beginning to make its way forward. When the foot has landed and the arm is at its peak, we call this the launch position. **(picture 8-9)**

8-9: Launch position

G. Acceleration Home:

1. Once the foot has landed, the arm's continuous motion is now accelerating forward toward its target.
2. The hips rotate open as the weight is fully transferred from the power leg to the lead direction leg. This weight transfer should be in a straight line to home plate.
3. The arm and elbow maintain their height, with the fingers remaining behind and on top of the ball to release point.
4. Glove hand rotates back toward the glove-side hip as lead elbow bends and leads the hand pulling back ¬toward second base.
5. The pitcher should envision putting his face in the catcher's glove. The head remains level with eyes focused on the target. **(picture 8-10)**

8-10: Acceleration forward

H. Release and Follow Through:

1. The ball is released with the hand extending forward and out in front of the body.
2. Throwing arm finishes low and outside the stride leg.
3. The weight has been transferred to the lead leg with the power foot rotating out and up as the foot leaves the rubber from momentum and effort of the pitch.
4. Back leg continues off the rubber as all weight is now totally transferred on the lead leg, Which balances the upper body. **(picture 8-11)**
5. Back is flat and parallel to the ground with proper arm extension out in front of the lead leg.
6. Back leg continues around, and finishes parallel or slightly in front of the lead leg.
7. Feet land near shoulder width apart, as pitcher is under control facing home plate ready for fielding responsibilities. **(picture 8-12)**

8-11: Release

8-12: Fielding position

Major League Pitcher Russ Ortiz on the Wind-up:

"The less movement in your delivery the better.
The more you stay around the rubber during your step back and pivot the better balance you will have and the easier it will be to deliver the pitch to home plate."

PITCHING FROM THE STRETCH

This delivery enables pitchers to get to the critical balance and gather position much easier than from the wind-up. The rest of the delivery is the same from the balance and gather position. The stretch delivery limits extra body movement, which can throw the pitcher's balance off track from the beginning. Extra body movement in the delivery does not result in more velocity or accuracy. A more efficient delivery will result in more velocity and control.

Expert Advice on Gaining Velocity and Command

Extra body movement in the delivery does not result in more velocity or accuracy. A more efficient delivery will result in more velocity and control.

Fundamentals Of The Stretch Delivery

A. Starting Position:

1. Pitcher places the power foot in front of the rubber.
2. Left-handers start power foot in middle to third-base side of rubber.
3. Right-handers start power foot in middle to first-base side of rubber.
4. Pitcher is resting comfortably with feet wider than shoulder-width apart.
5. Body is bent at the waist leaning slightly forward, looking in for sign.
6. Ball is in free hand with proper grip ready.
7. Head is level and eyes are focused for sign and target. **(picture 8-13)**

8-13: Starting position

B. Set Position:

1. Pitcher takes a step back with the lead leg to set the feet in a comfortable position and to bring hands to set position near chest.
2. Feet are perpendicular to home plate and parallel with the rubber. Feet are together or roughly shoulder width apart, with weight on the balls of the feet.
3. Knees are slightly flexed for balance.
4. Bend waist slightly, keep shoulders level and rounded.
5. Head is level with both eyes focused on the target. **(picture 8-14)**

8-14: Set position

C. Balance-and-Gather Position:

1. Lift lead leg and thigh to a height where the player is balanced and comfortable. Hips and shoulders are rotated and closed off together with the lifting motion from the front leg. Front knee is in line with back knee at height of leg lift. Shoulders are level to ground and in line to home plate. This lifting of leg should be smooth and controlled.
2. All movements and positions are identical to the wind up delivery from this point on.

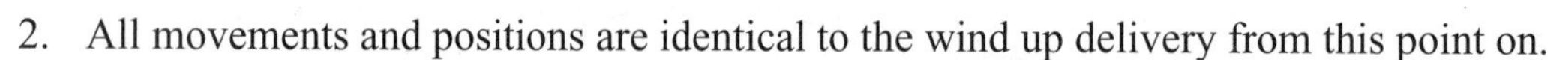

PITCHING DRY DRILLS

Below is a step-by-step progression of the wind-up delivery. These drills can be done with one pitcher or all the pitchers at once. The drills do not have to be performed on the mound.They can work on the flat ground as well with blocks of wood to simulate the rubber. 1-by-4 wood cut to 16 inches long will work well. Now all pitchers can participate together. **The dry drills are recommended for ages 8-16.**

1. **Starting Position Dry Drill:** Pitcher should stand upright and relaxed. Grip the ball and hold it in the glove, centered in front of the body, with the back of the glove facing the hitter. The feet should be positioned properly on the rubber. If the feet are not positioned as stated in the fundamental section A, the player will have a more difficult time performing the next moves in the delivery. **This drill can enhance the initial footwork of the wind-up delivery and help maintain balance.**
2. **Rocker Step Dry Drill:** Place pitcher on the rubber in the ready position. On verbal command, *step*, pitcher takes a small step back and raises his hands to the bill of his hat. Stop and repeat 5 times. Check for a small, controlled step that does not throw the pitcher off-balance or put him in an uncomfortable position. This is just a starter step to give the pitcher some rhythm. This step also allows the pivot foot to be placed in front of the rubber. The hands are moved slightly up for rhythm as well. The hands could remain still during the step back, if the player appears to do better with less movement.
3. **Foot Block Dry Drill:** Following the starter step, the next command is *block*. The pitcher places the power leg (back foot) in front of and parallel to the rubber. Middle to first-base side for righties. Middle to third-base side for lefties. The arms remain in the rocker step position. If the pitcher cannot perform this move easily. The starting positions of for the feet are not placed correctly, or the rocker step may be too big.
4. **Lift to Balance Dry Drill:** On verbal command, *lift*, the pitcher lifts his direction leg up into the balance-and-gather position. This is a controlled lift, not a kick up. Remind your players to lift the leg using the thigh muscles, which will help with control and balance. Simultaneously, the hands are brought down, settling in front of the chest. This position is key in the delivery. Check points: power foot weight is on the inside ball of the foot, not the heel. The lower part of the lift leg is relaxed. Hips and shoulders are rotated closed and in line with home plate, not over rotated. There is no arching of the back. Shoulders and head are level with eyes focused on the target.
5. **Down and Out to Launch Dry Drill:** Next command is *down and out*. The pitchers now begin their first movements toward the plate. Players break hands, with the direction leg moving down first. Arms continue with proper arm action, stopping the throwing arm at its peak. The leg continues down and out to its stride point, landing on the ball of the foot slightly closed for the drill and in line to the target. The player stops and holds this position (Launch Position) for critique. All points of fundamentals F (Arm action and Launch Position) should be checked. **Another important factor of the drill is for the player to understand the feeling of the leg going down slightly first. That helps keep the weight back longer so it does not get ahead of the arm. Head and body weight remain over the power leg throughout this drill.**

Expert Advice on the Balance and Gather Dry Drill

Players should be able to perform the first three moves in the wind-up delivery and get into a fundamentally sound balance and gather position. If this is difficult for them, they should be pitching out of the stretch.

6. **Acceleration and Release to Follow-through:** The pitcher is now ready to get his proper weight transfer and direction line moving to home plate. On verbal command, *throw*, pitcher simulates a pitch to home plate. The arm should transfer forward with the weight, keeping the elbow and throwing arm up in a strong position. The lead arm is pulling back in toward the pitcher's side, both arms working together. The pitcher should think about putting his face in the catcher's glove. This will ensure proper energy moving in the right direction to home plate. The ball is released out in front of the body, with throwing arm finishing across lead leg. The back is flat as the power foot comes up and off the rubber. The momentum of the pitch and weight transfer bring the back leg off the rubber, swinging up and around landing even or slightly in front of the stride leg into a fielding position. When a pitcher puts good effort into the pitch, and transfers the weight correctly, this will happen naturally. **The proper follow-through phase of pitching happens naturally when the pitcher does everything correctly.**

VARIATIONS OF THE DRY DRILLS

7. **Stretch Position Dry Drill:** Position pitcher in the stretch starting position. On the verbal command, *set*, pitcher moves into the set position. On the command, *lift*, pitcher lifts leg into the balance and gather position and holds that position for five seconds. Stop and repeat 5 times. Check each player for all fundamentals stated in section C. It is easier to get into a good balance and gather position out of the stretch than it is from the wind-up. This is why teaching pitchers to pitch from the stretch usually allows the pitcher to have more success.

   Recommended ages 8-10.

8. **Balance and Gather Dry Drill:** Place pitcher on the rubber in the ready position. Pitcher performs the first three moves in the wind-up on verbal commands, *step, block* and *lift*. Pause between step and block for two seconds. Example: At *step*, pitcher steps back and brings hands to bill of the hat. At *block*, pitcher picks up the power foot and places it directly in front of the rubber. At *lift*, pitcher lifts leg to the balance and gather position and holds that position for five seconds. Stop and repeat drill 5 times. Check each player's balance and gather position for all fundamentals stated in section C. Players need to be able to get into good balance and gather position to help them perform the next moves in the delivery. This is one of the key points in the wind-up. **This drill shows the coach if players are in a good position to deliver the ball home. It also works on their balance skills. If players are having a difficult time with this drill, they should be pitching out of the stretch.**

   Recommended ages 8-16

9. **Acceleration Direction Drill:** Position pitcher in the launch position. On verbal command, *throw*, pitchers simulate a pitch to home plate—but pitcher is to balance on the front foot for two seconds. Repeat drill 5 times. This drill can also be done with the baseball, letting the pitcher pitch the ball from the launch position. **This drill forces the pitcher to direct his energy and weight transfer straight toward home, not falling off to the sides. Pitchers should think about putting their face directly into the catcher's glove. (picture 8-15)**

   Recommended ages 8-16.

8-15: Balance on lead leg

DIRECTION DRILLS FOR BULLPEN WORK

10. **Direction Line Drill:** One of the best teaching tools is simply a straight line in the dirt. When pitchers are working on the side, or even pitching in the game, draw a line in the dirt from the arch of the power foot, straight toward home plate. The pitcher should land on the line or within two inches to the glove side of the line. If the pitcher is not within that area, he needs to improve his line to home plate. If a pitcher does not get open enough and is throwing across their body, it can hider their performance. It's more stressful on the arm. It is harder to finish the pitch out in front, and make it more difficult to locate the fastball to the outside corner consistently. **Drill shows pitchers where they are stepping on the pitch. (pictures 8-16 to 8-18)**
Recommended ages 8-16.

8-16

8-17

8-18

11. **Direction Drill:** Pitchers begins in the stretch position with a baseball in their throwing hand. Take the glove off and tuck the lead arm behind the pitcher's back. On the verbal command, *throw*, pitcher lifts leg and delivers a pitch to the catcher. If the pitcher does not move the lead-arm shoulder directly toward home plate, the pitcher's stride will not be in a straight line to home plate. **This drill teaches players to keep their front shoulder in when throwing the pitch home. Good drill for pitchers who fly open with their shoulders early. (pictures 8-19 & 8-20)**
Recommended ages 10-16.

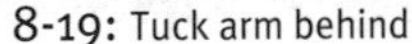
8-19: Tuck arm behind

8-20: Deliver the pitch

BALANCE DRILLS

12. **Eyes Shut:** Perform any or all of the dry drills with the player's eyes closed. This is a great way to increase a player's sense of feel. **The player will come away with a better understanding of their body and the importance of balance.**
Reccomended ages 8-16.

13. **Balance Drill:** Position pitcher in the stretch starting position. Coach takes a position to the side facing the pitcher. On the verbal command, *set*, pitcher moves into the set position. On the command, *lift*, pitcher lifts leg into the balance and gather position. Pitcher remains there as the coach tosses the pitcher a ball. Pitcher catches the ball keeping his balance, then pitches the ball to a catcher. **This drill teaches players how to gather and maintain their balance at a critical point in the pitching motion. (pictures 8-21 to 8-23)**
Recommended ages 10-16.

8-21

8-22

8-23

14. **Block Drill:** Pitcher begins in the stretch set position. Place a 1-by-4 block of wood under the heel of the pitcher's back foot. This will shift the pitcher's weight to the ball of the foot and off the heel. Now have the player lift his leg to the balance and gather position. The pitcher will be able to feel the proper weight distribution for the balance leg. This drill can be done dry, or let the pitcher continue with the delivery and pitch to a catcher with the baseball. **This drill is useful for all pitchers, but especially for pitchers who lean back or are always on their heel when getting into the balance and gather position.**
Recommended ages 8-12.

Russ Ortiz on Keys to Having Success on the Mound:
"Just throw strikes and work on hitting the catchers' glove.
Don't worry about throwing too hard or having a curveball. Location is the key."

ARM ACTION DRILLS

15. **Fence Drill:** Place a pitcher along a fence or wall as shown in the photo. Start pitcher from stretch position. The pitcher's back should be within several inches of the fence or wall. Let pitcher throw a baseball to a partner or simulate throwing a ball if a partner is not available. The pitcher's throwing arm or hand should not hit the fence. **This drill is designed to develop proper arm action for those players who wrap the ball or deviate from the straight line needed to throw most efficiently. (pictures 8-24 & 8-25)**

    Recommended ages 10-16.

8-24: Fence Drill

8-25: Straight lines

16. **Lead Arm Drill:** Place a ball in the pitcher's glove and start him in the set position. Place a bucket or coach eight feet in front of the pitcher directly in a line toward home plate. Pitcher begins from the set position. When pitcher separates his hands to throw the pitch, he tries to flip the ball out of his glove and into the bucket or to the coach. The pitcher must use his lead arm correctly to perform this drill – turning the thumb down and opening the glove directly to home plate. Many players throw their glove hand off to the side, which takes their body slightly in that direction. All energy should be directed straight toward home plate.

    Recommended ages 12-16

17. **Finish-The-Pitch Drill:** This drill is used from the back of the mound. The objective is to have a pitcher starting on flat ground throw slightly up hill when his stride leg hits the ground. Let the pitcher do the drill dry first to gain a feel for the drill. Pitcher starts in the stretch position and throws to a standing partner finishing the pitch to follow through. Distance is the same as their pitching distance. **In performing this drill the pitcher must emphasize the finish of the pitch to get proper follow through and get the throw down to his partner. (pictures 8-26 & 8-27)**
Recommended ages 12-16.

8-26: Behind mound

8-27: Finish the throw

NOTE: The following drills can be found in the throwing section and are valuable for developing pitchers as well.

Drills 1 and 2 Arm-Action Dry Drills.

Drill 6 Long Toss.

Drill 10 One-Knee Drill.

Drill 12 High-Elbow Drill.

Drill 13 Colored Ball.

Major League Coach Ron Wotus on Utilizing Drills:
"Find the drills that address your pitchers flaws.
Stick with the drill and give your player a chance to improve.
Don't change drills all the time just for the sake of change."

THROWING BULLPENS

Throwing bullpens before, during or after practice to a catcher or a coach is an important part of developing your pitchers. Knowing you do not have enough time to practice every phase of the game you would like, having your pitchers throw bullpens at least once a week is highly recommended. This is where a pitcher should work on their pitches and location of those pitches. We know most of you just want a fastball over the plate consistently. With that in mind, treat every pitcher's bullpen work and expectations a little differently depending on where they are in development. Remember, the philosophy—develop the fastball and work on locating the fastball. For pitchers who are ready for location, below is a routine to follow:

Release Point

A release-point adjustment is how a pitcher achieves control. When a pitcher throws a pitch too high or too low or outside or inside, the pitcher must make a minor adjustment to their release point. Granted, flaws in the delivery will cause pitches to be wild, and more difficult to adjust release point on a pitch, but we want you and your pitchers to understand that the release point is the major key to locating pitches. Remember to keep your instruction to one point at a time. If the delivery is out of whack, work on fixing that first. Either work on the delivery or the release-point routine. Combining the two will usually result in overload.

Think of the plate as three sections: middle, corner away and corner in. It is best to repeat a pitch and location a few times to find that release point, as opposed to randomly throwing different pitches to different locations. Do not move to other pitches or locations until the pitcher can repeat the pitch two or three times. So first off, fastballs down the middle. Next, throw fastballs away from their arm side. Example: right-handed fastball away to right-handed hitter. This pitch is more difficult to throw because you must hold on to the ball longer and make sure to finish the pitch. When pitchers are tired, they often miss high or on their arm side. Next, locate fastballs to the arm side. After pitchers can do so, move to your secondary pitches. Throw change-ups for location down in the zone. If you are using a breaking ball, throw that to the opposite arm side as well. Then pretend there is a hitter at bat as if you were in a game. This will help a pitcher with their game plan and awareness to get ahead of the hitter or you will not get to the other pitches. Finish the bullpen with a couple located fastballs down the middle. The most important part of this routine is locating the fastball within the strike zone.

Colored Plate

Color a throw-down plate into three equal sections as described in the release-point heading. This will provide the pitchers with a visual of where they are trying to locate their pitches. **(picture 8-28)**

8-28: For bullpens

Batters Stand In

When possible during bullpens, let a hitter or a coach stand in at the plate with a helmet on near the end of the session. One of a young pitcher's biggest fears is hitting the batter. That's why you see a lot of pitches being thrown outside to the hitters. This will give the pitcher more experience in dealing with this fear. Frankly, it's more game-like and will help with visual location whether the pitcher is concerned about hitting the batters or not. This will have a benefit for the hitter as well. The hitter should work on tracking the ball from release point to the plate. As we know one of a young hitter's biggest fears is getting hit, so you are killing two birds with one stone.

GAMES

Location Game: During a bullpen session, see how many fastball strikes a pitcher can throw out of 10. Set a number as a goal and if the pitcher obtains that number reward him in some manner.
Recommended ages 8-10.

For pitchers who are advanced, play a location game utilizing an inside corner or an outside corner. The same games can be played with their other pitches as well.
Recommended ages 11-16.

Eyes-shut Game: Perform the Balance-and-Gather dry drill with the eyes closed. If the player cannot perform it smoothly and balance for 5 seconds at the end, they must do 5 push-ups.
Recommended ages 10-16.

INTRASQUAD GAMES

It will be necessary to plan and keep track of when pitchers are pitching. Have a weekly throwing schedule to make sure pitchers get to pitch in games and at practice. Before the first game starts, it is important to give all pitchers a chance to pitch in an intrasquad game. Throwing a bullpen is very different from throwing to a real batter in a game. A pitcher needs to throw to a batter under game-like conditions. If you can get all your pitchers on the mound at least two times in this environment before their first game, it will be extremely beneficial.

Intrasquad games become even more valuable to the pitcher in leagues where leads and stealing are allowed. One of the most difficult aspects of pitching is when pitchers have to deal with baserunners who can steal. Now the pitcher's attention is divided between a batter trying to hit and a runner trying to steal. Pitchers encountering this for the first time will need lots of practice dealing with this.

PRE-GAME ROUTINE

The pre-game routine should vary depending upon the player's age. Preparing to start a game should take no more than 15 minutes. Less time is needed if the player is already loose and coming in after playing another position. Some thoughts to keep in mind when the starting pitcher prepares for the game are as follows:

- The pitcher should stretch and be warmed up properly to assure his body is ready to take the mound.
- There are advantages to throwing the ball farther than the distance of the mound to stretch the arm before the player takes the mound to start warming up.
- Many pitchers like to go through a few simulated pitches dry, so they can focus on their balance and rhythm. This sets the tone and gives them a mental picture of their delivery, which they can carry into their warm-up pitches and the game.
- Do not let the pitcher throw too many pitches in the bullpen. He is down there to get loose and find his release point for control and command of his pitches. Anywhere from 15 to 25 pitches should be adequate, depending on age.
- After getting loose, have the pitcher work on locating his pitches. It is best to repeat a pitch and location a few times to find that release point, as opposed to randomly throwing different pitches to different locations. Making adjustments with the release point will be a key in achieving control. The most important pitch to command is the fastball.
- Have a hitter stand in at the plate with a helmet on for the last five pitches. This will help both your pitcher and the hitter. This is when the pitcher can mix up his pitches as if it was the first hitter in the game. Remember, throwing strikes is the most important thing a pitcher can do.

PITCHES AND GRIPS

1. **Two-seam Fastball:** This pitch is gripped with the two narrowest seams together. This should be a pitcher's No. 1 pitch, and thrown the majority of the time. As players develop arm strength and throw the ball harder, this grip will allow for movement (sink, or run) on the pitch. This is the tougher of the two fastballs to hit because it has movement. As pitchers mature and improve command, they can throw this pitch for the corners. But because of the grip for movement, it is more beneficial that pitchers focus on throwing this pitch down in the strike zone. **(picture 8-29)**

8-29: Two-seam fastball

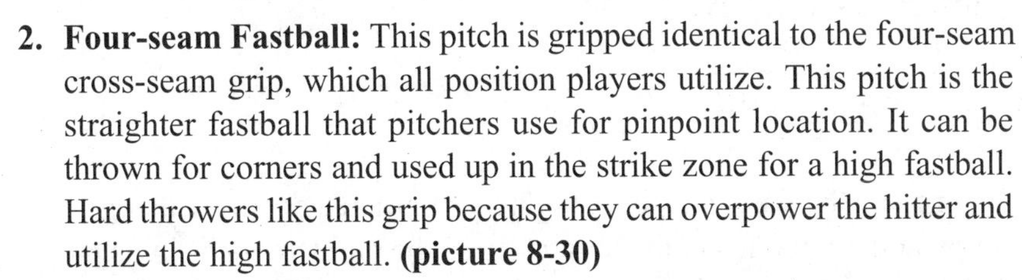

2. **Four-seam Fastball:** This pitch is gripped identical to the four-seam cross-seam grip, which all position players utilize. This pitch is the straighter fastball that pitchers use for pinpoint location. It can be thrown for corners and used up in the strike zone for a high fastball. Hard throwers like this grip because they can overpower the hitter and utilize the high fastball. **(picture 8-30)**

8-30: Four-seam fastball

3. **Change-up:** This pitch can be thrown numerous ways. The two most common you may be familiar with are the "circle change" and the "palm ball." The circle change is more difficult for a young player to throw and command. We advise throwing a variation of the palm ball. The grip can be varied to where a pitcher can control the pitch. If the pitch cannot be controlled, it does not have much value. Both change-ups are designed to look like a fastball and throw off a hitter's timing by removing speed from the pitch. When throwing the change-up the pitchers focus should be to keep it low in the strike zone.

   Three-Finger Change: This pitch is going to be easier to throw and command. This is just a variation of the palm ball but without moving the ball back towards the palm. **(picture 8-31)**

   Palm Ball: This pitch will be tougher to command but will remove more velocity. How far back in the palm the ball should go will vary with each individual pitcher. **(picture 8-32)**

   The great thing about throwing the change-up is it is thrown with the same arm action and arm speed as the fastball. That means pitchers can develop more consistency with their command, because they are throwing all three pitches the same way. The only difference is how the pitch is gripped.

8-31: Three-finger change

8-32: Palm Ball

4. **Curveball:** There are numerous grips for the curve, which can allow for different drops and breaks. We recommend gripping the pitch with the middle finger along the horseshoe part of the seam. The thumb rides the opposite seam below the ball. The pitch is designed to be a 12-to-6 drop like curveball. This pitch is recommended for players who are 13-years-old and above. Although the curveball is a safe pitch to throw for older players, the potential for injury increases with these pitches for young players. Most of the players' deliveries are not sound and consistent at the younger ages. Along with being a more difficult pitch to teach, if not taught correctly, often players are turning and twisting the arm, which makes an injury more likely. **(picture 8-33)**

8-33: Curveball

TEACHING THE CHANGE-UP

The beginner should first add a third finger to the ball and throw some pitches until he can throw that grip for a strike. The thumb remains in its proper position, underneath the baseball, and the pinky remains in its proper position. After the pitcher can throw that pitch for a strike, he is ready to start putting the ball deeper into his palm with the same three-finger grip.

When a finger is added, some velocity will be removed from the throw. When the pitcher begins to move the ball back in the palm, velocity will drop even more. Remember, the pitcher does not slow his arm on the throw, he tries to throw the pitch hard just like a fastball. If the arm speed changes, the hitter will recognize the difference and know it's a change-up.

How far back in the palm the pitcher eventually gets the ball for his final changeup grip – the grip he will use during the games—depends upon the individual. Let the command of the pitch determine the final grip position in the palm. What we are saying is, the player keeps putting the ball deeper into his palm until he reaches a point where he cannot throw the pitch for a strike. The point where he can get the ball back in his palm and still control the pitch the majority of the time is the position where that player should grip his changeup. The deeper the grip, the more speed taken away. But it is usually harder to command the pitch the deeper it goes into the palm.

San Francisco Giants Pitcher Russ Ortiz:
"Always have fun playing the game of baseball.
The older you get, the more competitive it gets.
If you can keep the perspective that baseball is a game,
I believe that will allow you to always have fun."

TAKING CARE OF YOUR PITCHERS

No matter what the pitcher's age, pitch counts must be taken into consideration. At the youth level, most leagues have criteria in place to protect the arms, usually a set number of innings per week. But that is not enough protection on its own. The total number of pitches thrown in an outing should be taken into consideration, not how many innings thrown. A player can throw as few as three pitches in an inning or as many as 50.

Also take into consideration how much throwing the player is doing at his other positions and the amount of practicing and throwing in general the player is doing. If unsure about how much a player is throwing, always err on the side of caution.

Regardless of the climate and weather, it is a good idea for pitchers to keep the throwing arm covered during and after games.

When developing a pitcher, don't just develop the physical aspects, help with confidence as well. Whenever possible, remove pitchers from the game when they have had success. If a pitcher has had a couple of good innings and you are not confident he will have another, seriously consider taking him out of the game on the positive note. If you send him back out anyway and you end up having to take him out in the middle of the inning the last taste the pitcher will have is negative. Often times we try to get to much water from the well. Be aware of which players are mentally strong enough to not let this affect them. Always do what you feel is right for the individual.

When possible, attempt to put your pitchers in situations where they can have success. And be aware of the pitchers who are better at handling pressure late in the game.

Expert Advice on Developing Pitchers

When developing a pitcher, don't just develop the physical aspects, help with confidence as well. Whenever possible, remove pitchers from the game when they have had success.

PITCH COUNTS

Pitch counts and how many pitches a pitcher should throw will depend largely on what part of the season it is. Most leagues today have pitch counts in place to protect the pitchers. Adhere to your league's guidelines and keep the following suggestions in mind:

- For your first pre-season scrimmages tell your pitchers they have 20 pitches. That could be two innings or it can be five batters, but when they reach 20 they are done.
- Hopefully all your pitchers will be able to pitch in a scrimmage at least two times at 20 pitches.
- For the first real game keep the pitch count to 30 pitches.
- If the pitchers arm is feeling fine you can increase the pitch count roughly 15 pitches every outing or two.
- Once the players arm is in shape and he has built up his pitch count properly, we believe the maximum amount of pitches a player should throw in one outing is 75. Remember, at the youth level many of your pitchers are playing short stop and catcher which are a demanding position on the arm as well. Take into consideration the warm ups before the game, pitches between innings and all the other throwing the pitcher is doing, and we believe this is in the best interest of the player.

CATCHING

Make the catching position a priority on your team. The catcher and pitcher will influence the pace and quality of the game more than any other players on the field. Not all players are cut out to be a catcher. If you are not sure who should catch, ask your players who would like to be a catcher. Give them a shot at it and then determine if this is a position they can handle safely. This position can be difficult for young players for several reasons. Lack of strength is just one. The catcher should have leadership qualities, be able to communicate with players on the field and should not be afraid to get dirty behind the plate. Look for a fearless blocker who possesses a strong arm to stop would be base stealers. A catcher should possess quick feet to come out of his crouch position to throw to bases. Look to develop a minimum of two capable catchers.

The catching position can easily be and is often overlooked during practice. As a coach, you should take the time to train your catchers at the numerous skills needed to have success at this position. We recommend getting your players into their catching gear more often. A great way to do this is to allow your catchers to catch coaches batting practice, whether it's on the field or in the cage. If you cannot create individual time for these two or three players during the regular practice, set aside 15 minutes with your catchers before or after practice at least once preferably twice a week. Take them through a routine of drills that will help them develop the skills needed at the position. Follow the "Catchers Drills and Practice Routine" at the conclusion of this section for a solid development program.

9-1: Target

9-2: Runners on base

9-3: No one on base

FUNDAMENTALS

A. Receiving Pitches

1. Feet are at least shoulder-width apart, for good balance.
2. Weight should be evenly distributed on the insides of feet with the right foot slightly open.
3. Knees are bent keeping the back side and body low.
4. Arms slightly bent and relaxed. The elbows point slightly outward and are above the knees. Elbow is never inside the knees when giving a target.
5. Glove is extended out in front. Give the target early **(picture 9-1)**.
6. With runners on base, the throwing hand is cupped with thumb inside fingers and behind mitt **(Picture 9-2)**. With no one on base, the throwing hand can be placed behind the back or for protection on foul tips if the player is strong enough to catch with one hand. **(picture 9-3)**

7. Turn the glove left slightly before the pitcher's release. This will help catch inside pitches and prevent getting handcuffed
8. For depth, set up as close as possible to the hitter, adjusting position depending on where the hitter is standing in the batter's box.
9. For location, set up down the middle of the plate unless well ahead in the count. Then set up on either corner. Strikes are at a premium at the youth level.
10. Receive pitches with soft hands never fully extending the arm and locking the elbow.
11. Receive pitches with your hand outside the baseball and the wrist turned toward the strike zone, or bring all pitches smoothly toward the chest settling to the closest part of the strike zone. This will help make pitches appear to be strikes.
12. On low pitches that could be called strikes, receive the ball palm down and bring the ball up.
13. On low pitches out of the strike zone, catch the ball palm up. **(picture 9-4)**

9-4: Low pitch, palm up

Expert Advice on Where to Set Up Behind the Plate

Many catchers stay in the same spot behind the plate regardless of the batter's position in the box. At all ages watch your catcher's distance from the batter. Too close and a catcher's interference call is probable, receiving too far back will hinder the pitchers. The catchers should adjust up in the box and back in the box according to the batter's position in the box.

Mike Lieberthal on Receiving Pitches:

"Having soft hands will help in framing pitches. Always let the ball come to you, so your legs can stay under you and you can maintain balance while receiving."

9-5: Giving signs

B. Giving Signs

1. Set up is the same as receiving pitches except for the following exceptions.
2. Knees are closed up slightly to keep base runners on first and third, and base coaches from getting a view of the signs being given.
3. Glove is draped over the left knee to block view of signs from third base coach and runner at third.
4. Hand position giving signs is directly between the legs. The fingers and hand should not be to low where they can be seen under the legs from the sides or from behind the catcher. **(picture 9-5)**

9-6: Blocking position

C. Blocking Balls in the Dirt

1. Balls inside the body frame: **(picture 9-6)**
   - Drop forward to both knees with weight slightly forward.
   - Keep shoulders rounded and chin tucked down.
   - Drop the mitt to the ground between the knees to block the hole between the legs.
     The glove pocket is facing the pitcher.
   - Tuck throwing hand behind the mitt and keep palm forward.
   - Attempt to block the ball in the center of the body with the chest.
   - The upper body is relaxed and not tense.

Mike Lieberthal on Blocking Pitches:
"Stay relaxed as possible with the upper body.
This will prevent the ball from rolling far away after it is blocked.
Staying soft will absorb the pitch."

2. Balls outside the body frame (move in half-circle motion)
   - Take jab step outward with near foot and drop knee. **(picture 9-7)**
   - Drop trailing knee to the ground and drag.
   - Turn near shoulder toward infield so chest is facing the plate.
   - Keep shoulders rounded, and chin tucked.
   - Drop the mitt to the ground between the knees keeping the wrist flexed and the pocket facing the pitcher.
   - Tuck throwing hand behind the mitt and keep palm forward.
   - Attempt to block the ball in the center of the body with the chest.
   - The upper body is relaxed and not tense. **(picture 9-8)**

9-7: Jab step with near foot

9-8: Smoother the ball

D. Throwing to Bases

1. Back side is up and thighs are level to the ground, for quicker release to bases.
2. Receive ball with the throwing hand cupped behind the mitt for quicker glove-to-hand transfer. **(picture 9-9)**
3. As ball is received, throwing hand and glove come together for grip. While securing grip, right foot takes a quick jab step in a half "c" towards second for momentum to throw. **(picture 9-10)**
4. The left foot steps directly toward the target as the hips and shoulders rotate in line to the base. As the left foot moves the mitt moves back across chest during the glove to hand transfer, which helps keep the catchers weight back. Catcher is square to throw with glove shoulder pointing to the target. **(pictures 9-11 & 9-12)**
5. The catcher should remain in an athletic position while shifting weight from right foot to left foot on throw and follow-through. Do not recoil; throw through the base. **(picture 9-13)**

Expert Advice on a Quick Throwing Release

Quick feet are critical for a quick release when throwing. Work on moving the feet up and down quickly utilizing the momentum of the feet and legs toward the base to make the throw.

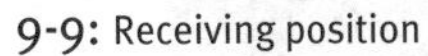

9-9: Receiving position

9-10: Block with quick step

9-11: Step directly towards base

9-12: Stay athletic

9-13: Finish the throw

Mike Lieberthal on Throwing Out Runners:

"Let the pitched ball travel to you so you can have your legs underneath you. This will help you stay in a powerful throwing position and have proper throwing mechanics."

E. Fielding Bunts

1. If time allows remove mask as moving to ball. **(picture 9-14)**
2. Approach ball in slight circle so momentum is moving toward target.
3. Position body so the ball is beneath the chest. **(picture 9-15)**
4. Align hips and shoulders with the target.
5. Keep knees and waist bent.
6. Use the glove as a backstop and pick up the ball with the throwing hand, looking the ball into the mitt. **(picture 9-16)**
7. Once secured, shuffle directly toward the target and throw. **(picture 9-17)**
8. Stay balanced throughout the play and do not panic.

9-14: Remove mask

9-15: Center the ball

9-16: Go down with two hands

9-17: Expect to throw

F. Fielding Pop-ups.

1. Turn to look for the ball in the direction of the pitch location.
2. Once ball is located, determine how high the pop-up is. If it's low, keep the mask on. If it's high, take off the mask with throwing hand and toss it away. **(picture 9-18)**
3. Move to anticipated point of catch while facing the backstop.
4. The ball rotation will cause it to curve toward the field. Allow for the deviation by staying in an athletic position and keeping feet active for an adjustment.
5. If underneath the ball, position the glove with palm up and catch ball directly above forehead **(picture 9-19)**. Otherwise, a one-handed Willie Mays-style basket catch is appropriate.
6. Keep knees flexed with good balance when receiving ball.
7. Cover the glove with throwing hand after catch.
8. Catchers should go for all pop-ups until called off by another player.

9-18: High pop-up

9-19: Receive ball in athletic position

Erik Johnson on Removing the Mask:

"The hockey style catching mask and helmet are very difficult for young players to remove quickly. If removing the mask slows the catcher down going for the ball on bunts and pop-ups, just have them leave it on."

G. Tag Plays at the Plate.

1. Position left foot in front of left -hand corner of the plate. Toe is facing towards third base. Always have the reference of where the plate is before the throw is made.
2. Verbally help position cut off man in a direct line between the throw being made and home plate.
3. Position the right foot open to the line of the throw. Face, chest and body should also be facing the line of the throw. **(pictures 9-20 to 9-22)**

9-20: Receiving throw from right field

9-21: Receiving throw from center field

9-22: Receiving throw from left field

4. Hands out front, keep knees flexed staying low as throw approaches.
5. Catch ball and secure it with throwing hand when time allows. **(picture 9-23)**
6. Right knee drops down as both hands reach to make tag. **(picture 9-24)**
7. Apply tag, clear and come up looking to throw to another base. **(picture 9-25)**

9-23: Secure ball

9-24: Apply tag

9-25: Tag and clear

Mike Lieberthal on Blocking the Plate:
"Always make sure your left knee is pointing towards third base. This will help to prevent knee and leg injuries."

CATCHERS DRILLS AND PRACTICE ROUTINE

9-26

The catcher is a pivotal player on the field. For one-on-one time, and to cover all techniques, catchers can come early or stay after practice to work on the skills explained above. When blocking balls, softer balls can be substituted. This will allow work on blocking mechanics without beating up the catcher. **The blocking drills are recommended for ages 10-16**. Ages 9-10 can perform these drills, but some will be a challenge.

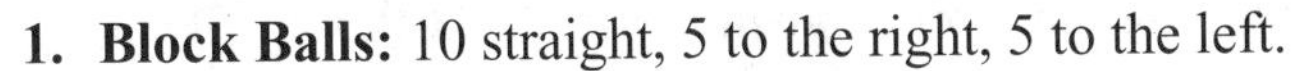

1. **Block Balls:** 10 straight, 5 to the right, 5 to the left.
2. **Receiving Pitches:** 20 repetitions.
3. **Borderline Strike (low strike):** 10 repetitions
4. **Throwing to Second Base:** 6 throws.
5. **Throwing to Third Base:** 6 throws.
6. **Fielding Bunts Throwing to First Base:** 3-5 throws. **(picture 9-27)**
7. **Fielding Pop-ups:** 5 pop-ups.
8. **Tag Plays at the Plate:** 5 from left field. 5 from center field. 5 from right field.

9-27: Coach's position for drills 6 and 7

Drills 1 through 5 can be performed from a distance of 20 to 30 feet. It is not necessary for the coach throwing the balls to be on the pitcher's mound. Be at a distance where balls can be thrown accurately to the desired locations so the catcher can repetitively work on technique. **(picture 9-26)**

DRILLS

1. **Blocking:** From a closer distance than the mound, toss balls in the dirt for the catchers to block. Start directly in front, then toss balls slightly to the left and right of the catcher. Toss 5 balls in each location. Remember, most players who are under 10 years old will have a difficult time blocking to their right and left. Blocking outside the body will be a challenge for any player under 12 years old. Remind catchers to keep their chin tucked down during this drill. Young catchers will have a tendency to look up as they block. When first teaching this drill to a catcher it is recommended to do this drill as a dry drill first allowing the catcher to get a feel for the technique of blocking before using the baseball.

   Recommended ages 10-16.

2. **Receiving:** This drill does not have to be performed from the mound. Get to a distance where you can throw the ball firmly to different desired locations. Throw 20 pitches to random locations while having the catcher softly receive the ball. Have the catcher smoothly bring bad pitches back to the closet point of the strike zone. This includes bringing the ball back to the top or bottom as well as the corners of the strike zone. If the pitched ball is well out of the strike do not attempt to frame the pitch.

   Recommended ages 8-16.

3. **Receiving Borderline Low Strike:** Follow the same principle as receiving above. Throw 10 pitches to the bottom of the strike zone, some near strikes and some clear balls. Catchers need to decide when to receive the ball palm down for a strike and when to receive it palm up (turning the glove over) for an obvious ball.
   Recommended ages 10-16.
4. **Throwing to Second Base:** Get to a distance where you can throw the ball firmly to the desired location. Place a player or coach at 2B to receive the throw. Throw balls to the catcher and have them go through their footwork throwing the ball to 2B. When first teaching this drill, let the catcher walk through the footwork first before introducing the baseball. Once the player can come up out of the crouch with proper footwork and body position in a dry drill it is time to try it using a baseball (refer to photos in fundamental section D, "Throwing to Bases"). Start the catchers in their crouch with a ball in their glove and let them throw to 2B. Finally progress to throwing the ball to the catcher. Remember, whenever a player struggles with technique or consistency you can always go back to a dry drill so the player can get a feel for and have success with the proper technique.
   Recommended ages 9-16.
5. **Throwing to Third Base:** Follow same drill set-up and progression as throwing to second base, But the mechanics and footwork are as follows. With a right-handed batter in the batters box, the pitch location will determine the catcher's footwork on the throw to 3B. On a pitch down the middle or on the inside corner, the catcher is to step with their right foot back and behind their left foot to clear a throwing lane. Then step directly towards 3B with the left foot as the ball is thrown **(pictures 9-28 to 9-30)**. On a ball that is thrown to the outside of the plate, the catcher is to step out toward the pitch with the right foot and step toward 3B with the left foot as the ball is thrown. Basically the catcher is clearing and throwing in front of the batter on an outside pitch as opposed to clearing and throwing behind the runner on a pitch down the middle or inside.
   Recommended ages 9-16.

9-28: Throwing to 3B

9-29: Step behind

9-30: Throw behind hitter

6. **Fielding Bunts:** Place a player or coach at first, second or third base. Start the catcher behind the plate in their crouch as if ready to receive a pitched ball. As shown in picture 9-27, get behind the catcher and roll a ball between the catcher's legs into fair territory at a speed and distance of a bunt. When the ball comes into view to the catcher he then reacts to the simulated bunt by fielding the ball and throwing to the desired base. Make sure the catcher approaches the ball correctly, gets over the bunt and uses the two-hand fielding technique as described in the fundamental section E "Fielding Bunts." When working on throws to first base, which will be the most common play, roll balls to three locations on the field. Roll to the first-base line area, directly in front of home plate and to the third-base line area. The bunt down the third-base line area is the only ball that is approached and fielded differently. The player must move directly to the ball by placing the right foot just to the right of the ball. Once the foot is in position, the catcher reaches down with the throwing hand, grabs the ball, pivots on the right leg and steps directly toward first with the left leg as he throws the ball **(pictures 9-31 & 9-32)**. Work on three to five bunts with each catcher. Players aged 9-10 should practice mostly throwing to first base. Ages 10 and above should work some to all bases. Remember when working on throws to second base that the simulated bunts must not be rolled down either line or too far out onto the field. In a game, the catcher will only have a play at second base on bunted balls or swinging bunts are closer to home plate. For plays working to third base, the ball should be rolled closer to the plate as well and not rolled down the first-base side. **Work on bunts that are common for your age group.**

   Recommended ages 9-16.

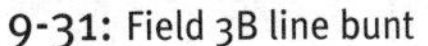

9-31: Field 3B line bunt

9-32: Turn and throw

7. **Pop-up Drill:** The most practical way to simulate a pop-up is to throw the ball for ages 9-12. This drill can be done anywhere; at home plate or in the outfield will work just fine. It can be done with the catcher's gear and mask on, which is more game-like, but is also effective to perform without. Place your catcher in their crouch. Stand right behind the catcher and underhand the ball into the air to the desired locations. Toss balls directly over the catcher first, then progress to tosses farther away, which will be more difficult to catch. Once you toss the ball into the air you yell *ball!* That's the cue for the catcher to spring up out of the crouch, turn around back to you looking up into the air for the tossed ball. Once the ball is located, the player attempts to make the catch. Try to simulate pop-ups that your age catchers are seeing in the games. If the ball is high enough, and the time and skill of the catcher allows, the catchers should attempt to catch the ball above the head. Follow fundamentals F "Fielding Pop-ups." Catching the ball Willie Mays style (underhand) is certainly acceptable and will be easier on pop-ups not high into the air. Remember, a lot of youth-league masks are difficult to remove quickly. In this case it will be easier to leave the mask on while making the catch. **For players 13-16, the coach should use a pop-up machine or learn to hit the pop-ups, which is no easy task.**

   Recommended ages 9-12.

8. **Tag Play Drill:** The coach should be positioned just beyond the infield dirt at the start of the outfield grass. The coach can throw balls or attempt to hit one-hop fungous to the catcher. Begin in left field, move to center field and finish in right field. The coach can move in closer and throw one-hop balls to the catcher if desired. Place the catcher at the plate in the proper fielding a throw position. Follow fundamental G, "Tag Plays At Plate." Throw or hit several balls from each field and look for the catcher to stay low and keep their fundamental position while attempting to field and tag the imaginary runner.

   Recommended ages 9-16.

BASERUNNING

Baserunning skills should not be overlooked. Youth players love to run and will enjoy baserunning drills whenever you plug them into your practice. A good baserunner can be developed with a little guidance from their coach. Teach your players to be alert and to know the situation before to every pitch. They should survey the defensive positioning of each player, know the number of outs and try to follow the ball at all times. If the ball is hit behind the baserunner, he should look to the third-base coach for assistance. The base coaches are there to assist the runners, not to control every move they make. The baserunner should never assume anything and run hard on all hit balls until the umpire makes a call. Runners should always think aggressively, trying to turn a single into a double or a double into a triple. By running hard, extra bases can be taken if the defense makes a mistake. Another rule to remember is to look to tag up on all foul balls with less than two outs.

Practicing baserunning techniques is important, but simulating game situations in practice is imperative to baserunning success. In setting up drills that re-create game situations, players learn what to look for and develop better instincts. Experience in a given situation can definitely help to alleviate the hesitations that keeps a runner from being aggressive.

Speed doesn't necessarily make a good baserunner. Being prepared before every pitch and good judgment on when to be aggressive will lead to good baserunning skills. Getting a good jump on batted balls can be learned and developed through practice.

As a coach, give players the freedom to succeed on the bases by giving them the freedom to fail. If runners are ridiculed for baserunning mistakes, they will run the bases with a safety-first attitude, never reaching their potential. Take pressure off baserunners by allowing them to be aggressive and understanding their decision-making abilities.

Erik Johnson on Developing Aggressive Baserunners:

"As a coach, give players the freedom to succeed on the bases by giving them the freedom to fail. If runners are ridiculed for baserunning mistakes, they will run the bases with a safety-first attitude, never reaching their true potential."

FUNDAMENTALS

A. Running Through First Base

10-1

1. Once the ball is hit, find where the ball is going. If the infielder has a play, run in a straight line on the foul side of the first-base line.
2. Keep focused on the first baseman to be ready to avoid a tag in case the throw is errant.
3. Run hard through first base, focusing on touching the middle- to front-third of the base with either foot. The only time a runner should slide or dive into first base is when avoiding a tag. **(picture 10-1)**
4. After touching the bag, look into foul territory in case there was a bad throw and advancing to second is possible.
5. If safe, turn into foul territory to return to first base. Never turn into the field to retreat to first base.
6. A few strides past first base, slow down to gain body control in case of a bad throw necessitating a quick change of direction. This is done by widening the feet beyond shoulders' width and taking short, choppy steps to enhance deceleration. Deceleration should never occur until past first base.

B. Rounding Bases

1. **Banana turn:** Once the ball has gone through the infield, veer into foul territory to create a better angle to advance to second base. A radius is created the shape of a banana. The bag is touched on the inside corner with either foot. Be careful not to get too wide in trying to create the angle. It should be just enough to maintain full speed and turn the corner without a wide swing to the next base. **(pictures 10-2 & 10-3)**

10-2: Foot position

10-3: Inside corner

2. **Point turn:** If the runner knows immediately that he is going to advance multiple bases, start the turn right away. This eliminates going straight up the line and then veering out, which is slower than picking a spot to cut the angle and running directly there. This holds true for all bases and is the quickest way to circle the bases.
3. After the base is touched, how far the runner advances on a turn is determined by where the ball is on the field. The farther the ball from the runner, the bigger the turn. An aggressive runner advances as far as possible toward the next base while still being able to retreat safely. The completion of a turn should be made with a shuffle breakdown to gain control while focusing on the play. The shuffle breakdown puts the baserunner in position to advance or retreat. **(picture 10-4)**

10-4: Break down position

C. Primary Lead

1. Before taking a lead, get the signs from the coach.
2. Find the ball and know the game situation—the number of outs, the score and strengths and weaknesses of the defense. Reviewing these facts before taking a lead will lead to good judgment on the bases.
3. Before the pitcher comes set, establish a lead off the back corner of the base. Use controlled side-to-side steps, never crossover steps, and watch the pitcher at all times. **(picture 10-5)**

10-5: Primary lead

4. Distance is measured with the number of steps taken, so steps must be controlled and consistent in length. Each individual will have a different distance for what is a good, safe lead. This can be determined in practice. Generally speaking this lead is normally two to three full side steps off the bag.
5. Depending on how quick or slow the pitcher's move to first is, runners can adjust their lead.
6. When leading off second base the third-base coach can verbally assist the runner by yelling out verbal commands. By saying OK, the runner takes one more step each OK and stays put when nothing is said. A careful means to shorten up one step per careful and on a back call a pick-off is on and the player must retreat as fast as they can back to the base.

10-6: Dive back

D. Diving Back to Base

1. When a pick-off attempt is made, retreat to the base with a push-off and crossover of the right foot and a forceful thrust off the left leg. Stay low on the dive, which is made with the right arm extending to the back corner of the base, farthest away from the fielder. Never leave contact with the base until positive the infielder no longer has the ball. **(pictures 10-6 to 10-8)**

10-7: Stay low on dive

E. Secondary Lead

10-8: Dive to back corner of base

1. **In leagues where leads are not permitted:** Once the ball crosses the plate, a couple of shuffles are taken toward the next base, anticipating an errant throw from the catcher. This routine will help players stay focused on the ball moving into the hitting zone, and be ready to advance on a ball in the dirt or a hit. Even though a primary lead is not allowed, it's still important for runners to go over the game situation before the ball is pitched.
2. **When leads are permitted:** Once the pitcher commits to home, 2 to 3 shuffles are taken toward the next base. The shuffles should be done in a controlled manner, always keeping the weight balanced underneath the legs. Time the shuffles so the right foot is down just as the ball enters the hitting zone. If the ball is hit, advance smoothly toward the next base. If the ball is not hit, a hard crossover step is made with the right leg to start the retreat back to the base. A good secondary lead puts the runner as far off the base as possible without allowing a catcher to pick him off. Using the crossover step and breaking back to the base at least two steps will deter the catcher from attempting a pickoff.

Lead off hitter Tony Womack on baserunning:
"An effective base runner has instincts just like a base stealer. The only difference could be the physical ability of the players that don't have that outburst of speed. If one understands the mental side of running the bases, their physical limitations will be overlooked by the sharpness of their decision making. The decision making and the mindset of the players on the bases will allow them to take advantage of weaknesses of the opposition."

F. Stealing

Look for tendencies: Take time to study the pitchers and to check out their pick-off moves, timing to the plate and any tendencies that tip commitment to a pitch. Things to look for are a slight lean toward home or a closing of glove-hand shoulder prior to committing to a pitch. Also look at their rhythm. Many players will come set and pitch, say, two seconds later every time. If this is the case then have your players break for a steal just before two seconds after the pitcher comes set. Left-handed pitchers, just like right-handed pitchers, have tendencies when throwing home or to first as well. For instance, a lefty may always turn their head to first when they throw to first. And keep their head turned home when going home. There are many other things a pitcher may do to tip a pick-off or commitment to a pitch. Keep your players active on the bench by having them watch for tendencies of opposing team's pitchers as well as their own.

Reading a righty: If no tendencies were found when reading the pitcher, there are still ways to get a good jump on a steal attempt. On a right-handed pitcher, the best place to focus is on their right foot. This foot will have to come up to start the pick-off move. Any other movement besides the pivot foot lifting up should key the runner to steal.

Reading a lefty: On a lefty, you have to hold until the pitcher commits to home plate. Commitment is constituted two ways: After coming set, if the pitcher's lead foot crosses back across the plane of the rubber as the pitcher lifts the stride foot up, the pitcher is committed to throw home. If the plane of the rubber is not broken with the stride leg, the runner must wait and determine when the pitcher is stepping home to pitch or stepping toward first base for a pick-off attempt. Pitchers who do not break the plane are tougher to steal on, as it forces the runner to wait longer before committing on a steal.

DRILLS

10-9: Proper breakdown

1. **Home to First:** Line up players at home plate. One at a time, players run through first base as if they have hit a ground ball to the infield. A coach is positioned near first base looking for correct foot placement on the bag, proper breakdown and players looking to foul territory for the ball after they have touched first base. After all players perform this drill correctly, the coach can randomly throw balls into foul territory after the runners touch first base, simulating an overthrow. Players react and advance to second when they see the loose ball. **(picture 10-9)**

   Recommended ages 8-12.

10-10: Banana turn

2. **Making a Turn:** Same as above, except have players run as if they have hit a single. If you have cones as in the photo, utilize them for ages 7-10. Otherwise, have one coach stand 10 feet in front of first base and 2 to 3 feet in foul territory. Have another coach stand 6 feet off first base and 2 to 4 feet behind the bag. With coaches in these two positions, have the players run around the first coach and in front of the second coach. This will help with the proper initial turn and make sure runners cut the corner correctly to get lined up toward second base. Coaches should watch to make sure base runners touch first base with either foot on the inside corner. **(picture 10-10)**

   Recommended ages 7-16.

3. **Turns Reading the Play**: Set a coach at an outfield position to simulate any given outcome of a fly ball, ground ball, or a thrown ball. Players start at home plate and run to first making a proper turn. Once the base is tagged, the player picks up the coach in the outfield to determine weather to try to advance to second or not. The coach is simulating different outcomes of plays. For example: coach comes up cleanly with ball in hand. Coach drops a fly ball that kicks away from him a few feet. Coach simulates ball slipping out of hand on an attempted throw back to the infield. The runner reads the coach acting as an outfielder and advances or retreats depending upon the situation. **This drill simulates game situations and gives players a chance to work on decision-making.**

   Recommended ages 7-16.

Tony Womack on baserunning items that win games:
"Knowing the arms and depth of the outfielders.
Good secondary leads to go from first to third and second to home on base hits.
Moving up to the next base on balls in the dirt.
Touching the corners of the bases correctly.
Advancing to third on a slow roller in front of you at second base."

4. **Balls in the Dirt:** Divide the team into three even groups. Place a group at all three bases, first, second and third. One player at each base takes a turn at the same time. Have a catcher with full gear working on receiving and blocking balls. A coach throws pitches to the catcher varying the tosses; some are good, some are in the dirt. The baserunners start from their primary lead and take their secondary lead as the coach makes the pitch. The runners are working on timing their secondary lead correctly. They are also reading the ball flight. As soon as they determine the ball will be in the dirt, they break for the next base. If the ball is caught, they utilize the crossover step and take three hard steps back to their base. Before the next pitch, runners jog to the next base and wait their turn in line there. If your league doesn't allow leads, starting position is on the base. Baserunners still read the pitch, and if it's in the dirt, they take off to the next base. If it's caught, they shuffle off the base two steps and watch the catcher throw the ball back to the pitcher. **This drill works on timing the secondary lead properly for the best jump to the next base. It teaches players to read a pitch in the dirt and to aggressively break to the next base when it is recognized.**
   Recommended ages 8-16.

5. **Picking up the Coach:** Line up all players at first base. When a coach yells, *Go!* one player runs from first to third base on a presumed ball hit to right field. The correct technique in running multiple bases when the ball is hit behind the runner is as follows: If the runner is not sure whether to advance, look to the third-base coach about halfway to second base. After seeing the coach, the runner should look at second base and focus on touching the bag and turning correctly. As soon as the bag is touched, the runner should pick up the third-base coach again. The third-base coach will give different signals to the baserunner. Examples: 1.Waving runners to third or stopping them at second on the first look. 2. Waving runners to third on the first look and stopping them at second on the second look. Throw out different signs so the runner has to react to different situations. **NOTE:** Time should be taken before this drill to establish a few simple hand signals to direct the runners. During games, use verbal commands along with the hand signals. **This drill will help both the runners and the coach.**
   Recommended ages 8-16.

Expert Advice on Picking Up the Coach

The "Picking Up the Coach" drill will help both the runners and the coach. It simulates game communication.

Stolen base champion Tony Womack on keys to basestealing:
"The most important key for being a successful base stealer is having instincts. Understanding the pitcher's move to first and to the plate as well as knowing the catcher's tendencies of their arm strength throwing to bases are major keys as well.
Finally, not being afraid of getting thrown out or picked off, will keep you hungry to get to the next base in a crucial situation."

6. **Reading Fly Balls:** Divide the team into three groups and put runners at all bases, and have three players in the outfield. Place coaches at bases to monitor and critique runners. Throw or hit different fly balls to the outfielders. Throwing balls will be more accurate and effective for the drill. Runners react to the simulated hits. Players need to learn in non-tag-up situations to get as far off the base as possible, but only to the point where they can return safely if the ball is caught. Runners should stay at that distance and watch to see if the ball is caught. If it is caught, they quickly retreat to the bag to tag up and watch for an errant throw. If it is dropped, they advance to the next base. This is a common situation, and players often don't get far enough off the base and are forced out at the next base when the ball is not caught. On balls that are deep enough, players should tag up and break for the next base as soon as the ball is caught. On all definite foul balls, baserunners should always tag up and look to advance.

   Recommended ages 8-12.

7. **Reading Balls at Second Base.** Put a full defense on the field and place everyone else at second base. One coach hits fungos to different locations on the infield and outfield. One coach critiques the baserunners at second base. Second base is a critical base to make good decisions. Players must learn when to break to third base on ground balls. Generally, runners can advance to third when a ball is hit to the right of second base. On balls hit to the left side of second base–in front of the baserunner–make sure the ball gets through for a hit. But that doesn't always hold true. The coach should hit balls just behind and just in front of the runners at different speeds to see how the runners react. There are no absolutes on when to advance. These situations need to be recreated in practice so runners experience when to stay and when to go. These same scenarios should be done with balls hit to the outfield as well. Have the defensive team make the plays on the hit balls as if it were a game.

   Recommended ages 8-16.

Tony Womack on Stealing Bases:

"The biggest key to stealing a base is the jump. Just because you are fast doesn't guarantee that you will consistently be successful at stealing a base. Speed helps but working at getting good jumps will solidify your success rate. Finally, your lead determines if you become a solid base stealer. A lead should fit the comfort level of each individual player. I feel that two steps and a dive is a level of comfort that can be easily mastered by all players. To me, it doesn't matter how you take your lead, but what kind of jump you get."

GAMES

1. **Stopwatch Games:** Bring a stopwatch to practice and time your players' speed to first base, their speed on doubles, triples and inside-the-park home runs. Keep a log of the times and see which players improve their running speeds throughout the season. This will motivate them to run faster and show them the importance of making a good turn, which saves time on doubles, triples and home runs. **We find that one of the favorite things players at all age groups enjoy is knowing how fast they can run the bases. For ages 7-8 keep it simple and time them to first base and second base.**

   Recommended ages 9-16.

2. **Relay Race Game:** Pick two captains and have them play rock, paper, scissors to determine who picks first. Alternating picks, captains choose players for their team. Place one team at second base and one team at home plate. The team at second starts on the base and goes third to home, while the team at home runs first to second. This is a relay race and the second player cannot start until his teammate touches the base he is running for. **Players will learn to cut the corners better and touch the base on the inside corner to save time rounding the bases. Adds excitement to practice.**

   Recommended ages 10-16.

Expert Advice on Spicing up Practice

If practice is not flowing as well as you expected, and you need to inject some life into your players, set up a baserunning game and have some fun!

COACHING THE BASES

Coaching the bases, especially third base, is a very important position on the field. Take charge when coaching the bases whether you are giving offensive signs or helping a base runner. The job of a base coach is to assist the baserunners and not to control every move they make. As a base coach your first priority is to stress to your players that they must be aware of where the ball is at all times. Another key is to give players reminders at the bases when play is stopped so that they are prepared mentally to react to what they see. The coach's job is to get into a position where the player can see the coach easily, and where the coach has more time to make a decision. When a runner is going from first to third, the third-base coach should be more toward left field so the player can see the coach easier when rounding second. When a player is going from second to third, the coach should be down the line toward home plate to give him more time to read the play and make a decision. It all happens very fast and the more time you have to read the play the better decision you can make.

Expert Advice When Coaching the Bases

During the games assist runners with their decision of whether to advance a base or stay put. When play is stopped remind baserunners of the number of outs, to be ready for a ball in the dirt, and to survey the field to see where the defense is playing. These reminders will allow them to use better judgment when they have to make a decision.

GIVING SIGNS

When establishing signs for the coach to give to the players, there are a few points to keep in mind. First of all keep them simple. Even at the professional level this holds true. It can be as simple as just touching a body part with two hands. Hat is hit-and-run, belt is bunt and shirt is steal. You may have noticed the signal touched started with the same letter as the task we want the player to perform. For example, belt is to bunt.

You can also use verbal signal. Select a word that you wouldn't say accidentally when cheering you players on. Possibly like the word "Dad." So when you say, "Do it for your Dad,'' that signifies bunt or whatever task you associate with that word.

Another way to give a signal is to have one body part hot, called an indicator. Once the coach touches a body part, the next touch is the live sign. You would have to establish what the live signs are for your team— possibly the hat, shirt or belt. In this system the player always watches for the hot sign. If touched, they know the next sign touched is the action the player needs to perform. Also establish a wipe-off sign in case you give the wrong sign and want to erase your last sign.

When giving signs, give them slowly and deliberately so the players can follow. Train your players to look to the third base coach right away to get the signs. Then they can survey the field and go over the reminders with the first or third base coaches. This will help the pace of the game as well. There is nothing that slows the game down more than players waiting until the last second to look for a sign. Lastly, have fun with your players by quizzing them frequently with the signs at practice. And always review them before games with any players you think need reminders and with players you expect to use plays with.

Expert Advice on Coaching Third Base

All good third base coaches use the scoreboard as a guide. The inning, the outs and the score all have a great influence on knowing when to be aggressive or cautious when it comes to sending runners.

SLIDING

Sliding is nothing more than controlled falling. Though it sounds easy, teaching sliding correctly can be difficult. Learning to slide properly will not only reduce the risk of injury but will cut down on skin abrasions. Head-first slides are dangerous and can damage fingers and shoulders. Do not encourage head-first slides and never slide head first into home plate. Head-first slides should only be used when a baserunner is avoiding a tag running to first base or when retreating back to a base. Take at least one day prior to your first game to practicing sliding for 10 to 15 minutes. Most players enjoy sliding, but you will have one or two that have fear that needs to be eased with sliding practice.

FUNDAMENTALS AND DRILLS

A. Establishing the lead foot is important. With players sitting on the ground, put both legs straight out and arms resting on the ground. **(picture 12-1)**

B. On the command, *slide*, have players fold one leg as quickly as possible under the other leg into a figure-four position. Do not tell them which leg to fold. Observe to see which leg they tuck under naturally. It is not necessary to teach players to slide on both sides at this level. Concentrate on proper technique using the side that is natural to each player. **(picture 12-2)**

C. After establishing the tucked leg, add the hands to the equation. Repeat the verbal command, *slide*. Players now tuck one leg and throw both hands into the air at the same time. The position they are in after the command is the same position to aim for when practicing. Players should be sliding on their buttocks, not their sides. **(picture 12-3)**

D. After slide, proceed to the next command, *back*. Players lean back, keeping their hands up. As players progress back in their lean players should tuck their chin forward towards chest. This will keep them from hitting their head on the ground. The extended foot is 2 to 3 inches off the ground, staying low enough to touch the base. **(picture 12-4)**

E. After players have gone through and understand the fundamentals A through D, the next step is to perform all the lessons at once. Set up players in the starting position again. On verbal command, *slide*, players tuck a leg and chin, raise hands and lean back simultaneously.

F. Have all players stand up at an arm's-distance apart. With their non-tuck leg, have them take a step forward as they tuck their other leg – as if sliding standing up. At the same time they raise their hands, tuck their chin and lean back to simulate a slide. This will help them to get the feeling of tucking their leg while moving.

12-1: Starting position

12-2: Establishing tuck leg

12-3: Hands up

12-4: Lean back

SIMULATING GAME SLIDE

After completing the figure-four slide fundamentals and the players have a complete understanding of what to do, it's time to slide at game speed.

There are three ways to simulate the game slide: on a sliding pad, on wet grass or on big pieces of cardboard. If using cardboard, get two pieces measuring about 6 feet by 7 feet and place them on top of each other. With two pieces of cardboard the top piece will slide on the bottom if a bad slide is made. A base is not necessary to teach the figure-four slide, but if one is available, players can practice touching the base with their extended leg.

Have players remove their shoes and line them up 45 feet away from the sliding area. One at a time, each player must run hard without slowing down when they start their slide. They should not jump into the slide; it should be a controlled fall. Just like in the sit-down drills, players should tuck one leg and raise the other as they pull their upper body back and raise their arms. The extended leg's foot should not hit the ground. If the lead leg is hitting the ground, have the players lean back a little more once their buttocks hit the ground. Have novice players wear a helmet when first learning to slide. **(picture 12-5)**

12-5: Figure four slide

GAME SITUATIONS

In this section there are a number of plays our experience tells us you will need to cover if you want to have a heads-up team. You want your players prepared for common and not-so-common baseball plays that are going to arise. Both players and coaches really enjoy this part of practice. As coaches, we get an opportunity to see if players can react properly when we give baseball strategy instructions. We find out what players have natural instincts and find out what players need to be assisted in this area.

The first key in getting players ready for all types of plays – common, fast moving or awkward – is to make sure players understand what is happening and what they do during these different plays. This means you must walk the players through the situation first and explain why you do this in that particular situation. Don't assume your players know what to do in all these situations.

- Start off by walking players through the situation without the ball. Move the players like chess pieces to make sure they are in the right spots.
- After you do this, place the ball where it is being hit and have players initiate the play on your command. Once this is accomplished to your liking, go back to home plate and hit the ball to the exact spot, and have the players react from their initial position.
- If players understand their responsibility, and are making plays successfully, then add a runner.

Remember that recording the out is not the most important goal in teaching these situations. The goal is to get players in the right spots and for them to understand their responsibility. If they record the out great, but players are human and will make physical errors.

In situation play we are training the mental aspect of the game. Our goal is to prepare them mentally so when situations arise they have been trained on what to do. This gives our players every opportunity to be in the right spot with a chance to execute the play.

Game Situation Plays

A. Infield

1. Balls hit to right side of the field in all the following locations:
   - Towards first base – First baseman and pitcher working together to get an out at first base.
   - Between first baseman and second baseman – Second baseman communicating whether he has ball so first baseman can retreat to first base. If both infielders commit to the ball then the pitcher has to cover first base.
   - To short right field – Right fielder and second baseman going after fly ball, communicating to make the play.
2. Man on second base, ball hit to infielders in the following situations:
   - Right side of field – Make sure second baseman and first baseman get the out at first base and don't try to throw to third base.
   - Left side of field – Both the third baseman and shortstop need to head check the runner then make a strong throw to first baseman. If the runner is way off of second base, get the runner. But players must be 100% sure they can get the lead out. If they don't, the batter will be safe at first and no outs will be recorded.
   - To the pitcher – Check runner at second base and just like previous play make sure you get an out.
3. Bases Loaded infield in, hit balls to all fielders.
   - With infield in, the priority is to go for the runner heading to the plate. If he does not go, get the out at first. First baseman should be ready to throw home after the out is recorded at first.
4. Runners at second base and third base.
   - Train your infielders as follows – If they are playing in, the priority is going home. If they are playing back, the priority is the out at first base. The exception is if the ball is hit to the shortstop and runner at second is going to third. He can go for the runner at third if he is sure to get him out.
5. Man on third base infield in.
   - Balls hit to every infielder: Directly at them, to the right, to the left – When the ball is right at the infielder, the priority is home. Balls to the sides become judgment plays and infielders need reps to improve judgment on whether to go home or get out at first base.
6. Man on first base.
   - Covering second base when ball is hit to right side of field.
   - Covering second base when ball is hit to left side of field.
   - Covering second base when ball is hit back to the pitcher.
   - Covering second base when ball is bunted to catcher.

ddddd

7. Infield seal defense.
   - Diving for balls with infield in and making plays at first base.
8. Run Downs.
   - Check rundown section page 154 for details.
9. Passed ball drill: Man on third base.
   - Work on technique for pitcher covering home plate on tag.
   - Work on technique for catcher retrieving ball and throwing to pitcher.

B. Outfield

1. Pop flies between outfielders and pop flies between outfielders and infielders – These are communication drills. Check pop-fly responsibilities on page 155.
2. One hopper or hard ground ball to right field – Right fielder thinks about getting the force out at first base.
3. Do-or-die plays, throwing runners out at home plate – Outfielders must charge ball as hard as possible and fight to make good throw to home plate.
   - Man on second base, routine single to outfielders – In this case the outfielder charges hard but breaks down under control to field ball and make good throw home.
5. Diving for balls, trying to make play before fly ball or line drive hits ground.
   Recommended ages 11-16.
6. Backing up bases and infielders.
   - When a play is being made in the infield, outfielders should be moving to get in line to back up the base the play may be at.
   - When ground balls are hit to infielders, outfielders must assume infielders will miss balls and be moving toward the ball before it passes the infield.

Bunt Plays

First off, teach your players when a bunt play is in order. They need to understand when a bunt play is probable so that they are not caught off guard. As the coach calling the play, you must know what your team is capable of and identify what out is most important. Understanding the situation, the time of the game and how it affects the outcome will determine what defense to run. Whether it is getting the lead out or the sacrifice out, you must teach the players to understand their starting positions on each play and most of all to remain calm and record an out. Make sure you get an out in order to make these plays successful. Let your players know, if they are unsure of where to throw the ball, to always get the sacrifice out (the batter who bunted the ball/the out at first base). If the offensive team advances the runner and you record an out then it's a success for us as a defense.

Because of limited time at practice for these situations and because younger players are still developing decision making abilities, getting the lead runner is an added bonus. It can be done with the right personnel and lots of time spent working on these situations. The bottom line is, know your players' abilities and the value of which out is most important at the time.

TEACHING BUNT PLAYS IN PRACTICE

Decision making plays are some of the more difficult plays any player has to make. At all levels of baseball, players make wrong decisions executing bunt plays. It goes without saying that you must take time in practice to teach your basic plays and give players as many repetitions possible if you want them to be better decision makers. Having said that, let's keep in mind our teaching progression philosophy from chapter one and follow these bullet points when teaching your players the bunt plays at practice:

- Keep it simple. Only go over one or two bunt plays per week.
- On a particular play, put players in their starting bunt play position and walk through the play in a dry drill. (show each position player where they go on a particular bunt)
- Next, call out the play and have a coach roll out the bunts and have players react. (Repeat the same play if players are confused or did not make the correct decision)
- Lastly, perform the drill live at game speed. There are three was to perform this drill: 1. With the coaches bunting and players working on the defensive side. 2. With the coach pitching and players executing the bunts and the defense reacting. 3. With players pitching and bunting just like in a game.

NOTE: With the coaches pitching, you will get more quality repetitions for the bunters and fielders in a short time. But at some point the drill should be done "all live," with the players pitching and bunting. This has great value but is best to be done once the plays and responsibilities are understood.

Man on first base bunt play or base hit bunt attempts

In this situation the players move in following fashion:

- P Covers or fields any bunts from first base line to third base line area.
- C Fields ball or calls out where ball should be thrown in a loud command two to three times so all players can hear. (Example: "One, one, one!")
- 1B Stays at first and covers the bag unless ball is bunted extremely hard. Then the player leaves the base, fields ball and tags the base unassisted.
- 2B Backs up first base.
- SS Breaks to cover second base anticipating a play at second. If the bunt was good and there is no play, the shortstop sees the throw to first base and retreats to protect third base.
- 3B Starts in on grass. Charges in hard to field bunt when pitcher lifts leg to deliver pitch. If he does not field ball, he immediately retreats back to cover third base.
- LF Backs up third base.
- CF Backs up second base.
- RF Backs up first base.

Men on first and second basic bunt play

In this situation the players move in the following fashion:

- P Covers or fields any bunts from first base line to third base line area.
- C Fields ball or calls out where ball should be thrown in a loud command two to three times so all players can hear. (Example: "One, one, one!")
- 1B Starts in on grass. Charges in hard to field bunt when pitcher lifts leg to deliver pitch.
- 2B Starts closer to first base anticipating the bunt. Covers first base.
- SS Starts at normal position. Covers second base there is a play. If not, then player sees throw to first base and retreats to cover third base.
- 3B Starts in on grass. Stays at third base and covers the bag unless ball is bunted extremely hard. Then the player leaves base to field ball and gets the out at first base.
- LF Backs up third base.
- CF Backs up second base.
- RF Backs up first base.

Men on first and second rotation bunt play

In this situation the players rotate in the following fashion:

- P Keys off shortstop. Waits for him to break two steps toward third base then delivers the pitch home. His responsibility is to field any bunts from mound area to third base line.
- C Fields ball or calls out where ball should be thrown in a loud command two to three times so all players hear. (Example: "Three, three, three!")
- 1B Starts farther in on grass. Looking to get the out at third base, he charges in hard to field bunt when pitcher lifts leg to deliver pitch. If no play is at third, first baseman throws ball to second baseman covering first base to record the out.
- 2B Starts two steps closer to first base anticipating the bunt, breaks to cover first when pitcher lifts leg to deliver pitch.
- SS Starts behind runner's left shoulder and holds him close. Once pitcher is set, breaks hard to third and covers third base.
- 3B Starts in on grass. Charges in hard to field bunt when pitcher lifts leg to delivery pitch. If there is no play at third he throws the ball to first base to record an out.
- LF Backs up third base.
- CF Backs up second base.
- RF Backs up first base.

First and Third Defense

As the coach calling the play, you must know what your team is capable of and identify what out is most important. Understanding the situation, the time of the game and how it affects the outcome will determine what defense to run.

Because of limited time at practice for these situations and because younger players are still developing decision making abilities, coaches must provide guidance. Expecting players to instinctively be able to read a throw to second base and decide whether to tag the runner at second or to abort that out and return the throw home to get the runner trying to score on a double steal is not probable. The bottom line is: You as the coach must decide what play to run and what outcome you want. Get an out, not let the runner at third score, or try to bait the runner at third to score and try to get him out, or let the runner steal second and play from there.

TEACHING FIRST AND THIRD PLAYS IN PRACTICE

Decision making plays are difficult plays at this level for many players to execute. It goes without saying that you must take time in practice to teach your basic plays and give players as many repetitions possible. When beginning to teach your defensive plays, keep in mind our teaching progression philosophy from chapter one and follow these bullet points when teaching your players first and third defensive plays at practice.

- Keep it simple. Use plays your players can remember and execute. Three plays maximum with an objective for different results is more than enough.
- Go over your plays once a week.
- Walk through plays in a dry drill and make sure players understand their responsibilities and objectives.
- Next, call out plays and have team perform them without base runners. (Repeat the same play if players are confused or did not execute properly)
- Lastly, add base runners at first and third and play it live. The runners should work on stealing and the fielders on defending.

1. **Play 1-**Catcher throws ball back to the pitcher. Pitcher than checks the runner at third and anticipates a play at third. Third baseman must yell home if runner breaks towards home. The objective is to not let the runner from third base score, while still attempting to make a play on him. Play is useful if coach believes the offense may be trying a double steal.

2. **Play 2-**Catcher throws the ball to second base to get out at second. Second baseman does not react if runner from third goes home. Just record out at second base. The priority is to get an out. Play is useful when you do not care if the runner at third scores or not.

3. **Play 3-**Catcher throws ball immediately to third base. Middle infielders do not break to cover second base but hold ground in case ball is hit. The priority is to not let the runner at third base score. Play is useful when a speedy runner is at third and you believe he may try to double steal.

4. **Play 4-**Catcher throws to shortstop, who comes running straight in from the shortstop position. The objective is to bait the runner from third into trying to score. The play has a higher margin for error but is effective in baiting the runner to try to score.
5. **Play 5-**Catcher throws ball to second base and the second baseman or shortstop comes across in front of second base 10 feet and cuts throw anticipating a play at home. The objective is to bait the runner from third into attempting to score. Play is effective in baiting runner but the risk is that the infielder must vacate his position early and batter may hit the ball.
6. **Play 6-**Catcher throws the ball to second baseman, who comes running straight in from his position and returns throw to home. The objective is to bait the runner from third into trying to score. The play has a higher margin for error and second baseman may be affected by runner stealing second if not performed properly, but is an effective way of baiting the runner to try to score.

Expert Advice on Deciding First and Third Defense

As the coach calling the play, you must know what your team is capable of and identify what out is most important.

Rundown Fundamentals

Pickle: This is the proper way to handle a rundown when a runner is caught between bases. The goal is to get the runner at full speed so he has a hard time changing direction. Ideally, the runner should be pursued back to the base last occupied.

For simplicity, the chaser will be the defender with the ball and the receiver the defender making the tag. Once the chaser receives the ball, his job is to get to one side of the baseline to create a throwing lane and get the ball out of his glove and into a dart-throwing position. The receiver clears himself to the same side as the chaser to keep the throwing lane.

It's best to work on the pitcher's mound side of the baseline to cut down the throwing distance, but it can be done on either side. The chaser pursues the runner at full speed to get him running hard. The receiver slowly cuts down the distance and flashes his hands and verbally calls for the ball when runner nears.

As a dart-like throw is made, the receiver steps to the ball to make the catch and apply the tag. The chaser must be careful not to fake a throw, which might also fake out his receiver and make his job more difficult. After the throw is made the chaser will follow their throw (making sure to avoid the runner) and take the spot the receiver just vacated. This is in case the rundown comes back. If the runner takes off early, and the chaser has to make a long throw, then the chaser stays put. This is in case the rundown comes back his direction.

The main problem youth players have with rundowns is lack of experience and judging when to throw and when to call for the ball. Take time at practice to recreate different rundown scenarios and get players familiar with how to communicate and the timing in a rundown.

Pop Fly Responsibility

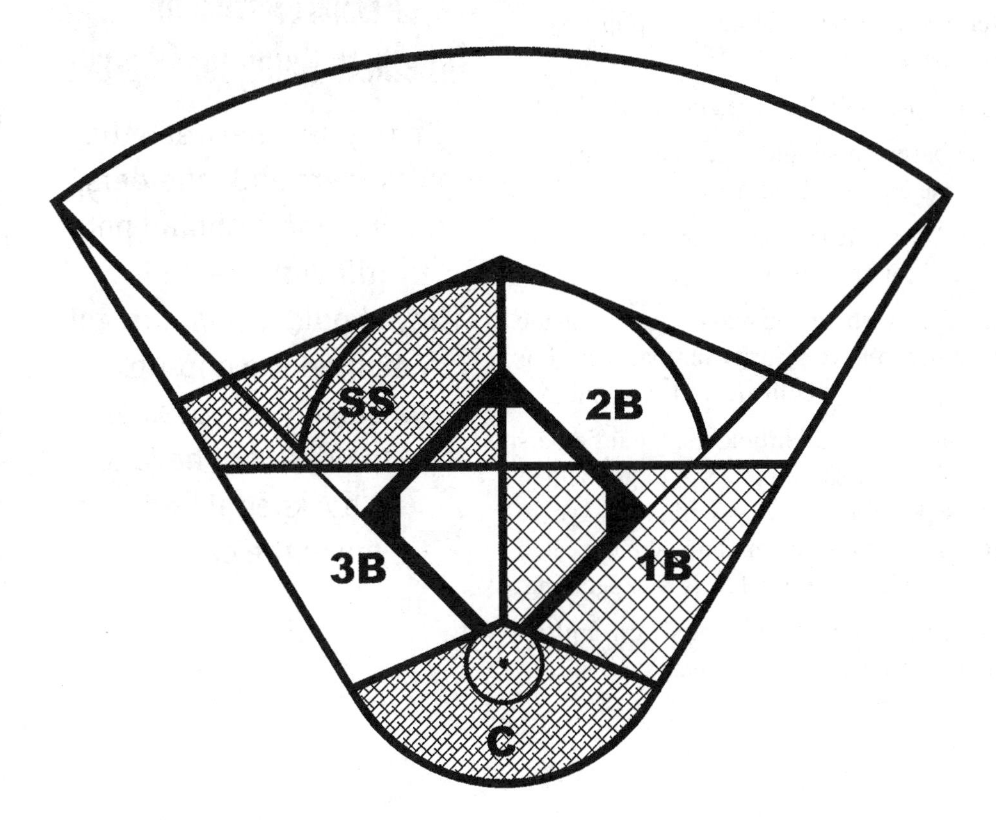

PRIORITIES FOR THE DIAGRAM

1. Out fielders have priority over the infielders.
2. The center fielder has priority over the left and right fielders.
3. Infielders have priority over the catcher and the pitcher.
4. Second baseman has priority over the first baseman.
5. Shortstop has priority over the third baseman and second baseman.
6. Second baseman can be given priority over the short stop if he is better at taking charge and catching pop-ups.

FUNDAMENTALS AND PRINCIPLES

1. When a pop fly goes up in the infield, all infielders should expect to make the catch until one player takes charge by calling for the ball loudly two times: "I've got it, I've got it!" Or: "Ball, Ball" can also be used for the younger players.
2. An infielder should take charge when the ball is in his area and not look for someone else to make the catch. Want the ball.
3. If the pop-up is really high on a windy day, the infielder should not call for the ball to soon. Wait until the ball starts to descend before calling for the ball.
4. If the sun is in line with the pop-up, use the glove to shade the sun.

5. Once a player with priority calls for the ball, the other players should give way to him.
6. When an infielder determines he will not catch a pop-up, he should retreat to cover his base.
7. Catchers should go for all pop-ups in their area until called off.
8. The shortstop and second baseman should take charge on pop-ups that are behind third base and first base, respectively.
9. On short pop-ups near the mound area which no other player can get to, the pitcher should call for and catch the ball.
10. On pop-ups near the mound area where two players can reach the ball, designate the best fielder to have priority on that play. For example, the shortstop has priority on balls over the mound.
11. On pop-ups between the outfielders and infielders, the infielders should not drift with the ball. They should attempt to get behind the pop-up as quickly as possible so they will not have to backpedal to make the catch. If an outfielder can make the catch easily, he should always call off the infielder if he is backpeddling.
12. All players should stay in a good athletic position and be ready to move their feet when camped underneath a pop-up.

Expert Advice on Infielders Going for Pop-ups

On pop-ups between the outfielders and infielders, the infielders should not drift with the ball. They should attempt to get behind the pop-up as quickly as possible so they will not have to backpedal to make the catch.

Joe Millette on Catching Pop-ups:
"The most important point about being good at catching pop-ups is, you have to want to catch the ball! Teach your players to take charge in their area and expect and want the ball."

CUT-OFFS AND RELAYS

Cut-offs and relays are the most important fundamentals your team will perform. They are utilized every game and can almost always affect the outcome. Their purpose is to keep the double play in order and to stop runners from advancing an extra base. When in doubt about multiple runners, always make sure the lead runner is stopped before trying for a trail runner.

TEACHING CUT-OFFS AND RELAYS

Proper positioning on all the different scenarios takes time to develop and can be overwhelming for younger players. But players need to have an understanding of where to be on the field in order to play the game correctly. Regularly expose your players to different situations that arise. Don't overload players with too much information at one time. Teach them where to go and how to communicate so they are prepared as a group when a play develops.

- Be patient and do it dry first. Explain the situation and walk the players through their positioning of that play.
- Then introduce a ball and cover the same situation without runners and watch for proper alignments and spacing of players.
- Lastly, add a base runner or two and play it live.
- Remember to have a runner start at home plate when doing live cut-off situations. This is the batter/runner that is often forgotten by the defense in a multiple-runner scenario.
- Over a few practices, slowly build on the different cut-offs and relay situations.
- Review the old situation briefly and then add a new one.
- The more players are exposed to these situations, the better they will become in handling them.

In any given play, every player has a place to be. Remind players never to get caught spectating and to cover their responsibility when a ball is hit. Make sure all bases are covered and all potential plays are being backed up. Watch for proper spacing between the outfielder, relay man and the player who represents the cut-off man.

Important Points for Outfielders

- The outfielders need to communicate with each other where the ball should be thrown.
- The throws should be good, low hard throws so they can be handled by the relay men.
- Outfielders should throw to hit the lead relay man, not the trailer. The throw should be chest high.

The Relay Man

The relay man needs to make his presence known to the outfielder by giving a visual target with his hands up, and yell for the ball, *Ball, ball.* As the throw is made, the relay man attempts to gain momentum to the base he is throwing and rides the throw for a quicker release. On tandem relays, he listens for help from the trailing infielder about where to throw the ball. But as he goes into the outfield and lines up for the play, he peeks at the runners himself to know where he has a play. He only uses the trailer for assurance. **(pictures 13-1 & 13-2)**

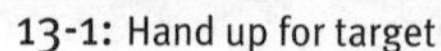

13-1: Hand up for target

13-2: Ride the throw

Important Points for Infielders

- Get in position early and get hands up to be visible for the outfielder.
- Players working in tandem should make sure they are lined up.
- Let the outfielder make the long throw and be aware if the outfielder is throwing from a dead-stopped position or with some momentum from the play.
- Lead man should know what he wants to do with the ball and use trail man for assurance
- When the balls are hit into the gaps, you have to want to throw the runner out.
- Be ready to move to adjust to the throw. Do not jump for throws. Get the long hop, if necessary, to keep momentum going toward the play.
- Trail man should be 7-15 yards behind the relay man, depending on age, and should help with communication.
- If the lead man gets an in-between hop, let it go for the trail infielder to handle.
- Shortstop stays 5-10 yards off the left-field line when getting a throw from down the line.
- Do not short hop the catcher or receiving player on throws. Know when you can reach the target all the way through the air and when you must make a one-hop throw.

Cut-off Man

- Cut-off men on a good throw, fake a cut to stop batter/runner.
- First basemen and third basemen position themselves on the inside of the base lines and watch to see if the passing runner touches the base.
- Cut-off men should adjust their depth to the arm strength of the outfielder or relay man and position themselves deep in the infield when the arm allows.
- The last point is key. Positioning deep when possible will freeze the batter/runner longer and allow you more time to read the play to make a decision about whether to cut the ball, go for the batter/runner or let it go.
- If it's a weak throw or off line, go get the ball.

COMMUNICATION OF VERBAL COMMANDS

The player covering the base where the throw is headed communicates to the cut-off man. His decision right or wrong should be emphatic. If the throw is on the money and doesn't need to be cut, the player yells go, go, go loud three times. If the ball needs to be redirected, the call is three, two, one or home—wherever the ball needs to be thrown. When calling out a redirection, it should be said at least three times as well. For example three, three, three, would be the call on a ball being relayed to third base. If there is no play and you want the ball cut and held, then say, *cut, cut, cut*. The key is to get the players talking and learning to make a decision. Below are the verbal calls in a cut-off situation for big or small diamond.

Terminology

1. *Go, Go, Go!* — Let the ball go.
2. *Cut, Cut, Cut!* — No play, cut and hold the ball.
3. *One! Two! Three! or Home!* — Cut and throw to base called.

SMALL DIAMOND (see diagrams on pages 160-167)

When teaching cut-offs and relays on the small diamonds (fields with 60-foot base paths) there are a few things to look out for. Because the typical fence is set at 225 feet, the relay man should only go out a few feet onto the outfield grass on balls in front of the outfielder. That is about 15-20 feet from the base. Too often the relay man gets way too close to the outfielder. On routine balls to the outfield, have the relay man leave a throwing lane for the outfielder to throw the ball all the way to the bag. Too often we see the outfielder throw the ball to the relay man even though he is only 20 or so feet away. It takes time to relay the ball, which allows the runner a better chance to advance. Get your players used to throwing the ball all the way to the base when they are close enough.

On balls past the outfielder, the relay man will go out further depending on how deep the ball is and should let the outfielder make the longer throw.

Plays develop fast on the small field, so keep it simple by having the pitcher and shortstop due most of the relaying. This is the best approach and, besides, they are usually your two best athletes on the field. It is best to have the ball in their hands when possible. On almost all plays to third base, the shortstop is the relay man. With regards to plays at home, the pitcher is always the cut-off.

BIG DIAMOND (see diagrams on pages 168-177)

When teaching on the bigger diamonds (base paths greater than 60 feet) cut-offs and relays can get much more complex. Because of the size of the field, we can't just count on the shortstop and the pitcher to do the majority of the relays and cut-offs. More movement and proper spacing comes into play because the field's increased size.

The first baseman and third baseman are now the cut-offs to home on a routine ball. On balls beyond the outfielders a double-cut may come into play. This is when the shortstop or second baseman is the first relay man. He then throws the ball toward home through the first or third baseman that has set up as cut-off men in the infield. The pitcher's sole responsibility is to back up home or the base where the ball is being relayed.

NO ONE ON : BASE HIT TO LEFT FIELD

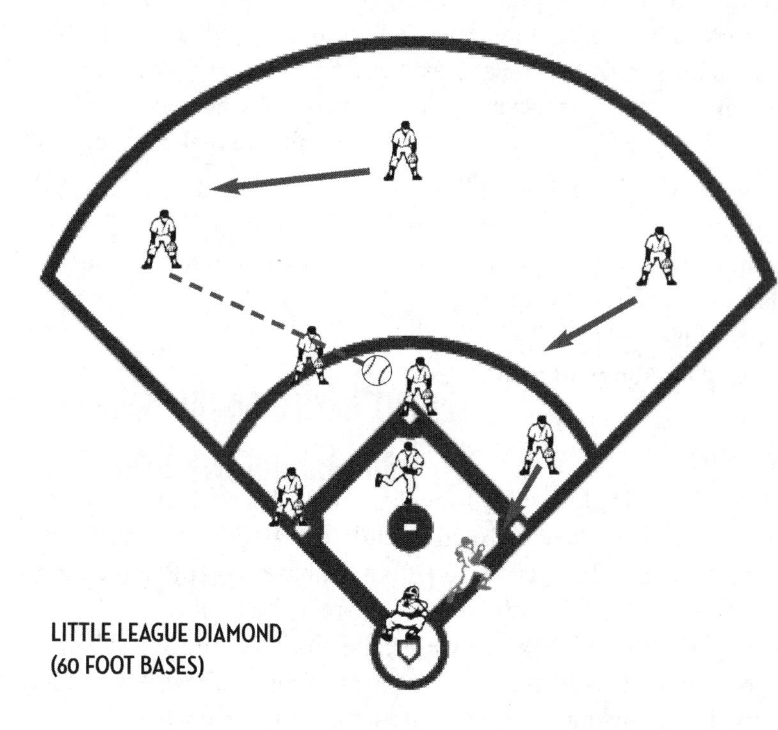

LF: Makes a good low, hard throw to second base. Low enough for relay man to handle.
CF: Backs up left fielder.
RF: Backs up second base.
3B: Covers third base.
SS: Goes out a few feet from regular defensive position toward left field and in line to second.
2B: Covers second base
1B: Avoiding runner, gets to inside part of the field between first-base bag and cut of grass. Watches runner touch base. Moves back to base in order to create a throwing lane for possible return throw.
C: Gets out in front of home plate and yells second base
P: Stays behind mound anticipating bad throw or a deflection off an infielder's glove.

NO ONE ON : BASE HIT TO CENTER FIELD

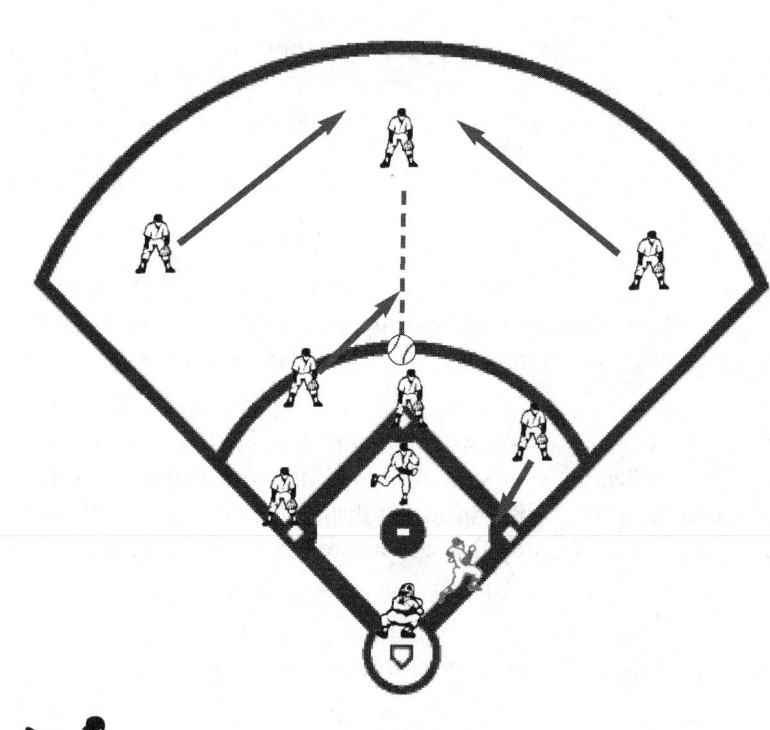

LF: Backs up center fielder
CF: Makes a good low, hard throw to second base. Low enough for relay man to handle.
RF: Backs up center fielder
3B: Covers third base.
SS: Goes out roughly 15 feet from second base toward centerfield and gets in line with second base.
2B: Covers second base
1B: Avoiding runner, gets to inside part of the field between first-base bag and cut of grass. Watches runner touch base. Moves back to base in order to create a throwing lane for possible return throw.
C: Gets out in front of home plate and yells second base
P: Stays behind mound in line with throw from center fielder at second base.

NO ONE ON : BASE HIT TO RIGHT FIELD

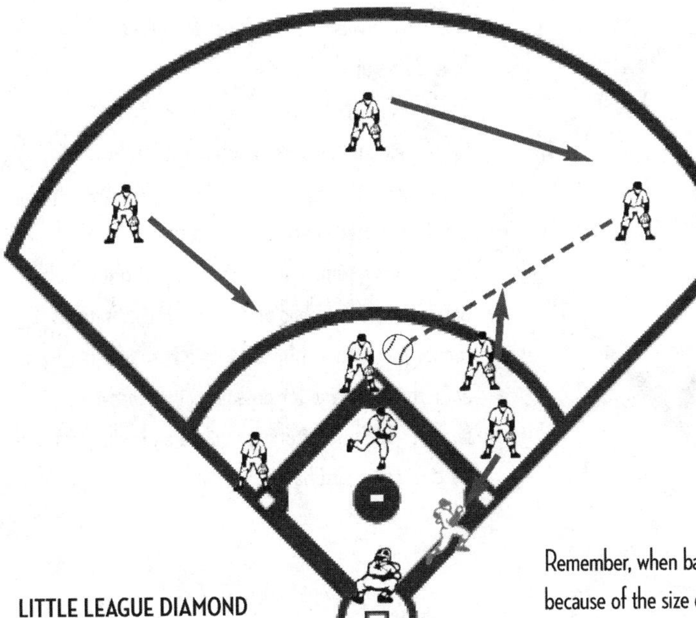

LITTLE LEAGUE DIAMOND
(60 FOOT BASES)

LF: Backs up second base

CF: Backs up right fielder.

RF: Makes a good low, hard throw to second base. Low enough for relay man to handle.

3B: Covers third base.

SS: Covers second base.

2B: Goes out a few feet from regular defensive position toward right field and in line to second.

1B: Avoiding runner, gets to inside part of the field between first-base bag and cut of grass. Watches runner touch base. Moves back to base in order to create a throwing lane for possible return throw.

C: Gets out in front of home plate and yells second base

P: Stays behind mound anticipating bad throw or a deflection off an infielder's glove.

Remember, when balls are hit over or past the outfielders, you are using one relay man because of the size of the field. The relay man needs to go out according to his arm strength and the outfielder's arm strength. Distances will vary depending on location and depth of a ball, as well as the players' abilities.

NO ONE ON : EXTRA-BASE HIT DOWN LEFT-FIELD LINE

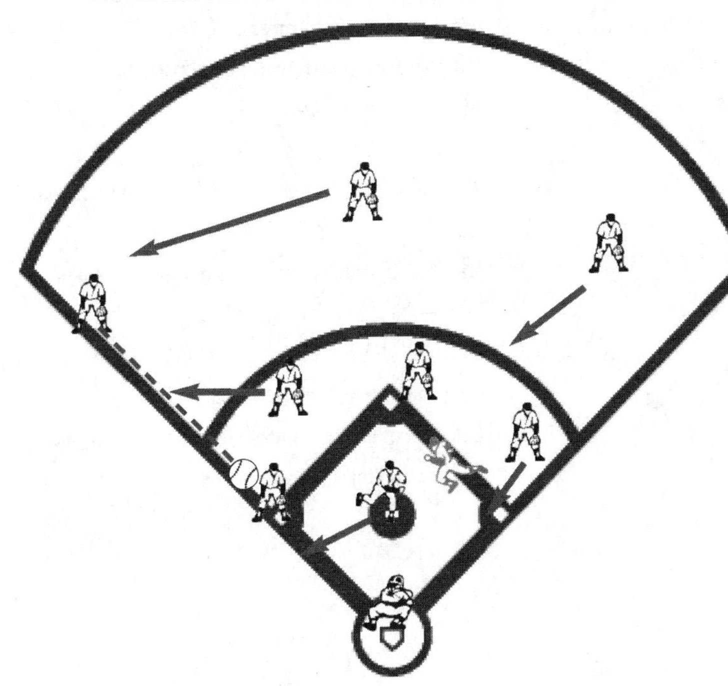

LF: Fields ball and makes a good, low hard throw into relay man (shortstop).

CF: Backs up left fielder.

RF: Backs up second base.

3B: Covers third base.

SS: Goes in line with left fielder and third base as relay man.

2B: Covers second base

1B: Avoiding runner, gets to inside part of the field between first-base bag and cut of grass. Watches runner touch base. Moves back to base in order to create a throwing lane for possible return throw.

C: Gets out in front of home plate and yells third base.

P: Backs up third base.

NO ONE ON : EXTRA-BASE HIT TO LEFT-CENTER

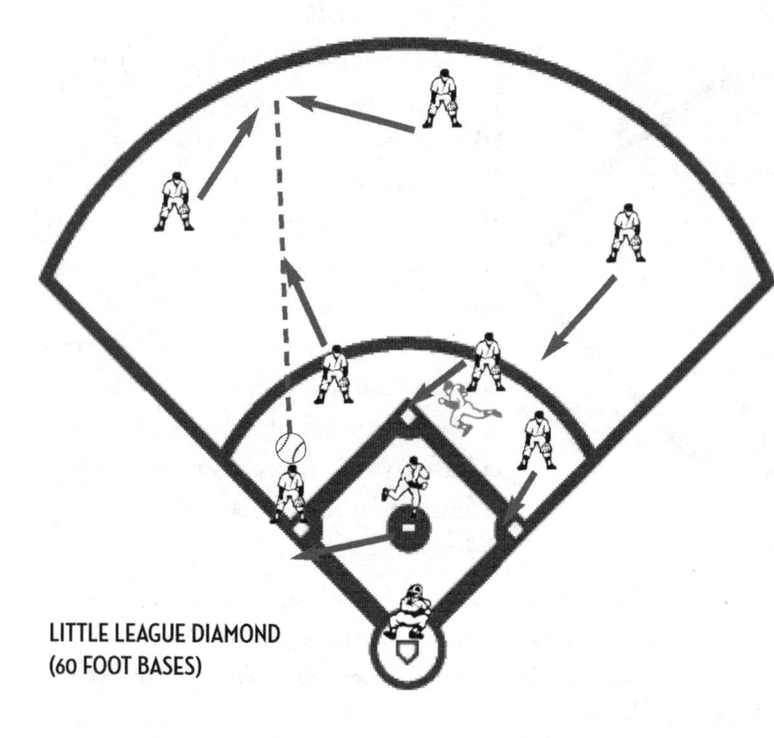

LF: Fields ball and makes a good, low hard throw into relay man (shortstop).
CF: Goes toward ball and tries to make the play.
RF: Backs up second base.
3B: Covers third base.
SS: Goes out in line with outfielder and third base as relay man.
2B: Covers second base
1B: Avoiding runner, gets to inside part of the field between first-base bag and cut of grass. Watches runner touch base. Moves back to base in order to create a throwing lane for possible return throw.
C: Gets out in front of home plate and yells third base.
P: Backs up third base.

NO ONE ON : EXTRA-BASE HIT TO RIGHT-CENER

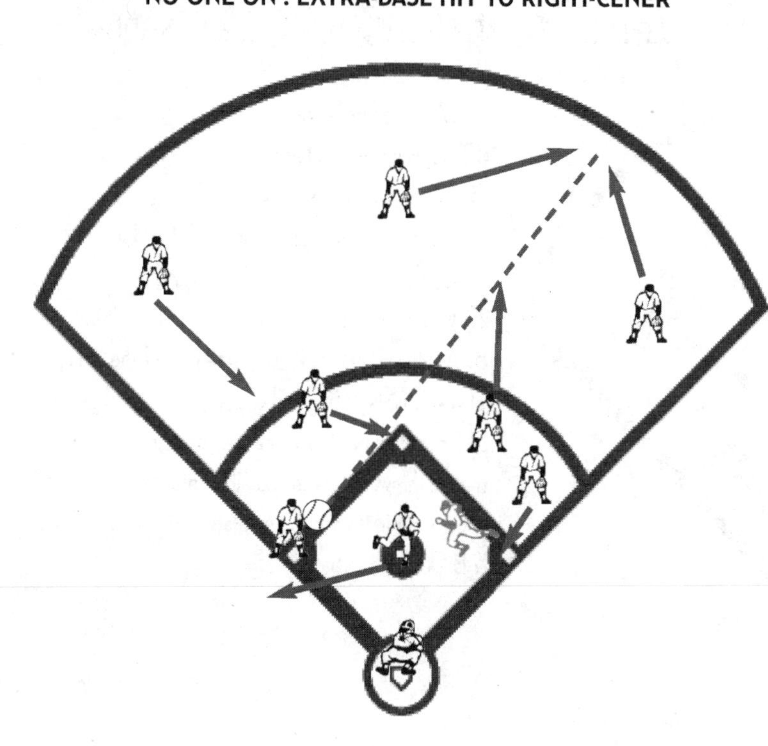

LF: Backs up second base.
CF: Fields ball and makes a good, low hard throw into relay man (second baseman).
RF: Goes toward ball and tries to make the play.
3B: Covers third base.
SS: Covers second base.
2B: Goes out in line with outfielder and third base as relay man.
1B: Avoiding runner, gets to inside part of the field between first-base bag and cut of grass. Watches runner touch base. Moves back to base in order to create a throwing lane for possible return throw.
C: Gets out in front of home plate and yells third base.
P: Backs up third base.

NO ONE ON : EXTRA-BASE HIT DOWN RIGHT-FIELD LINE

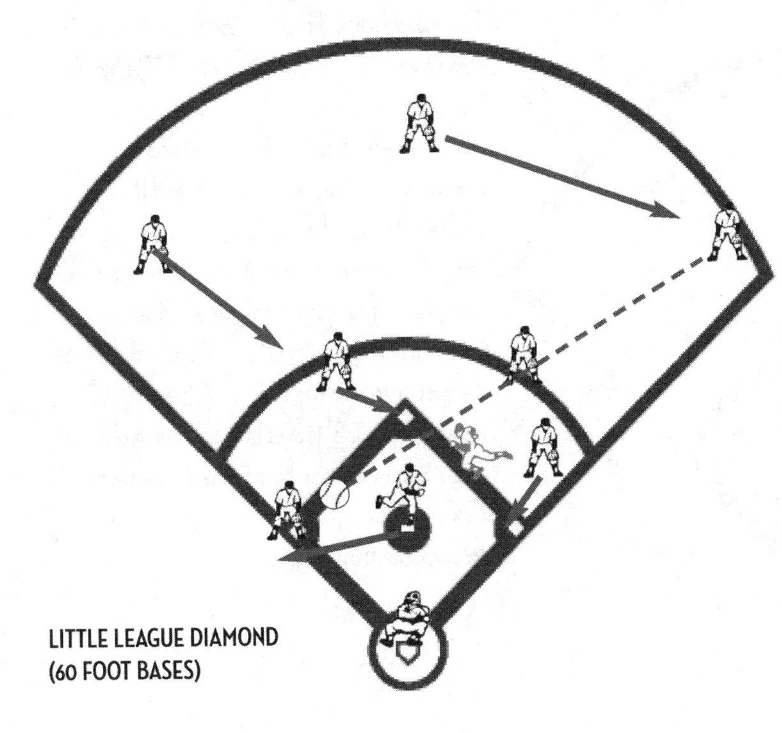

LF: Backs up second base.
CF: Backs up right fielder.
RF: Fields ball and makes a good, low hard throw into relay man (second baseman).
3B: Covers third base.
SS: Covers second base.
2B: Goes out in line with right fielder and third base as relay man.
1B: Avoiding runner, gets to inside part of the field between first-base bag and cut of grass. Watches runner touch base. Moves back to base in order to create a throwing lane for possible return throw.
C: Gets out in front of home plate and yells third base.
P: Backs up third base.

MAN ON FIRST : BASE HIT TO LEFT FIELD

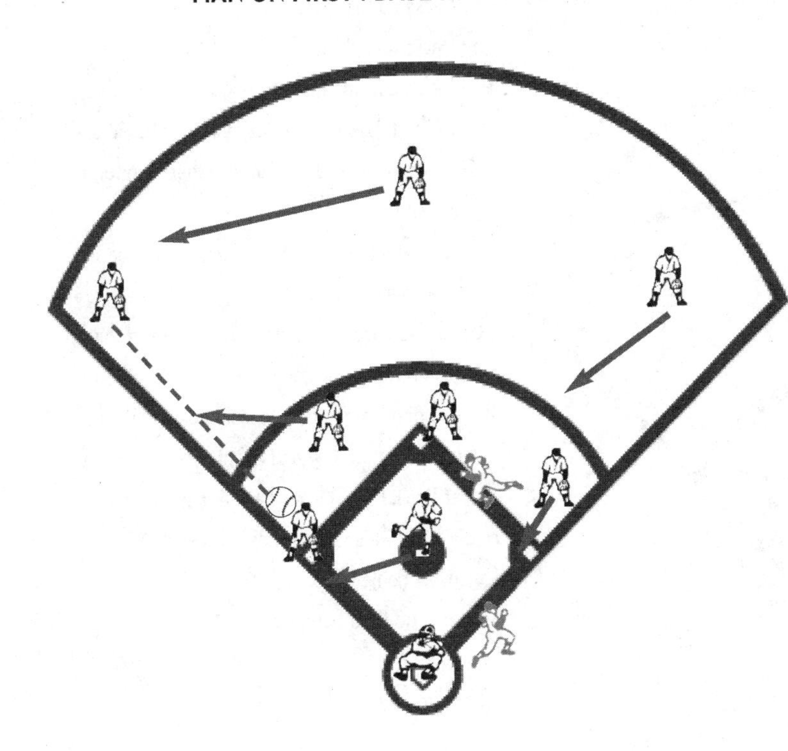

LF: Fields ball and makes a good, low, hard throw toward third. Low enough for relay man to handle.
CF: Backs up left field.
RF: Backs up second base.
3B: Covers base and lines up shortstop.
SS: Gets in line with left fielder and third base as a relay man to third.
2B: Covers second base and communicates with shortstop and second baseman if runner is trying to advance.
1B: Avoiding runner, gets to inside part of the field between first-base bag and cut of grass. Watches runner touch base. Moves back to base in order to create a throwing lane for possible return throw.
C: Covers home plate.
P: Backs up third base.

MAN ON FIRST : BASE HIT TO CENTER FIELD

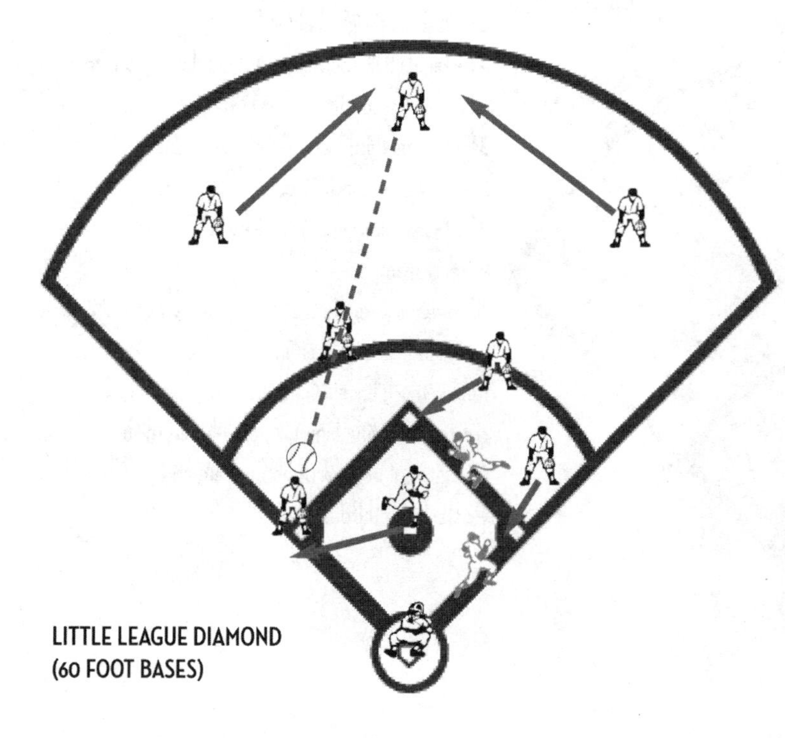

LF: Backs up center fielder.
CF: Fields ball and makes a good, low, hard throw toward third. Low enough for relay man to handle.
RF: Backs up center fielder.
3B: Covers base and lines up shortstop.
SS: Gets in line with center fielder and third base as a relay man to third.
2B: Covers base and informs shortstop and third baseman of if runner is trying to advance.
1B: Avoiding runner, gets to inside part of the field between first-base bag and cut of grass. Watches runner touch base. Moves back to base in order to create a throwing lane for possible return throw.
C: Covers home plate
P: Backs up third case.

MAN ON FIRST : BASE HIT TO RIGHT FIELD

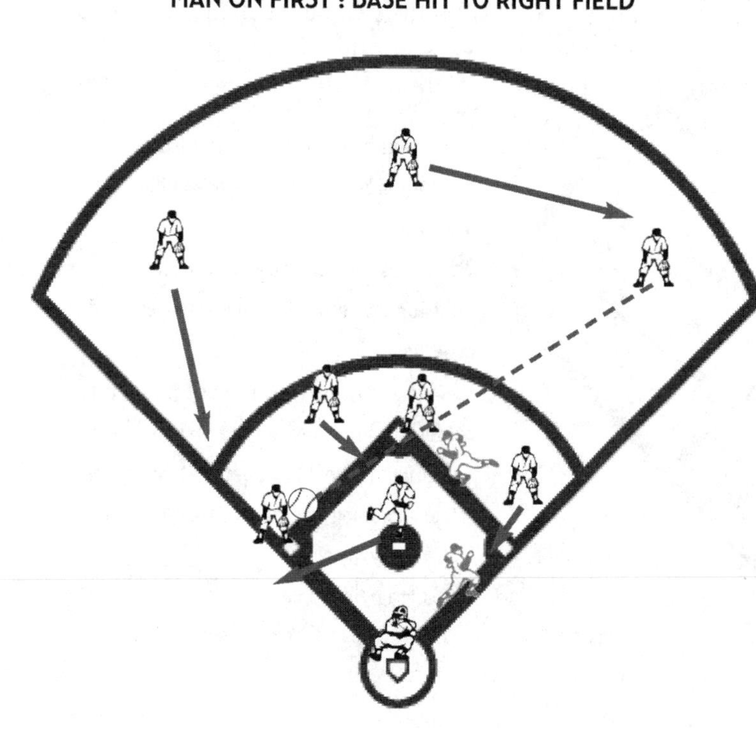

LF: Backs up third baseman.
CF: Backs up right fielder.
RF: Fields ball and makes a good, low, hard throw toward third. Low enough for relay man to handle.
3B: Covers base and lines up the shortstop for a possible throw.
SS: Gets in line with right fielder and third base as a relay man to third.
2B: Covers base and informs shortstop and third baseman if runner is trying advance.
1B: Avoiding runner, gets to inside part of the field between first-base bag and cut of grass. Watches runner touch base. Moves back to base in order to create a throwing lane for possible return throw.
C: Covers home plate.
P: Backs up third base.

MAN ON SECOND OR RUNNERS ON SECOND AND THIRD : BASE HIT TO LEFT

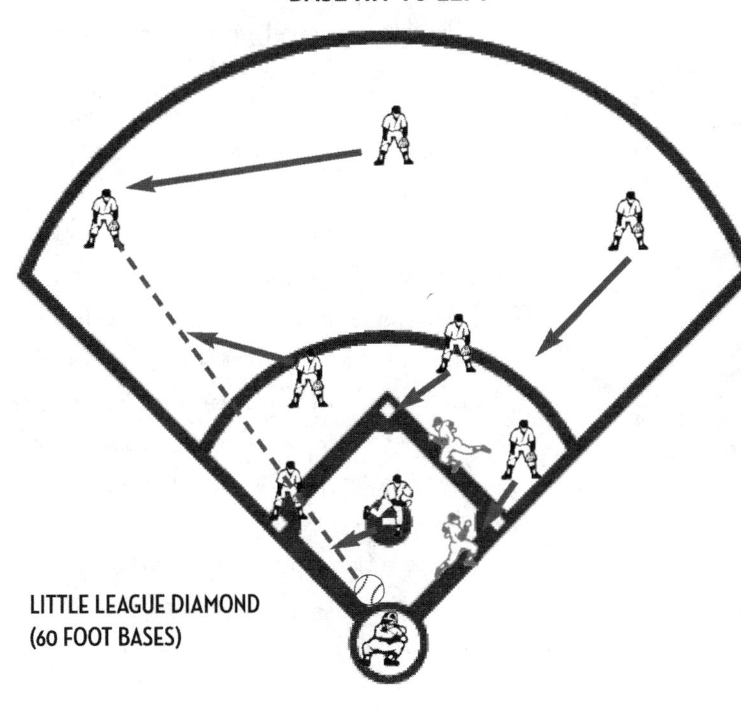

LF: Makes a good low, hard throw toward home plate so cut-off man can handle throw.
CF: Backs up left field.
RF: Backs up second base.
3B: Covers third base.
SS: Goes out a few feet from his position toward left field and points and yells home.
2B: Covers second base.
1B: Avoiding runner, gets to inside part of field between first-base bag and cut of grass. Watches runner touch base. Moves back to base for possible return throw.
C: Lines up the pitcher and communicates whether to cut the ball, redirect the ball to another base or let the ball go through.
P: Gets in line between left fielder and the catcher as cut-off man, setting up between the pitcher's mound and base path.

MAN ON SECOND OR RUNNERS ON SECOND AND THIRD : BASE HIT TO CENTER

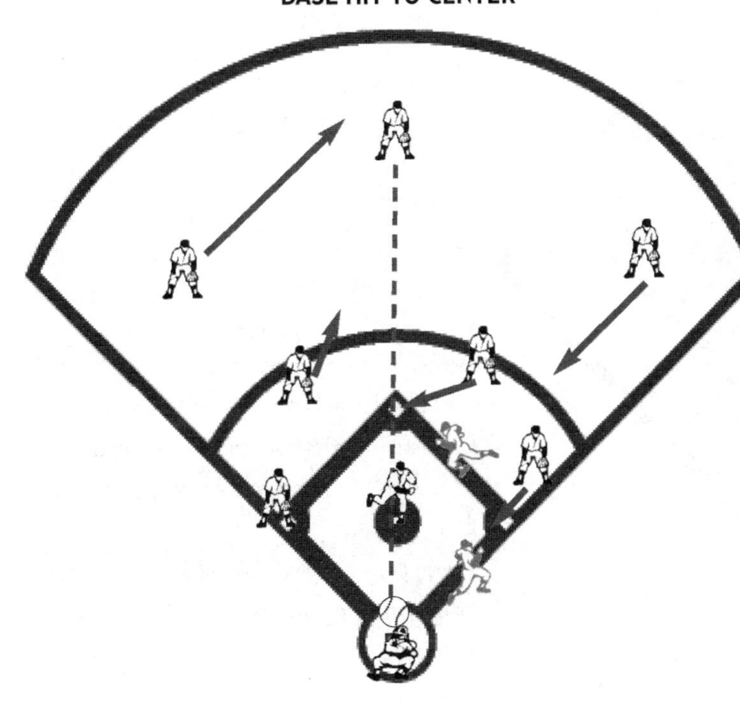

LF: Backs up center field.
CF: Makes a good low, hard throw toward home plate so cut-off man can handle throw..
RF: Backs up second base.
3B: Covers third base.
SS: Goes out a few feet from his position toward left field and points and yells home.
2B: Covers second base.*
1B: Avoiding runner, gets to inside part of field between first-base bag and cut of grass. Watches runner touch base. Moves back to base for possible return throw.
C: Lines up the pitcher and communicates whether to cut the ball, redirect the ball to another base or let the ball go through.
P: Gets in line between center fielder and home near back of mound as cut-off man.
* Second baseman stays out of line of throw then moves in to cover second base.

MAN ON SECOND OR RUNNERS ON SECOND AND THIRD : BASE HIT TO RIGHT

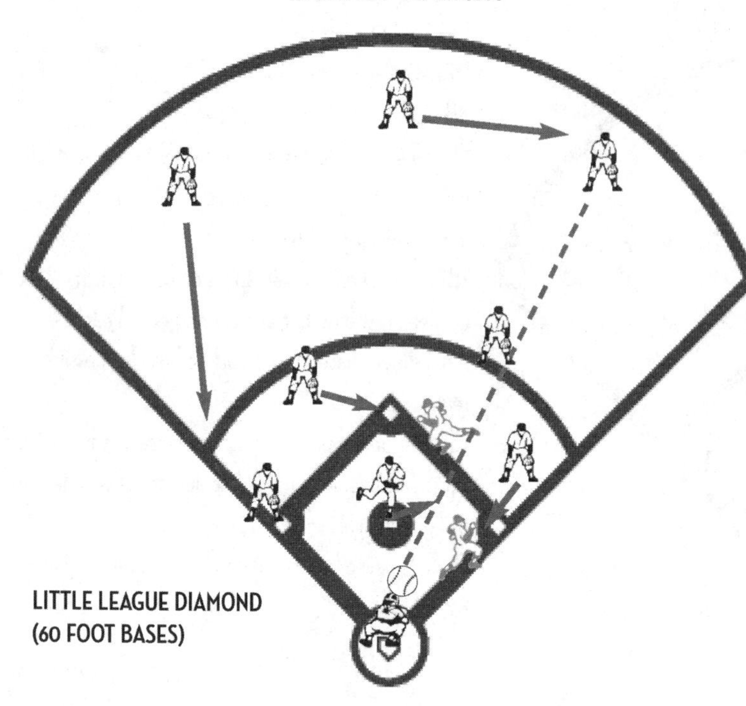

LF: Backs up third base.
CF: Backs up right field.
RF: Makes a good low, hard throw toward home plate so cut-off man can handle throw.
3B: Covers third base and informs fielders of whether the runner is rounding third or not.
SS: Covers second base.
2B: Goes out a few feet from position toward right field and points and yells home.
1B: Avoiding runner, gets to inside part of the field between first-base bag and cut of grass. Watches runner touch base. Moves back to base for possible return throw.
C: Lines up the pitcher and communicates whether to cut the ball, redirect the ball to another base or let the ball go through.
P: Gets in line between right fielder and the catcher as cut off man, setting up between the pitcher's mound and base path.

RUNNERS ON FIRST AND SECOND OR BASES LOADED : BASE HIT TO LEFT FIELD

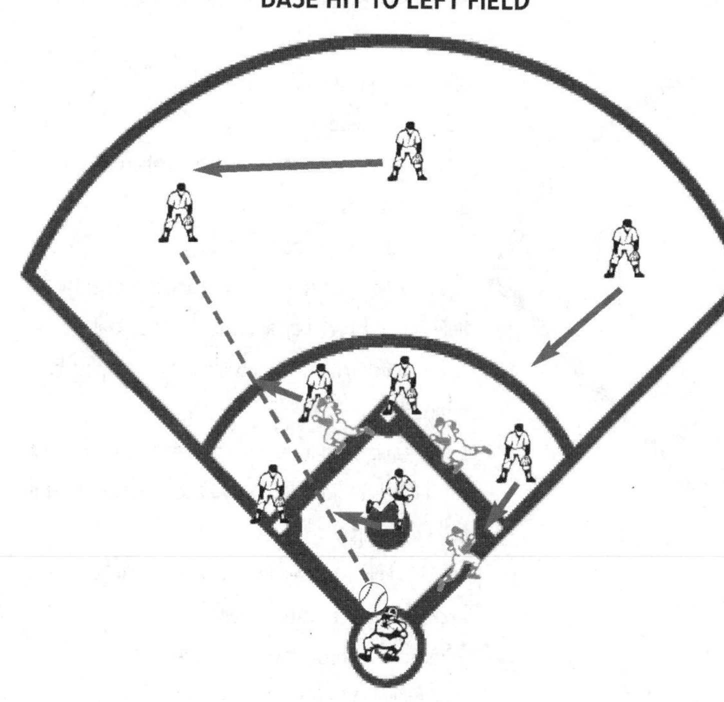

LF: Makes a good low, hard throw toward home plate so cut-off man can handle throw.
CF: Backs up left field.
RF: Backs up second base.
3B: Covers third and informs fielders of whether or not the runner is rounding third.
SS: Gets in line with third base in case outfielder throws ball towards third.
2B: Covers second base.
1B: Avoiding runner, gets to inside part of the field between first-base bag and cut of grass. Watches runner touch base. Moves back to base for possible return throw.
C: Lines up the pitcher and tells him whether to cut the ball, backdoor the runner on first or let the ball go through.
P: Gets in line between left fielder and the catcher as cut-off man, setting up between the pitcher's mound and base path.

RUNNERS ON FIRST AND SECOND OR BASE LOADED: BASE HIT TO CENTER FIELD

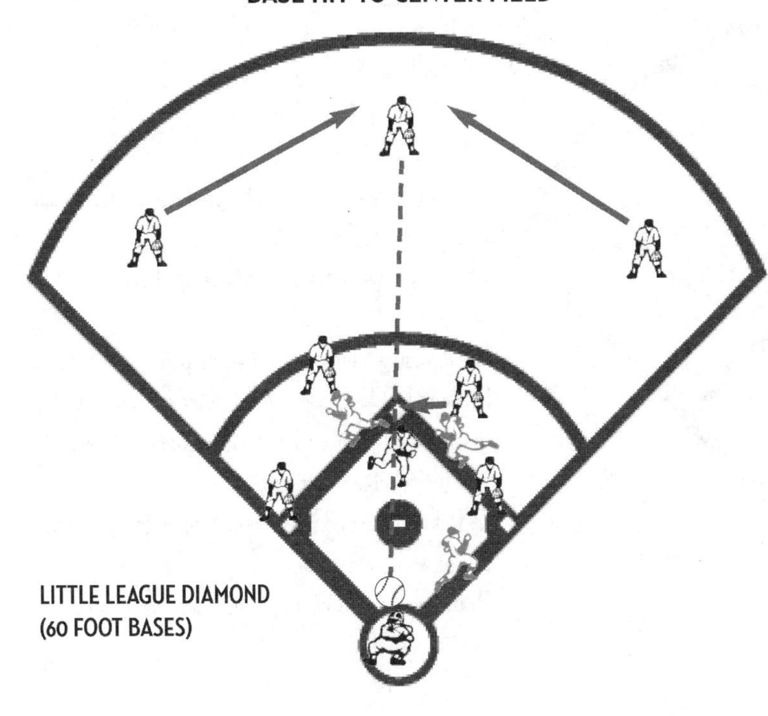

LF: Backs up center field.
CF: Makes a good low, hard throw toward home plate so cut-off man can handle throw.
RF: Backs up center field
3B: Covers third and informs fielders of whether or not the runner is rounding third.
SS: Gets in line with third base in case outfielder throws ball toward third.
2B: Covers second base once center fielder has thrown ball toward home. Waits until the ball passes the bag before covering the base.
1B: Avoiding runner, gets to inside part of the field between first-base bag and cut of grass. Watches runner touch base. Moves back to base, for possible return throw.
C: Lines up pitcher and communicates whether to cut the ball, redirect the ball to another base or let it go.
P: Gets in line with center fielder and catcher, 5 feet behind back edge of the pitcher's mound, as cut-off man.

RUNNERS ON FIRST AND SECOND OR BASES LOADED: BASE HIT TO RIGHT FIELD

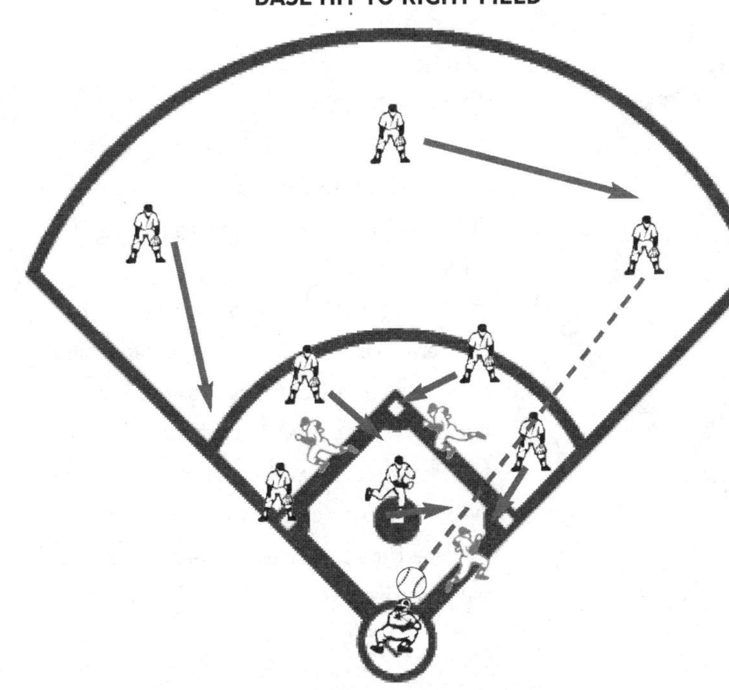

LF: Backs up third base.
CF: Backs up right fielder.
RF: Makes a good low, hard throw toward home plate so cut-off man can handle throw.
3B: Covers third and informs fielders of whether or not the runner is rounding third.
SS: Gets in line with third base in case outfielder throws ball toward third.
2B: Points and yells home to right fielder then covers second base.
1B: Avoiding runner, gets to inside part of the field between first-base bag and cut of grass. Watches runner touch base. Moves back to base for possible return throw.
C: Lines up pitcher and communicates whether to cut the ball, redirect the ball to another base or let it go.
P: Gets in line between right fielder and the catcher as cut off man, setting up between the pitcher's mound and basepath.

NO ONE ON : BASE HIT TO LEFT FIELD

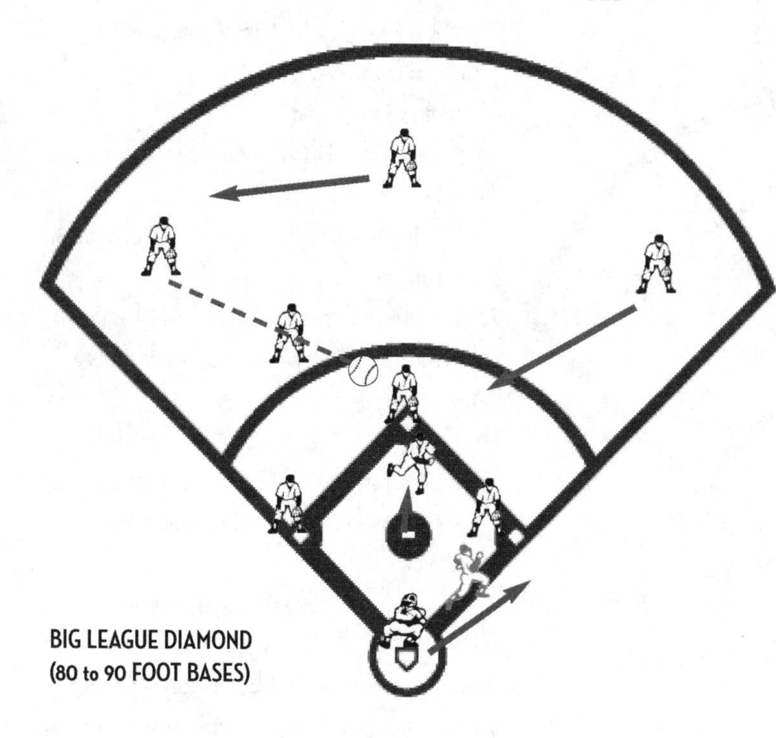

LF: Fields ball and makes a good, low, hard throw to second base.
CF: Backs up left fielder.
RF: Backs up second base.
3B: Covers third base.
SS: Gets in line with left fielder, acting as a relay man to second base if needed.
2B: Covers second base and lines up shortstop if needed.
1B: Avoiding runner, gets to inside part of the field between first-base bag and cut of grass. Watch runner touch base. Moves back to base, creating a throwing lane for possible return throw.
C: Calls out second base loudly from in front of plate and backs up first base.
P: Moves into a back-up position between mound and second base.

NO ONE ON : BASE HIT TO CENTER FIELD

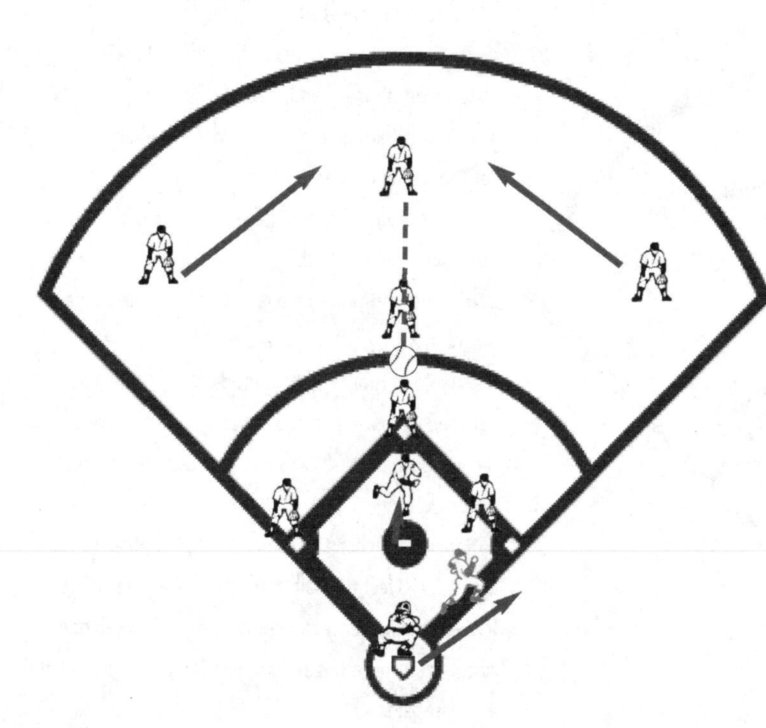

LF: Backs up center fielder.
CF: Fields ball and makes a good, low, hard throw to second base.
RF: Backs up center fielder.
3B: Covers third base.
SS: Gets in line with center fielder acting as a relay man if needed to second base.
2B: Covers second base and lines up shortstop if needed.
1B: Avoiding runner, gets to the inside part of the field between first base bag and cut of grass. Watches runner touch base. Moves back to base, creating a throwing lane for possible return throw.
C: Calls out second base loudly from out in front of the plate and backs up first base.
P: Moves into a back up position between the mound and second base.

NO ONE ON : BASE HIT TO RIGHT FIELD

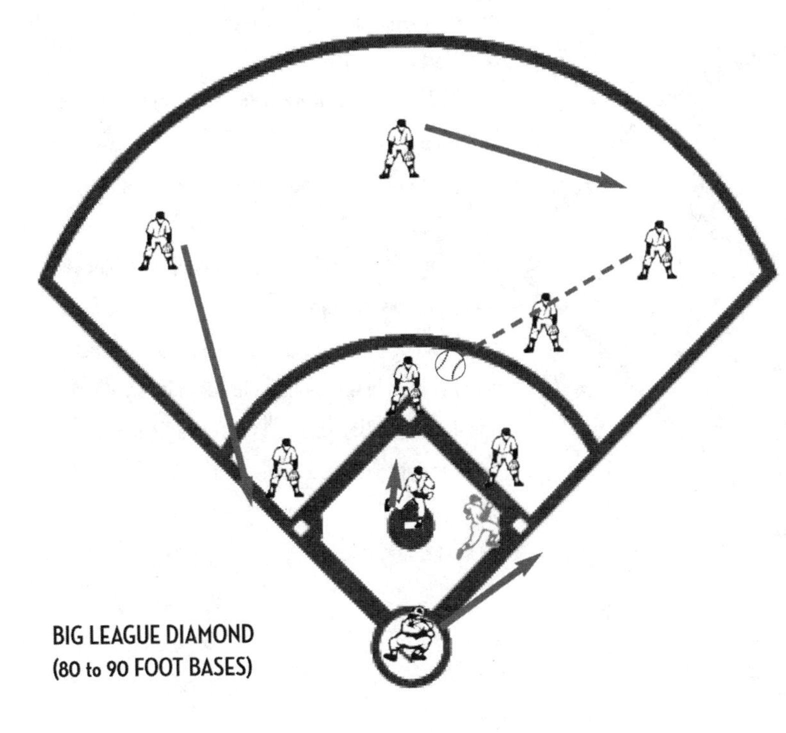

LF: Backs up third base in a direct line with right fielder and the second-base bag.
CF: Backs up right fielder.
RF: Fields ball and makes a good, low, hard throw to second base.
3B: Covers third base.
SS: Covers second base and lines up second baseman if needed.
2B: Gets in line with right fielder acting as a relay man to second base if needed .
1B: Avoiding runner, gets to the inside part of the field between first-base bag and cut of grass. Watches runner touch base. Moves back to base, creating a throwing lane for possible return throw.
C: Calls out second base loudly from out in front of the plate and backs up first base.
P: Move into a back up position between the mound and second base.

NO ONE ON : EXTRA-BASE HIT DOWN LEFT FIELD LINE

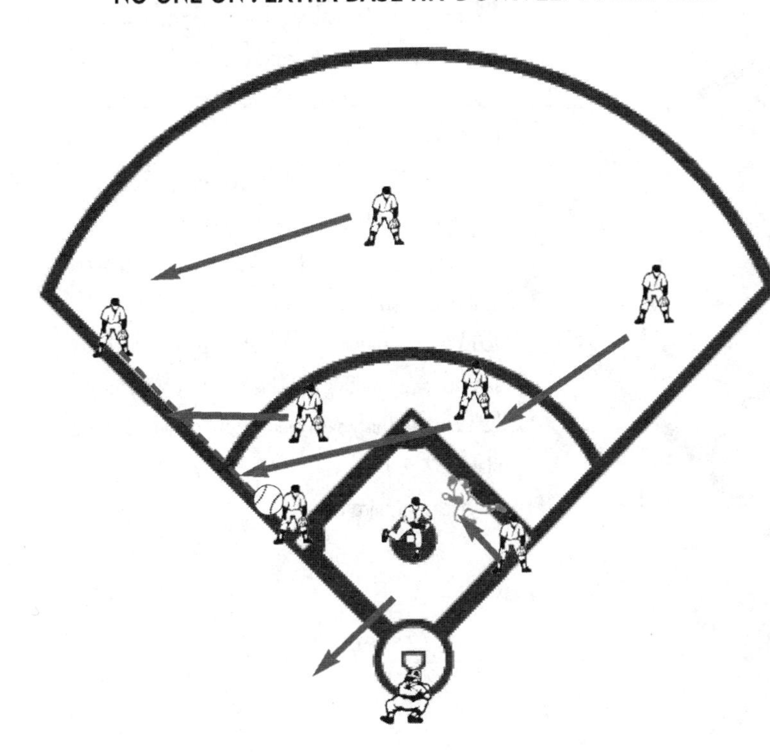

LF: Fields ball and makes a good, hard throw into relay man (shortstop).
CF: Backs up left fielder.
RF: Backs up second base.
3B: Yells third base three times lining up the shortstop to third base.
SS: Gets in line with outfielder, acting as a relay man to third base .
2B: Runs 20 feet behind shortstop as trailer in case ball is overthrown.
1B: Avoiding runner, gets to the inside part of the field between first-base bag and cut of grass. Watches runner touch base. Then follows runner to second base.
C: Calls out third base loudly from in front of the plate .
P: Backs up third base.

NO ONE ON : EXTRA-BASE HIT TO LEFT CENTER

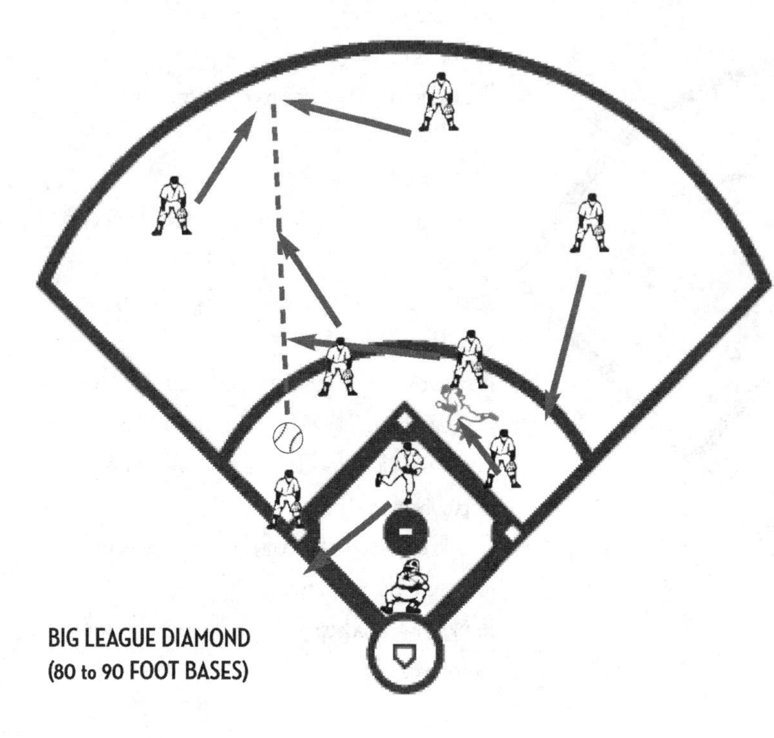

LF or CF: Fields ball and makes a good low, hard throw into relay man. (shortstop)
RF: Backs up toward first base.
3B: Yells third base three times lining up the shortstop to third base.
SS: Gets in line with the outfielder, acting as relay man to third base.
2B: Runs 20 feet behind the shortstop as trailer in case ball is overthrown.
1B: Avoiding runner, gets to the inside part of the field between first base bag and cut of grass. Watches runner touch base. Then follows runner to second base.
C: Calls out third base loudly from out in front of the plate.
P: Backs up third base.

NO ONE ON : EXTRA-BASE HIT TO RIGHT CENTER

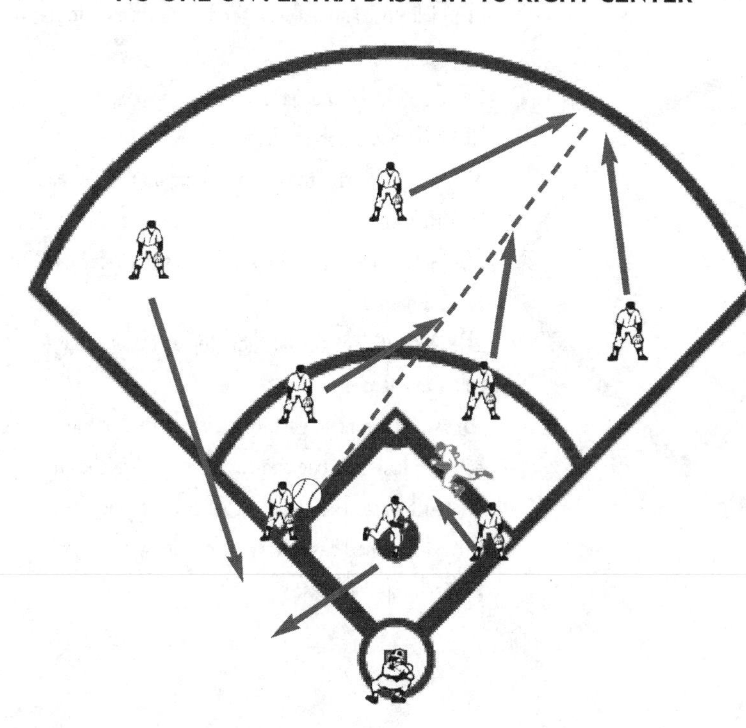

LF: Backs up toward third base.
RF or CF: Fields ball and makes a good low, hard throw into relay man (second baseman).
3B: Yells third base three times lining up the second baseman to third base.
SS: Runs 20 feet behind the second baseman as trailer in case the ball is overthrown.
2B: Gets into a straight line with the outfielder, acting as a relay man to third base.
1B: Watches runner touch first base, trails batter to second base awaiting possible throw at anytime.
C: Calls out third base loudly from out in front of the plate.
P: Backs up third base.

NO ONE ON : EXTRA-BASE HIT DOWN RIGHT-FIELD LINE

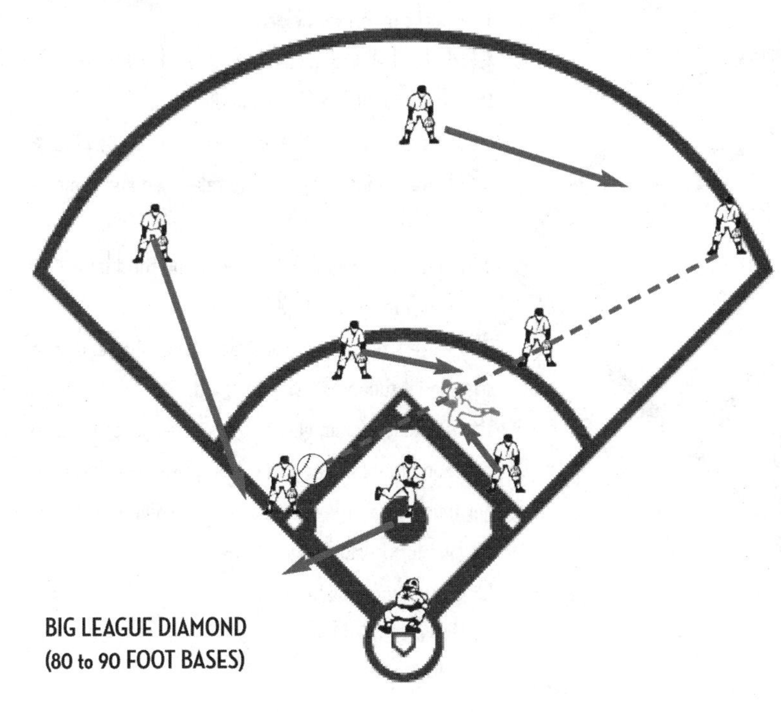

LF: Backs up toward third base.
CF: Moves toward right field.
RF: Fields ball and makes a good low, hard throw into relay man (second baseman).
3B: Yells third base three times while awaiting throw from relay man.
SS: Runs 20 feet behind the second baseman as trailer in case the ball is overthrown.
2B: Gets into a straight line with the RF, acting as a relay man to third base.
1B: Watches runner touch first base, trails batter to second base awaiting possible throw at anytime.
C: Calls out third base loudly from out in front of the plate
P: Gets between home plate and third base, waiting to get into back-up position depending where the ball is being thrown. Man on first, balls in front of the outfielders.

MAN ON FIRST : BASE HIT TO LEFT FIELD

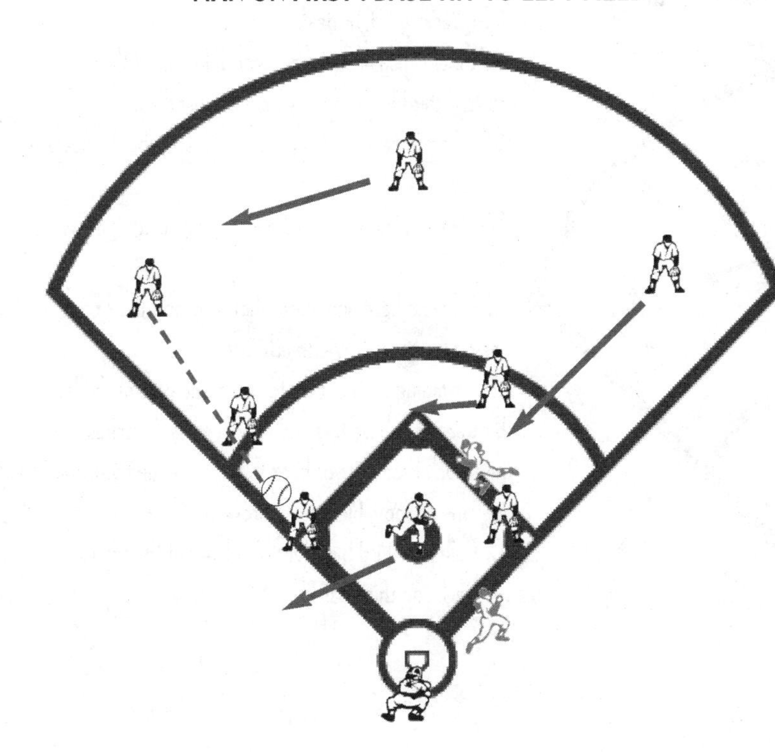

LF: Fields ball and makes a good low, hard throw to third base so relay man can handle it.
CF: Backs up left field.
RF: Backs up second base.
3B: Covers third base, lines up relay man and communicates play.
SS: Gets in line with third baseman, acting as a relay man to third.
2B: Covers second base and alerts shortstop and third baseman if runner is trying for third.
1B: Avoiding runner, gets to the inside part of the field between first base bag and cut of grass. Watches runner touch base. Moves back to base, creating a throwing lane for possible return throw.
C: Covers home plate.
P: Backs up third base.

MAN ON FIRST : BASE HIT TO CENTER FIELD

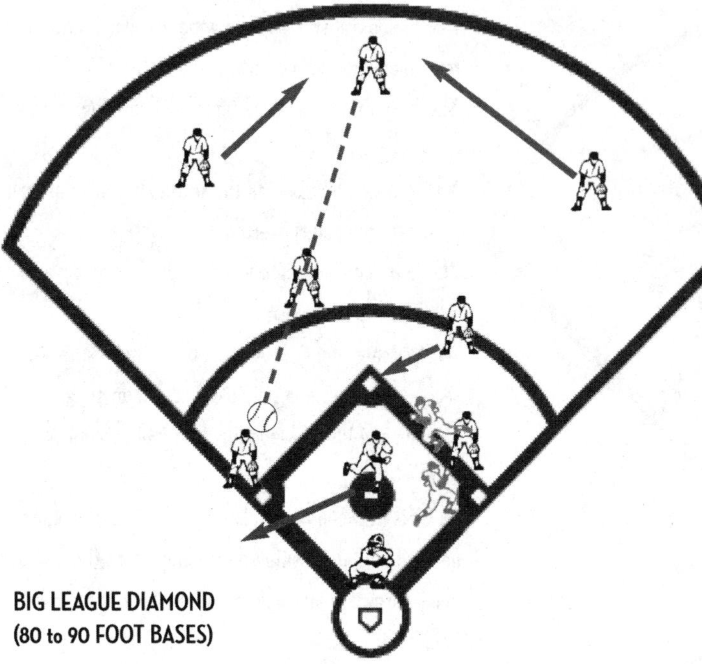

LF: Backs up center fielder.
CF: Fields ball and makes a good low, hard throw to third base so relay man can handle it.
RF: Backs up center fielder.
3B: Covers third base, lines up relay man and communicates play.
SS: Gets in line with center fielder and thrid base, acting as a relay man to third.
2B: Covers second base and alerts shortstop and third baseman if runner is trying for third.
1B: Avoiding runner, gets to the inside part of the field between first base bag and cut of grass. Watches runner touch base. Moves back to base, creating a throwing lane for possible return throw.
C: Covers home plate.
P: Backs up third base.

MAN ON FIRST : BASE HIT TO RIGHT FIELD

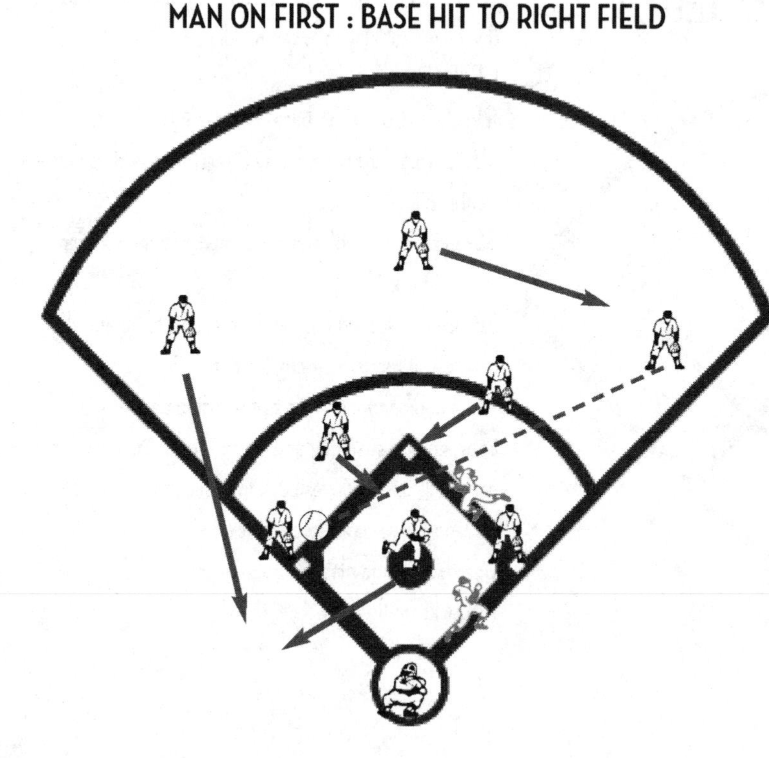

LF: Backs up third base.
CF: Backs up right field.
RF: Fields ball and makes a good, low, hard throw toward third base so relay man can handle it..
3B: Covers base, lines up relay man and communicates the play.
SS: Gets in line with third base, acting as a relay man to third.
2B: Covers base and alerts shortstop and third baseman if runner is trying to advance.
1B: Avoiding runner, gets to the inside part of the field between first-base bag and cut of grass. Watches runner touch base. Moves back to base, creating a throwing lane for possible return throw.
C: Calls out third base loudly in front of the plate.
P: Backs up third base.

MAN ON FIRST : EXTRA-BASE HIT DOWN LEFT-FIELD LINE

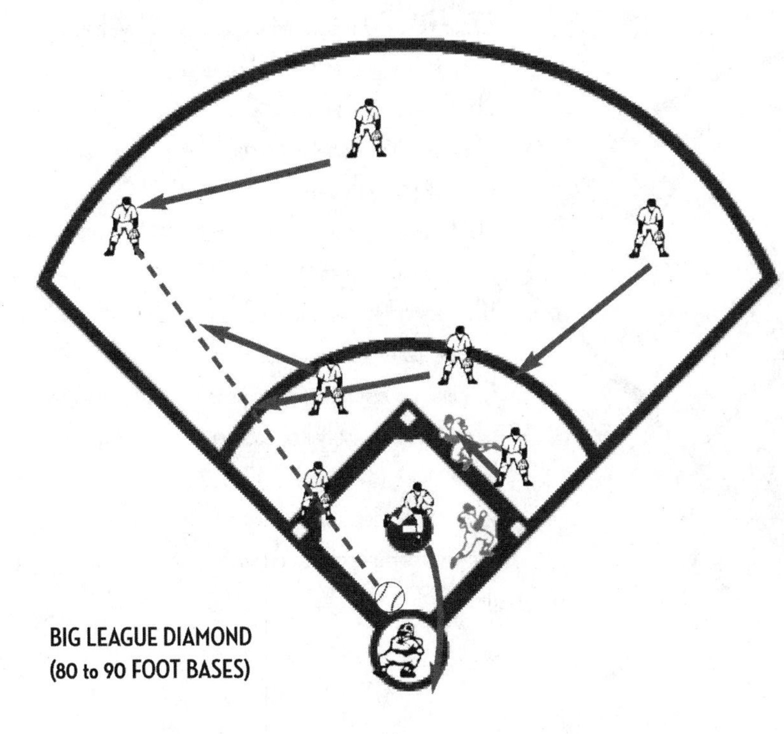

LF: Fields ball and makes a good, hard throw into relay man (shortstop).
CF: Backs up left fielder.
RF: Backs up second base.
3B: Gets in line with relay man and home between mound and base path as cut-off man to home and is responsible for covering third if play is at third instead of home.
SS: Gets in line with left fielder and home, acting as relay man to home. Stay in fair territory.
2B: Runs 20 feet behind the shortstop as trailer in case ball is overthrown.
1B: Watches runner touch base, then trails runner to second base and covers the bag.
C: Lines up third baseman and communicates whether to cut ball, relay ball home or direct play to third instead of home.
P: Backs up home plate.
Note: On this play, third baseman reads play. He is both cut-off home and responsible for covering third if the play is there instead of home.

MAN ON FIRST : EXTRA-BASE HIT DOWN LEFT CENTER

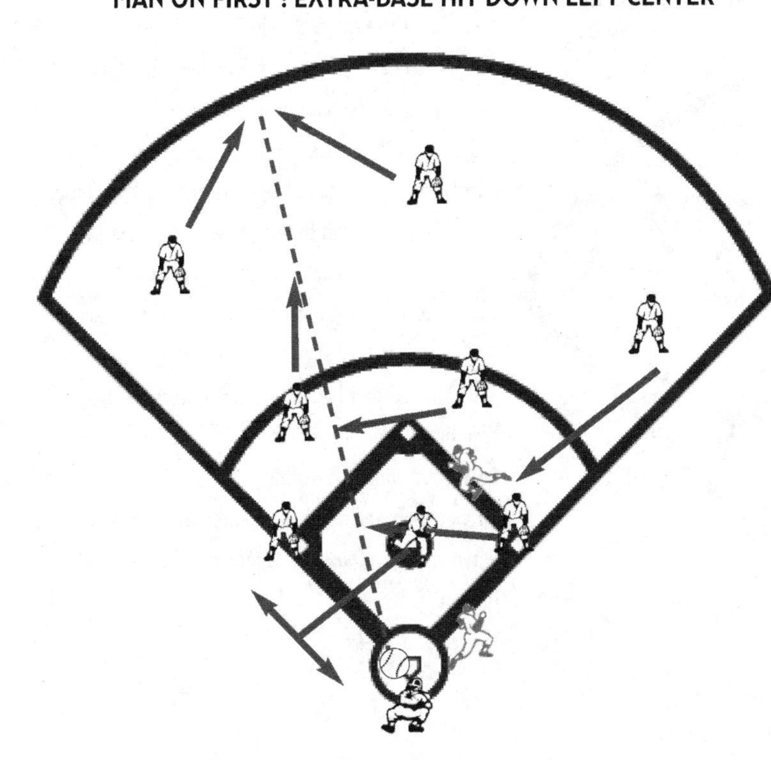

LF or CF: Fields ball and makes a good low, hard throw into relay man (shortstop).
RF: Backs up second base.
3B: Covers third base.
SS: Gets in line with outfielder and home, acting as relay man to home.
2B: Runs 20 feet behind the shortstop as trailer in case ball is overthrown.
1B: Gets in line with relay man and catcher between mound and base path as cut-off man.
C: Lines up first baseman and communicates whether to cut ball, redirect ball to another base or relay ball home.
P: Gets between home plate and third base, waiting to get into back-up position depending where the ball is thrown.

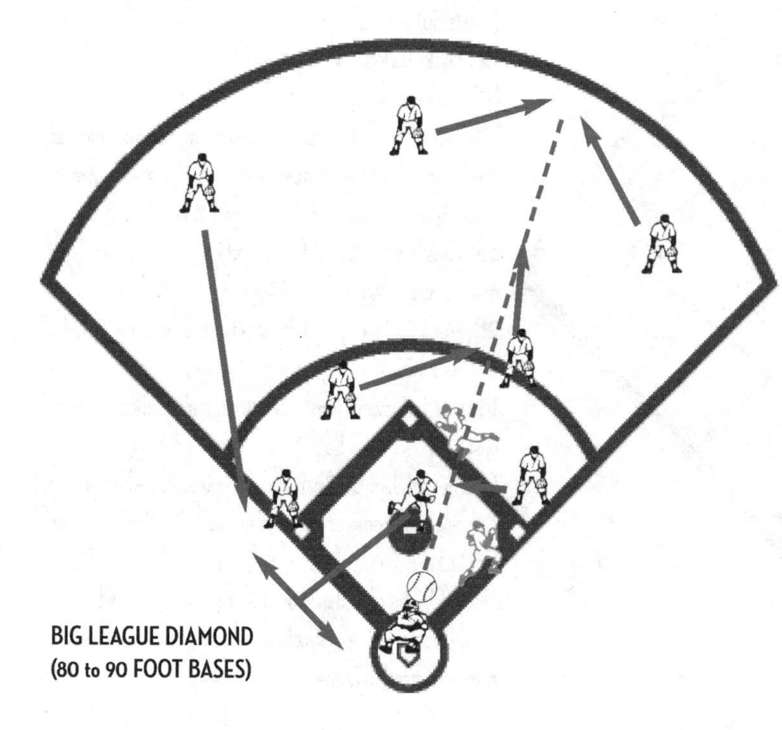

LF: Backs up toward third base.
CF or RF: Fields ball and makes a good low, hard throw into relay man (second baseman).
3B: Covers third base.
SS: Runs 20 feet behind second baseman as trailer in case ball is overthrown.
2B: Gets in line with the outfielder and home plate, acting as a relay man to home.
1B: Gets in line with relay man and catcher between mound and base path as cut-off man.
C: Lines up first baseman and communicates whether to cut ball, redirect ball to another base or relay ball home.
P: Gets between home plate and third base, waiting to get into back-up position depending where the ball is thrown.

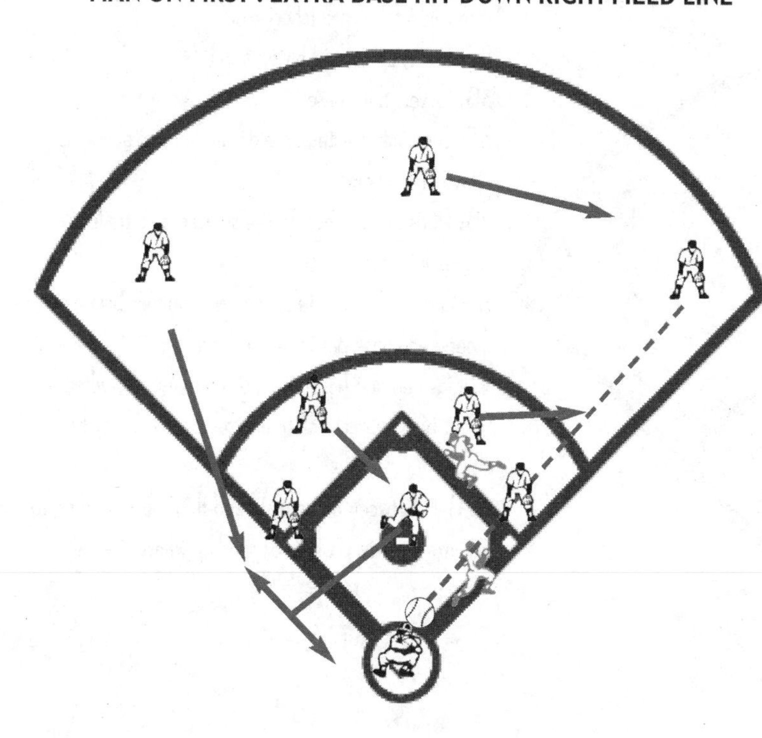

LF: Backs up towards third base.
CF: Moves toward right field.
RF: Fields ball and makes a good low, hard throw into relay man (second baseman).
3B: Covers third base.
SS: Gets in line between right fielder and third base, acting as cut-off man to third base. Also is alert in reading play as possible cut-off man to home.
2B: Gets in line with catcher and right fielder, acting as a relay man to home.
1B: Runs 20 feet behind second baseman as trailer in case ball is overthrown.
C: Covers home.
P: Gets between home plate and third base, waiting to get into back-up position depending where the ball is thrown.

MAN ON SECOND OR RUNNERS ON SECOND AND THIRD : BASE HIT TO LEFT

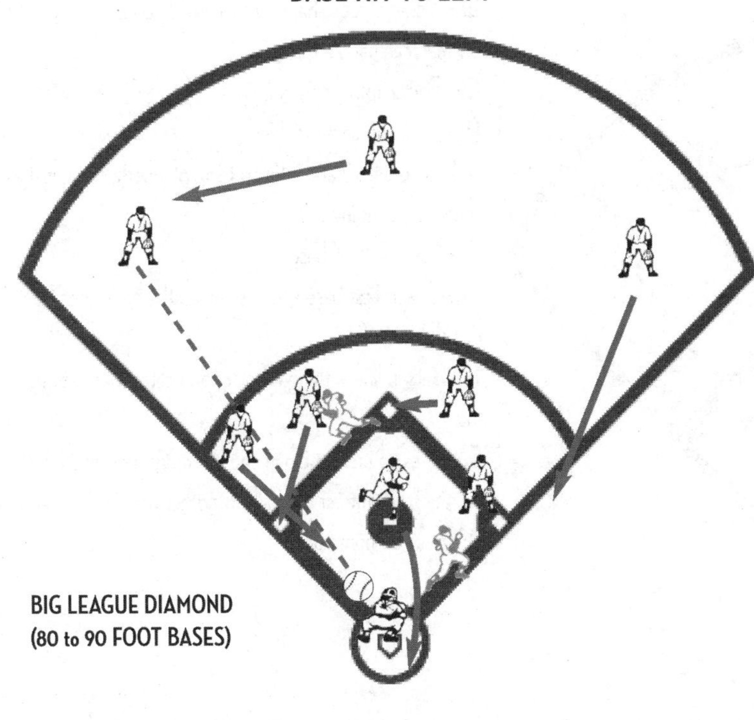

LF: Makes a good, hard throw toward home plate so cut-off man can handle throw.
CF: Backs up left fielder.
RF: Backs up toward first base.
3B: Gets in line with left fielder and catcher between mound and third-base area as cut-off man.
SS: Covers third base.
2B: Covers second base.
1B: Covers first base.
C: Lines up the first baseman and communicates whether to cut the ball, redirect ball to another base or let it go.
P: Backs up home plate.

MAN ON SECOND OR RUNNERS AT SECOND AND THIRD : BASE HIT TO CENTER

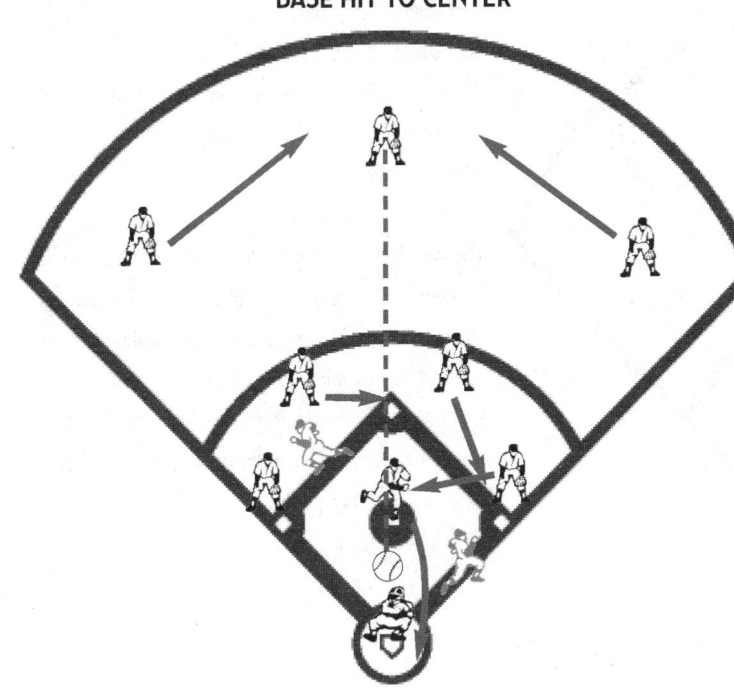

LF: Backs up center fielder.
CF: Makes a good, hard throw toward home plate so cut-off man can handle throw.
RF: Backs up center fielder.
3B: Covers third and informs team of whether or not the runner is rounding third.
SS: Cover second base.
2B: Covers first base and anticipates the back door from cut-off man.
1B: Gets in line with center field and catcher between mound and second base as cut-off man.
C: Lines up first baseman and communicates whether to cut the ball, redirect the ball to another base or let it go.
P: Backs up home plate.

MAN ON SECOND OR RUNNERS AT SECOND AND THIRD : BASE HIT TO RIGHT FIELD

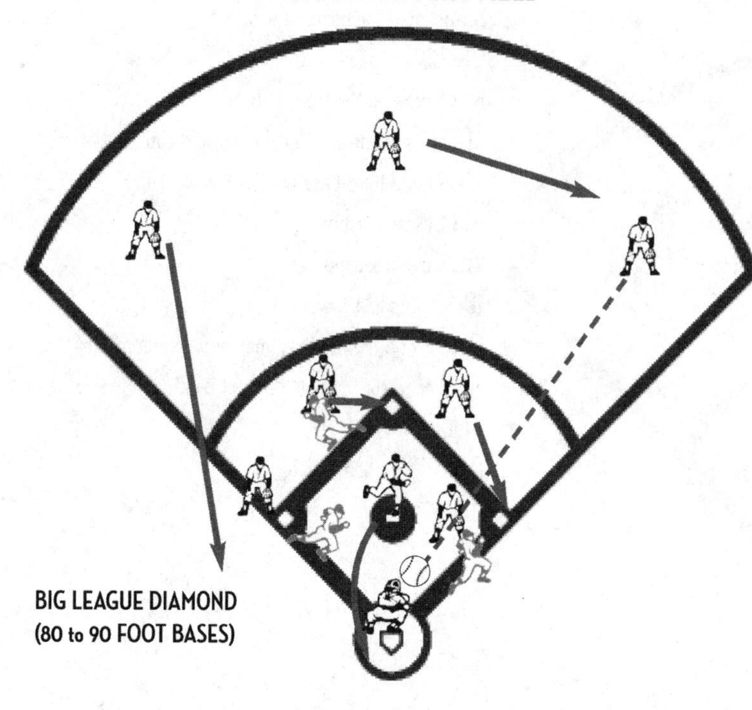

LF: Makes a good, hard throw toward home plate so cut-off man can handle throw.

CF: Backs up right fielder.

RF: Backs up center fielder.

3B: Covers third and informs team of whether or not the runner is rounding third.

SS: Cover second base.

2B: Covers first base and anticipates the back door from cutoff man.

1B: Gets in line with right fielder and catcher as cut-off man.

C: Lines up first baseman and communicates whether to cut the ball, redirect the ball to another base or let it go.

P: Backs up home plate.

MAN ON SECOND OR RUNNERS ON FIRST AND SECOND OR BASES LOADED : BASE HIT TO LEFT FIELD

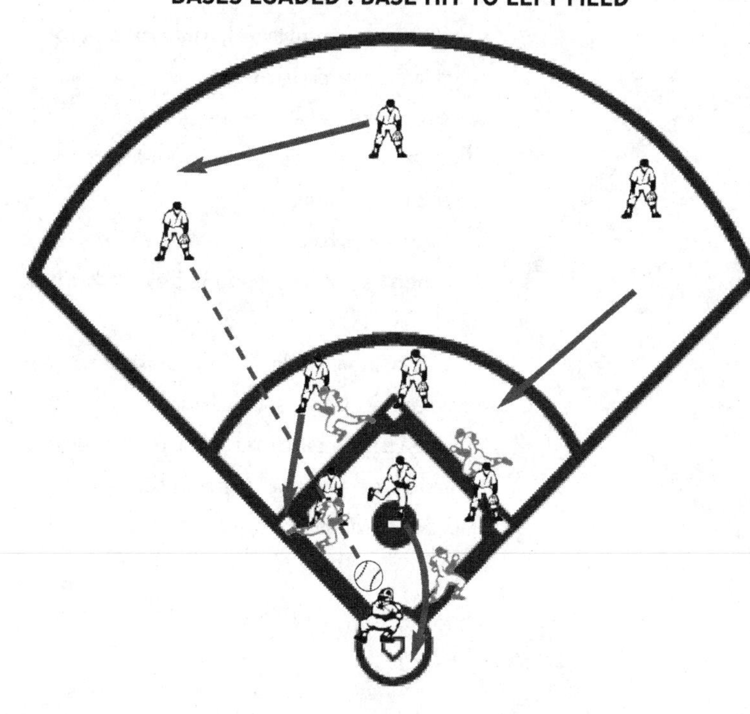

LF: Makes a good low, hard throw toward home plate so cut-off man can handle throw.

CF: Backs up left field.

RF: Backs up second base.

3B: Gets in line with left field and the catcher, between mound and third base, as cut-off man.

SS: Covers third base.

2B: Covers second base.

1B: Avoiding runner, gets to the inside part of the field between first-base bag and cut of grass. Watches runner touch base. Moves back to base, creating a throwing lane for possible return throw.

C: Lines up the third baseman and communicates whether to cut the ball, redirect the ball to another base or let the ball go through.

P: Backs up home plate.

RUNNERS ON FIRST AND SECOND OR BASES LOADED : BASE HIT TO CENTER

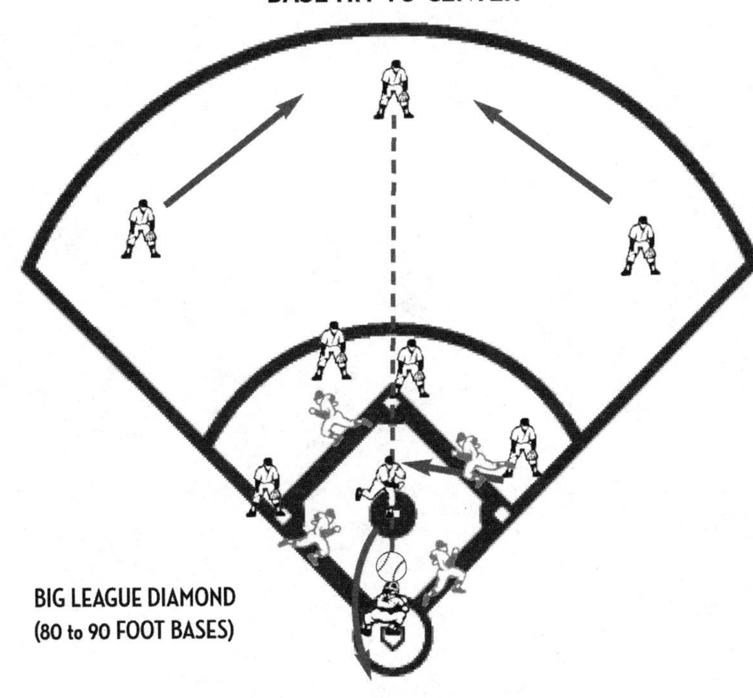

LF: Backs up center fielder.
CF: Fields ball and makes a good low, hard throw toward home so cut-off man can handle throw.
RF: Backs up center fielder.
3B: Covers base and lines up the shortstop for a possible throw.
SS: Gets in line with third base and center fielder, acting as a relay man.
2B: Covers second base.
1B: Gets in line with center fielder and catcher, between mound and second base, as cut-off man.
C: Lines up first baseman and communicates whether to cut the ball, redirect the ball to another base or let it go.
P: Backs up home plate.

RUNNERS ON FIRST AND SECOND OR BASES LOADED : BASE HIT TO RIGHT FIELD

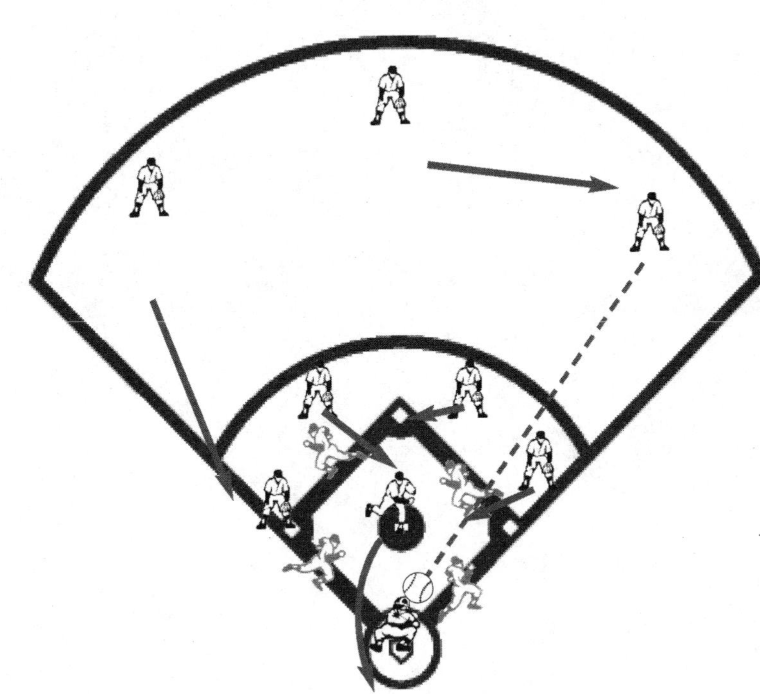

LF: Backs up toward third base.
CF: Backs up right fielder
RF: Fields ball and makes a good low, hard throw toward home so cut-off man can handle throw.
3B: Covers base and lines up the shortstop for a possible throw.
SS: Gets in line with third base and right fielder, acting as a relay man.
2B: Covers second base.
1B: Gets in line with right fielder and catcher as cut-off man.
C: Lines up first baseman and communicates whether to cut the ball, redirect the ball to another base or let it go.
P: Backs up home plate.

PRACTICE PLANNING

Youth league coaches face numerous considerations in planning a team practice. How many players will show up? How many coaches or parents will be there to help? Is there a field available to use? What baseball skills should be covered? The list goes on and on.

Remember these two points:

1. You get what you emphasize, and
2. Players feed off a coach's organization and preparation for practice.

If the coach is prepared, players will perform better, enjoy practice and, most importantly, want to come back again because the routine was fun and energetic. If the goal is to provide a positive youth-league experience, it will be much easier achieved with preparation and a practice plan.

KEY ITEMS TO REVIEW FOR AN EFFICIENT, PRODUCTIVE AND MOTIVATING PRACTICE.

1. **Where Should the Practice Be?**
   Often, baseball diamonds are not available for practice. If there is an available diamond, great. But even if there isn't, productive practices are possible if they are planned correctly. Below is a list of some possible practice locations and some suggestions on what can be accomplished.
   - **An Open Field**
     Whether it's a soccer field or any level, open field, a lot can be accomplished. Throwing drills, outfield drills and games will not be affected. Infield drills and games can be done on the grass. All hitting (live batting, soft toss and tee work) can be done with whiffle balls. With throw-down bases, base-running drills and team situations like cutoffs, relays and rundowns can be worked on. There aren't many drills that can't be done. Other than a baseball diamond, an open field is the best place to hold a team practice.
   - **Blacktop**
     This is a common place to practice when it has been raining and grass is slick and wet. It is a must that all players bring their tennis shoes to practice. This is an adequate place to work on throwing, controlled fielding of ground balls and hitting drills. It's actually a great place to work on bunting drills. Go through a controlled infield and outfield practice, simulating proper positioning with cutoffs and relays. We recommend staying away from any game-speed activity where running and fielding are involved. Falling on the blacktop can be dangerous.
   - **Batting Cages**
     Batting cages cost some money, but most have group rates for teams. Check with the local batting cages beforehand to find out the cost and how many players can be hitting at one time to figure out how long it will take for every player to get his swings. This is a valid option on rainy days or when hitting is the main goal.

Expert Advice on Where to Practice

Often, baseball diamonds are not available for practice. If there is an available diamond, great. But even if there isn't, productive practices are possible if they are planned correctly.

2. **How Many Players Are Going to Show Up?**
   This helps plan the practice, determines where the practice can be and how much help will be needed to run practice effectively. Estimate a best-case scenario and a worst-case scenario so that no matter how many players show up, the practice is still efficient.

3. **How Many Teaching Coaches Will Be At Practice, and How Many Parents Are Willing to Help?**
   Once establishing the number of coaches, determine how to effectively break up the practice into smaller groups. Smaller groups are the most efficient way to keep players active and get them more repetitions. Even if parents have never coached baseball and may not be comfortable enough to run a drill, encourage them to help if the alternative is running practice alone. At the very least, they can provide more repetitions by hitting, rolling or throwing balls in drills.

4. **Always Be Prepared to Run Practice Alone.**
   If there is no one to help, plan a practice that can be effective with just one person in charge. Here are some examples: Cover drills that involve the whole team, like throwing (cutoffs and relays) partner ground balls or baserunning. Dry hitting drills also keep everyone involved, as do infield and outfield practice or defensive bunt situations. It's important to keep the players active as a group so there is a minimal amount of time spent sitting and waiting. This is not an ideal situation, but practice can still be effective if the coach is prepared and chooses the right drills to cover.

5. **What Needs to be Addressed in Practice?**
   There are two thoughts to keep in mind when preparing a practice. They are team and individual players needs. Evaluate your team and individual players from past games and practices. Know what area of the game the team needs work on and incorporate those situations into practice. But also be aware of what adjustments individual players need to make to improve their game.

6. **Prepare a Practice Plan to Use as a Guide.**
   Before practice, write down what areas of the game are going to be covered and the drills to cover them. Determine how long to spend on each drill, and keep track of how long it actually took to get the benefits out of the drill. Having this information will help plan the next practice.

   Be prepared to utilize some extra drills if the practice you have planned moves quicker than you expected. Prioritize what areas are most important to work on that particular day and do not leave them to the very end. Remember, this is only a guide, and often a plan may take longer than expected.

Expert Advice on Being Prepared to Run Practice Alone

It's important to keep the players active as a group so there is a minimal amount of time spent sitting and waiting. Being alone is not an ideal situation, but practice can still be effective if the coach is prepared and chooses the right drills to use.

7. **Utilize Controlled Reaction Drills.**
   Time and space are always an important factor when developing a player's skills at practice. Controlled reaction drills take up less space than practicing skills at game speed. Numerous drills can be done at the same time during practice, because there is more space to practice them. Most importantly, players will be more active at practice, get in more repetitions and will often be in better fundamental positions than game speed. (Refer to Chapter 1, "Coaching Philosophy" for more on controlled reaction drills.)

8. **Set Time Aside Before or After Practice to Work with Individuals on Position-Specific Work.**
   Having 1 to 4 individuals arrive before or stay after practice allows coaches to give personal attention and help players with their needs. Give all players a chance to get one-on-one time throughout the year. It helps get to know the players better and will do wonders for the coach-to-player relationship.

   To help develop your pitchers, catchers, and infielders it will be imperative to spend one-on-one time with them working on plays and skills that are needed to have success at the position, especially since it is so difficult to work on specific positions during a team practice.

   Allow assistant coaches some time during practice to work with individuals. We realize there is never enough time in the day to do it all. But we truly believe some of the best coaching is done in smaller groups and one-on-one.

Expert Advice on Working with Individuals

Allow assistant coaches some time during practice to work with individuals. We realize there is never enough time in the day to do it all. But we truly believe some of the best coaching is done in smaller groups and one-on-one.

9. **Make an Effort to Keep Practice Fun and Moving at a Productive Pace.**
   Players want to be active and enjoy practice. They are at an age where trying to get better should not feel like work. Not all activities will be fun. There will be some things that have to be covered which will involve some standing around and patience. Be aware of that fact, and attempt to keep other areas of practice enjoyable and moving at a productive pace. Make drills short so players won't lose interest. Implement competitive drills into practice. Friendly games between teammates adds excitement and motivates players to perform. Quality in drills is much more important than quantity.

10. **Develop a Routine at Practice that Incorporates the Basic Skills Needed to Have Success at Baseball.**
    Utilize the drills and games that seem to work best for the team on a regular basis. Don't feel like all the drills in the book are necessary for all players. Find a sound routine for every facet of the game and put it to use. Add or delete certain drills on occasion for specific skills or just for fun. But stick with what works. The players will understand the drill and the expectations when performing it.

11. **Take Time to Recreate and Practice Game Situations.**
    Before games start and throughout the season, simulate game situations during practice. Individual skills will naturally be in every practice whether planned or not, but the more experience and knowledge players have at handling different situations when they arise will determine the team's success.

    At first, players will have a difficult time with decision making on the field because they have very little experience. But players will be much more comfortable and prepared for game situations they have worked on in practice.

    Baserunning illustrates this point well. Some players get on base very few times throughout a season. When they do reach base in a game, they need to have the experience from practice on how to be a good baserunner.

12. **Before Your First Game, Have a Couple of Intrasquad Games.**
    This is very important for several reasons. Pitchers need experience throwing to live hitters. Conversely, hitters need the same experience of facing live pitching. This gives everyone the opportunity to experience a game atmosphere. Coaches can use this to evaluate what needs to be worked on and which players are confused and need guidance.

    The beauty of a scrimmage is that the coach can stop the game and instruct to show players correct positioning when they are confused. Intrasquad games will prepare a team as much as possible for the first real game.

13. **Where Should Players Play? Should They Play Multiple Positions?**
    Most players have a desire to play a specific position. Try to accommodate or at least expose the player in practice to the position they prefer. This will not always be possible. Safety must be given consideration when determining a player's position. Coaches should attempt to place players in positions where they can have success.

    Your league may have requirements on players playing different positions. Players benefit if they can learn more than one position. Having said that, don't move players around too often because they will get confused and won't be able to grasp the responsibilities that go along with each position. This is not putting the player in a position to have success. Don't expect the average player to successfully play more than three positions.

Expert Advice on Playing Multiple Positions

Attempt to place players in positions where they can have success. Don't move young players around too often because they will get confused and won't be able to grasp the responsibilities that go along that position.

14. **Take Time to Bring the Team Together to Formally Begin and End Practice.**
    This is a good time to talk with players and connect with the team. Utilize this time to go over any points you want to make from the last practice or game. Be positive and try to address something good they have done or are improving on. This improves morale and confidence. Tell them what to expect in the current practice and what should be accomplished.

    Also try to end practice in a group. Let players know about the next practice or game. This is another opportunity to connect with the team or individuals. Let players know about something positive they did or are improving on.

15. **Proper equipment will help tremendously in running an efficient practice.** First off get a lot of baseballs– 60 to 100. You don't want to waste valuable practice time gathering baseballs. Get 25 wiffle balls so you can work on hitting in other areas besides the field. 3 to 4 batting tees. Ask your players to bring theirs to practice. Throw down bases. Now you can create another field, which is great for drills and teaching bunt plays, first and third defense, etc. Small soccer cones help with organization and reference points. Your practice will be very difficult to run if you don't have the right equipment.

16. **Always Stretch and Warm Up as a Team Before Players Take the Field.**
    Take the time to stretch and warm up before every practice or game. This will help prevent injuries and aid in ones flexibility. Refer to the Dynamic Warm Up/Stretching section for more details..

Practice Plans

Here are some examples of different practice plans. Obviously, drills and simulated game situations should be planned out according to time of season and the players' skill development.

Our goal is to give you a core practice plan in length and structure that would be appropriate for the different age groups. We are also guiding you on what areas need to be covered fundamentally throughout the year. Remember pre-season practices will be different from mid- to late-season practices. Refer to the coaching philosophy chapter for more clarification. Most importantly, write practice plans based on how the team is developing.

Remember to utilize stations in your practices. Smaller working groups will give players more repetitions and limit the standing around, which makes for a boring practice if there is a lot of it.

Expert Advice on a Coaches Persona

Players feed off a coach's energy level and organization. Come prepared and exude positive energy to get the most out of your players.

Each practice can last 60 to 120 minutes depending on age and skill level. Keep in mind that having a solid throwing and receiving routine is important for any youth league team. The game of baseball is an exaggerated game of catch.

Throughout the season, your core practices should cover the following areas: Throwing and receiving skills, catching ground balls and fly balls, pitchers and catchers practice, hitting and base running. Continue to work in game situations, so that players understand where to go and how to handle the games.

Sometimes you may want to have specialized practices. Possibilities include offensive practice, defensive practice, game-situation practice, pitching practice, scrimmages or 6-on-6 baseball games. As practices proceed and skills improve it will be important to spend additional time on situations and to incorporate more game-like environment into your practices. Sharpening the focus of practice will help your team get better in responding to a given game situation. Remember, you can always go back to the skill teaching and drills for those who need them.

Ron Wotus on Using your Assistant Coaches:
"Utilize your coaches wisely.
Find out what areas of the game and drills they are comfortable teaching.
Let them be in charge of those areas, and lead those drills when you use them.
The more you coach a particular skill the better you become at teaching it."

PRE-SEASON

You will not have a lot of time to cover everything before your first game. At your first practices, cover the basic skills. Begin with responsibilities of positions, recording outs at first and getting the ball in from the outfield. Start developing your pitchers and catchers so they will be better prepared for the first real game. Before the first game, get your players into a preseason scrimmage or two. Scrimmage against another team or, if necessary, scrimmage among yourselves by using a defense on the field and three extra men as hitters. Rotate fielders in to hit once the first three hitters get two at-bats each. This game should be played with your pitchers pitching in pre-season, but it is also very effective to play during the season with the coach pitching. It is a great opportunity to stop play and correct mistakes on defensive decisions, cutoffs and relays, etc. After each scrimmage, write notes on plays the team was having trouble with and review them at the next practice.

Keep things moving. Have your practice set up before you start, even if you have the players wait a few minutes to set up your stations. This is important. Do not rush or look unprepared. Have everything set up so you can transition through each phase of practice. Make sure all players have their gloves, batting gloves, batting helmets and bats outside of the dugout, resting against fence. This allows you to keep players moving. Players waste a lot of valuable practice time looking for their equipment. If each player took an extra two minutes to get their gear that is 24 minutes of wasted practice time.

The tempo of your practice can make it more enjoyable. Get players jogging from station to station. This approach helps to develop the proper mindset of what it means to be in athletics. Younger age groups are not ready for this but for the older age groups, 11-16, it sets a tone for how you want things done. It can be empowering for your players to be accountable for their team's philosophy on how to practice and play the game the right way.

PRACTICE PLANNING: AGES 7-9 (75-90 Minute Practices) NON-PITCHING

Priority areas for this age group during the year:

1. Throwing and receiving skills.
2. Ground balls.
3. Receiving skills above player's head.
4. Batting.
5. Base running.
6. Situational baseball play. Primarily infield situations.
7. First-base receiving skills and tagging technique.

Additional areas that need to be covered as the year moves forward:

8. Outfield relays on routine singles to outfield.
9. Relay technique on transferring the ball.
10. Base running knowledge on pop-ups and fly balls.

Expert Advice on Practice Groups

Working in groups of four with players that have similar skills will help drills and teaching much more than working in larger groups of players who have very different abilities.

Practice Plan (Ages 7-9)

Read through this practice plan even if this age level doesn't apply to you. This plan spells out a core practice in greater detail.

A. 5 minutes – Stretching Routine

Light jog around the bases

Jumping jacks

Arm circles

Shoulder stretch

Wrist and forearm stretch

Trunk twists

Toe touches

Reach through

Hamstring stretch

Quadriceps stretch

Groin stretch

Sprint to fence and back

B. 20 minutes – Throwing Drills (This is the most important part of practice for this age group)

1. Grip: Demonstrate and have each player show their grip to you. (This needs to happen every three practices throughout the year)
2. Dry-Drill Routine for Throwing
   a. Arm-Action Break.
   b. Arm-Action Throw.
   c. Catch, Block, Break, Throw.
3. Coach Catch Drill: Block and Throw Drill
4. Coach Catch Reaction Drill
5. Warm-up Drill: Coaches control the first three minutes to make sure players are blocking their feet and crow-hopping correctly during the following progressions.
6. Have Players Play Catch and Progress to Long Toss
   a. 30 feet: 2-3 minutes.
   b. 45 feet: 2-3 minutes.
   c. 60 feet: 2-3 minutes.
   d. 80 feet or to players' maximum distance. 5 Throws.
   e. Move back to a routine game-throwing distance and toss for one minute.

NOTE: Length of time throwing and throwing distance should vary according to age group and arm condition of each player. But this is the standard for this age group. First three weeks throwing is roughly 7 minutes. Once arms are in shape extend throwing program three more minutes.

7. Throwing and Receiving Games to Play after Long Toss
   a. Accuracy Throwing and Receiving Game.
   b. Foot Ball Game.
   c. Four-Corner Game.
   d. Reaction Game.

NOTE: Pick one or two of these games for each practice.

C. 10 minutes – Dry Hitting Drills

These drills are recommended every other practice. If you see your team struggling then incorporate them every practice until you see improvement

D. 30 minutes – Stations

(Four players per group with 8-minute rotations. Allow two minutes between stations to get players to next stop.) If you only have two coaches, use only two groups with two different stations. You may do two sets of stations to cover four different skills. Keep the coaches at their teaching station and just rotate the players.

Group 1: Glove-work drills: First drill — Toss fly balls to themselves. Each player throws ball 10 feet above their head and tries to catch it in the correct fundamental position (see: outfield section). Ball should be caught in front of head with two hands. Second drill: Football Drill or tossing fly balls and throwing to a base or coach.

Group 2: Split-hitting station. One coach throws golf-sized wiffle balls to two players. The other coach is working with two players hitting off batting tees or soft toss. Switch and rotate players within the group.

Group 3: Ground ball station: Drills: Ready position and triangle drill. Coach rolling ground ball drill and coach Short-Hop Drill. End with Live Fungo Drill.

E. 12 minutes – Game Situation: Recording Outs

Make two six-person teams. You need two sets of bases or cones. Make two fields away from each other. Put each six-man team at its own separate field. Put six players at the various infield positions, including catcher. At the first practice or two you will have to walk players through these situations. We strongly recommended you do this before you start hitting the ball. It might take a little time, but you want players to know what to do when this arises in the game. Focus on one position and one play at a time when you explain and walk through. You have to explain and re-create situations for them in order for them to learn and retain the information. Keep instruction clear and simple. Do not complicate things.

1. **First Situation: No one on base.** Recording the out at first base. Perform for all infield positions. One position and one play at a time. (First two or three practices.) Have players communicate out loud before each play. For example coach yells out Runner at first and no outs: Where can you make the play? The team yells back, first or second.
2. **Second Situation:** Man on first base. Force out at second base. Same procedure in terms of walking players through situation without hitting the ball right away. This cannot be stressed enough.

Other Game Situations You Need To Cover During The Season

1. How to get the ball in from the outfield.
2. Pop-fly responsibilities.
3. Tagging runners between bases.

F. 10 minutes – Team Drill: Base Running

1. Home-to-first drill.
2. Making-a-turn drill.
3. Reading fly balls.

Base-running drills should be done at most every practice, even if it's just 5 minutes covering just one of above base-running drills. Once players understand technique, they need to continue to get repetition on reading balls and making decisions.

Remember to adapt to the situation to the intelligence of the team. If your team understands these skills, then advance to the next lesson. But always make sure they are strong in these three base- running drills by the time they complete their season.

G. 2 minutes – Bring Players Together for Conclusion of Practice

1. Give next practice time.
2. Positive feed back on practice.

PRACTICE PLANNING: AGES 8-10 (90-120 Minute Practices) WITH PITCHING

Priority areas for this age group during the year:

1. Throwing and receiving skills.
2. Ground balls.
3. Receiving skills above player's head.
4. Batting.
5. Base running and sliding.
6. Situational baseball play (Infield situations).
7. Situational baseball play (Outfield relay situations).
8. Proper tagging technique.
9. First-base receiving skills.
10. Pitching and catching position skills.

Additional areas that need to be covered as the year moves forward:

11. Base-running knowledge on pop-ups and fly balls.
12. Bunt coverages.
13. Covering bases on steals and throws from the outfield.

Practice Plan (Ages 8-10)

A. **5 minutes – Stretching Routine.**

B. **20 minutes – Throwing**

Same routine and games as 7 to 9-year-old non-pitching, except add accuracy drill game from throwing routine.

C. **7 minutes – Dry Hitting Drills**

These drills are recommended every other practice. If you see your team struggling, incorporate them into every practice until you see improvement.

D. **33 minutes – Stations** (Four players per group, 10 minute at stations and 1 minute to move to each station.)

If you have only two coaches at practice, split into two six man groups, with one coach working infield and one coach working outfield for 8 minutes. After the groups switch and cover both areas, do hitting all together. Perform dry drills as a group for 5 minutes. Then split into two groups again and work a soft-toss station and a tee or live-hitting station for 6 minutes each.

Group 1: Hitting tees/Soft toss: One coach soft tossing with two players and two players hitting off tee with wiffle balls or hard balls. Each player hits 20 balls off the tee and 20 balls from soft toss.

Group 2: Drop step and communication: Drop-Step Drills 5 minutes, Communication Drill for the remainder of time. After catching balls during the drills, make a strong throw to a base.

Group 3: Ground balls and tags: Coach rolling Ground Balls Drills, Cross-Over Step Drill and Live Fungo Drill.

E. **15 minutes – Pitching Practice and Ground Balls**

Bullpens: Each pitcher throws for 5 minutes. Three pitchers at a time and the others catch for them with mask on. Also, utilize your catchers here in full gear to get them familiar with their equipment. After 5 minutes switch players and have the other three pitchers complete their bullpens. Throwing bullpens must happen once a week. Never the day before a game.

Ground Balls: While the six pitchers are participating in pitching practice, the other six players are fielding ground balls from their positions in the infield and throwing to first base. Or do any other of your favorite drills or games, such as the triangle-rotation drill.

F. **10 minutes – Game Situations: Recording Outs**

These two fundamental skills need to be covered once a week. Use base runners in the drill. You can substitute situational baseball play the other day you have practice.

1. Man on first base: Getting the force out at second base
2. Man on second base: Hitting ground balls to various infield positions with players recording the out

G. **10 minutes – Game Situations: Base Running**

Cover what to do in the following situations based on how many outs there are. Set up an infield and have the rest of players as runners at second base. Coach hits ground balls and runners play the situations live. When players react incorrectly, explain the play and have player repeat the situation.

1. Runner at second, ball hit to left side of infield.
2. Runner at second, ball hit to right side of infield.
3. Runner at second, ball hit to all outfield positions.

Other Game Situations You Need To Cover During The Season

1. Infield in, play at the plate
2. Base hit to outfield, no one on base
3. Base hit to outfield, runner on first base
4. Runners at second base ball hit to the infield

H. 15 minutes – Catchers Practice and Sliding Practice: Catchers are off to the side with catching coach working on stance and receiving pitches. Also working on footwork for throwing to bases or for fielding bunts. All others are with coach practicing sliding.

I. 2 minutes – Bring Players Together for Conclusion of Practice

---

PRACTICE PLANNING: AGES 9-12 (90-120 Minute Practices)

Priority areas for this age group during the year:

1. Throwing and receiving skills with a quicker glove-to-hand transfer.
2. Ground balls.
3. Batting.
4. Judging fly balls.
5. Base running when ball is put in play in various situations.
6. Situational baseball play: Extensive cut-offs and relays, balls in alleys and down the lines. Runners on first base and first and second base.
7. Covering bases and making tags.
8. Pitching and catching.
9. Offensive plays: Sacrifice and base-hit bunting.
10. Covering bases on steals and throws from the outfield.

Additional areas that need to be covered as the year moves forward:

11. Bunt coverages.
12. Understanding throwing lanes in rundowns and on plays in general.
13. Understand first-and-third stealing situation, defensively and offensively.

Practice Plan (Ages 9-12)

A. 5 minutes –Stretching Routine

B. 20 minutes – Throwing

1. Review Throwing Dry Drills and perform Coach Catch Drill
   (Once these drills are performed well and not needed routinely, start your throwing practice with the Warm Up Drill progress into Long Toss).
2. Warm-up drill.
3. Long toss.
4. Move back to routine game distance and throw for one minute.
5. Quick toss drill.
6. Quick toss speed game.

Throwing Games to Play after Long Toss

a. Accuracy game.
b. Relay-drill game (this game is described in the infield section).
c. Reverse four-corner speed game.

C. 5 minutes – Dry Hitting Drills

D. 45 minutes – Stations (Four players per group, 12 minutes per station with 2 minutes to rotate between stations).

Group 1: Coach rolling balls or partner-roll drills. All types, regular, short hop, backhand and forehand. Crossover-Step Drill and Live Fungo Drill (throwing to first base, second base and home)

Group 2: Hitting in batting cages. If you have a fourth coach, he can run the soft-toss station and make this a split group.

Group 3: Start with the drop-step drill then progress to hitting fly balls and line drives at players. Have one player act as second baseman catching throws from outfielders. Rotate players at second base. Hit balls from 100 feet away and work balls slightly over their heads. Watch for proper drop step.

E. 25 minutes – Game Situations

1. Put players at each infield position. Leave the remaining players in to be base runners. Vary runners at different bases for different situations. There is always a runner at home running to first base. Coach hits balls to various infield positions. Rotate runners with defense after 15 minutes.
2. Load bases with runners. Hit balls to each infield position, making an out at home plate or possibly a double play by throwing home and then to first base. Make sure you bunt balls to the catcher and pitcher so they stay involved.
3. Substitute these other team-drill situations
   a. Man on second base, base hit to outfielder, play at home.
   b. Man on first base, base hit to outfielder.
   c. Introduce rundowns.
   d. First-and-third defense.
   e. Bunt defense.
   f. Defensive passed ball drill with pitcher covering home plate.
   g. Pitchers fielding practice (PFP).

F. 5 minute – Team Drill: Sliding

G. 15 minutes – Pitching Practice and Ground Balls

Each pitcher throws for 6 minutes. Three pitch at a time and the others catch for them with a mask on. After 6 minutes switch players and have the other three pitchers complete their bullpens. While the six pitchers are participating in pitching practice, the other six players are fielding ground balls from their positions in the infield and throwing to first base.

Throwing bullpens must happen once a week, never the day before a game.

PRACTICE PLANNING: AGES 10-12 (90-120 Minute Practices)

Priority areas for this age group during the year:

1. Throwing and receiving skills with a quicker glove-to-hand transfer.
2. Ground balls and introducing how to turn a double play.
3. Batting drills.
4. Judging fly balls to side and directly at the player.
5. Base running when ball is put in play in various situations.
6. Situational baseball play. Cutoffs when runners are on first base and first and second base.
7. Outfield relay on balls hit the in alleys and down the lines.
8. Covering bases and making tags.
9. Pitching and catching.
10. Pitchers fielding practice (PFP).
11. Infield and outfield pop-fly responsibility.

Additional areas that need to be covered as the year moves forward:

12. Bunt coverage.
13. Covering bases on steals and throws from the outfield.
14. Rundowns and understanding throwing lanes in rundowns and on plays in general.
15. Understand first-and-third stealing situation. Both offensively and defensively.

Practice Plan (Ages 10-12)

A. 5 minutes – Stretching Routine

B. 18 minutes – Throwing

1. Follow same routine as age 9-12 practice; add four-corner game in a different direction.

C. 2 minutes – Infield Drills

1. Partner ground balls with a throw back. After 1 minute, switch and other partner tosses ground balls from 40 or so feet away. Player catches and throws ball back.

D. 33 minutes – Stations (10 minutes each group with 1 minute between to rotate groups)

Group 1: Outfield: Drop-Step Drill and Foot Ball Drill. Then hit or throw different fly balls when performing the Communication drill.

Group 2: Partner rolls, short hops, backhand and forehand drills, 1 minute each. Then hit ground balls and have players throw balls across diamond. Turn double plays for the last two minutes.

Group 3: Base running: Explain rules for tagging up from second base and third base on all types of fly balls. Then re-create groundball and fly-ball situations for the runners to execute from those bases. End station with the Ball-In-The-Dirt Drill.

E. 12 minutes – Pitching Practice

Each player throws a 5-minute bullpen. Utilize your catchers with their gear on. Players who are not a catcher pair up and one acts as a catcher. The receiving player semi-squats down with a mask on as his partner executes his pitches. Pitchers work on throwing to a specific location for roughly 1-minute intervals. Example would be: outside fastball (first minute), inside fastball (second minute) and change-up (third minute).

Players not involved with pitching or catching perform the Triangle-Rotation Drill with another coach.

F. **34 minutes – Batting practice (three groups of four players)**

10 minutes each group with 1 minute allotted for rotating. Remember to tell players to get helmets, bats and batting gloves out of bags and in front of dugout so transition in between groups is smooth.

Group 1: Soft toss. Also, have two tees set up for players waiting their turn to soft toss.

Group 2: Bunting. Practicing both sacrifice and bunting for a base hit.

Group 3: Live hitting group on field. Have one player hitting and the rest shagging balls. If you have another coach, he can hit ground balls between batting practice pitches to a shagger.

G. **15 minutes – Game Situations:**

(Cutoffs and relays, first-and-third defense, bunt defense coverage, covering bases on steals and catchers throwing runners out, performed with live base runners.) Pick one or two situations each practice.

Other Game Situations You Need To Cover During The Season

1. Pitchers fielding practice.
2. Base-running situations for different scenarios.
3. Passed Ball Drill with pitchers and catchers.
4. Rundowns.
5. Other cutoffs and relay situations that occur in games.

PRACTICE PLANNING: AGES 13-16 (90-120 Minute Practices)

Priority areas for this age group during the year:

1. Throwing and receiving skills.
2. Every type of possible ground ball and double plays.
3. Infielders holding runners on base and pickoff play.
4. Batting and bunting skills.
5. Situational hitting, hit-and-runs, moving runners over and sacrifice flies.
6. Judging fly balls, liners and catching balls with momentum into a throw.
7. Primary and secondary leads, how to dive back to the bag.
8. Pitcher holding runners on base and pickoff moves.
9. Pitcher fielding practice (PFP).
10. Situational baseball play. Double cuts on balls past the outfielders.

Additional areas that need to be covered as the year moves forward:

11. First-and-third offense and defense.
12. Bunt coverage.
13. Multiple runner rundowns.
14. How to hit a curveball or off-speed pitch.
15. Base stealing from first and second and third-base coach's verbal commands.

Practice Plan (Ages 13-16)

A. 10 minutes – Stretching.

As players get older and have more muscle mass stretching becomes even more important. Stretching gets players loose before activity and limits injuries.

B. 10 minutes – Primary and secondary leads with coach as pitcher.

Also, getting steal breaks and diving back to first base. Set up four first-base bags that are 5 feet apart. Have players break into groups behind each base, with one player per group getting a read on the coach (who is acting as the pitcher). The coach will pitch to home or attempt a pickoff throw.

C. 17 minutes – Throwing

1. Extension Forward and Backward Drill on one knee. (2 minutes)
2. Have players play catch and progress to long toss. (8 minutes)
3. Quick Toss Drill. (2 minutes)
4. Play the Point Game. (5 minutes)

D. 20 minutes – Position Specific

Group 1: Infielders. Partner rolls, short hops, backhand and forehands. (30 seconds each). Go to their infield position to take live fungos. Or Rapid-Fire Fungo Drill. Last few minutes work on double plays.

Group 2: Outfielders. Drop-Step Drill. Fielding fly balls and ground balls and finishing the play by making a strong throw to a relay man. Line Drive Drill and Fly Ball Correction Drill.

Group 3: Catchers. Do catching routine, with extra emphasis on blocking balls and proper throwing footwork to second and third base.

E. 34 minutes – Batting Practice (three groups of four players) 10 minutes each group with one minute to rotate.

Group 1: Soft Toss. Remember to mix in a little slower lobbed throw to simulate an off-speed pitch once in a while.

Group 2: Live Hitting. First round: bunt the first two pitches, then one swing as if it's hit and run and one swing as if attempting to move a runner over to third base. Then five regular swings with emphasis on hitting the ball to the opposite field. Run the bases and react at first on bunt and advance to second on hit and run. Then advance to third on ball hit to right side. Then practice taking walking leads at third and reacting to batted balls. Second round: Take eight swings and then run to second base and react to batted balls of next hitter. If there is time for a third round, present different offensive situations or do a base-hit round.

Group 3: Shag. Spread out evenly and have one player as the ball boy in center field gathering balls in a bucket. Other players play balls live and collect balls and throw toward the ball boy. If you have an extra coach, he can be hitting fungos to one of the shaggers for extra work.

F. 20 minutes – Game Situations.

Set up a defensive team and have the rest of the players as base runners. Work in the base runners to their defensive positions as time goes on.

1. Cut offs and relays on singles with men on base, and double-cut relays on extra-base hits past outfielders.
2. Set base runners at each base and have player get picked off and practice a pickle situation. For the first sequence, pick runner off first base. Then proceed to pick players off second and third.
3. Substitute these other team drills:
   a. First-and-third offensive and defensive situations.
   b. Bunt defense.
   c. Pitcher fielding practice (PFP).
   d. Pop fly responsibilities for infield and outfield.
   e. Pitchers holding runners at first base, and next practice at second base, while base runners are trying to steal. Use a full infield, including a catcher and batter at the plate. Let hitters hit when the pitcher throws home.

Expert Advice on the Big Diamond

At the older ages the game becomes more involved. Plays in place for first and third defensive situations, bunt plays, and pick off plays become more valuable. Pitchers learning to hold runners and base stealing reads and breaks are other important areas to address.

G. 2 minutes – Bring team together and go over your signs and conclude practice.

H. 15 minutes – Pitching Practice.

Keep pitchers and catchers and have pitchers throw a 25-40 pitch bullpen.

Specialized Practices

These next series of practice plans are subject-specific. They are built for you to narrow the focus of practice when you want to work on specific skills or when the facility for practice limits what you can accomplish. These practices are different from your core practice and sometimes a change in the routine will help spark the interest of your players. One thing we know from working with teams and coaches is that you need to keep things fun or competitive to keep the attention of players. And at times players like to come to practice and experience something new and exciting. We feel you can achieve this by changing your routine periodically.

DEFENSIVE AND BASE RUNNING PRACTICE

This practice is set up for those coaching 9-12 year-olds. If your age group is older or younger, adjust the drills and game situations to apply to the correct level. This is just a sample of how to set up a defensive practice.

A. 5 minutes – Stretching Routine

B. 20 minutes – Throwing

1. Follow same routine, as 9-12 practice except add Relay Game.

C. 20 minutes – Position Specific (utilizing four coaches)

1. By now, the coaches should have a feel for where players can play. If players are at multiple positions, do not move them from position to position too quickly. If you do, they may not retain their responsibilities at each position. Try not to do too much too fast. Players have trouble retaining too much information in a short period of time.
   a. Catchers with coach doing catching-routine practice (receiving balls, working on catching ball correctly and teaching blocking skills).
   b. Outfielders with coach doing outfield drill practice (Drop-Step Drill and Foot Ball Drill).
   c. Infielders with coach doing infield drills (Triangle-Rotation Drill and Game and Live Fungo Drill).

D. 20 minutes – Infield Situations

Work on infield in with a runner at third. Runner at second no outs, and runner at third base executing play on a passed ball. Make sure players know what to do when a ball is hit to them. If players have difficulty, we recommend that you walk through the situations without balls and runners first. Then you can proceed to hitting the balls and having live runners.

1. Group 1: These players are running.
2. Group 2: These players are at their infield positions. This includes a pitcher and a catcher.
3. After 10 minutes have runners and defenders switch.

E. 10 minutes – Rundowns

Set up an infield defense with a couple of pitchers and have the rest of the players as base runners. Put base runners at first, second and third and re-create a run down between each base. Start by picking a runner off first and recreating a rundown between first and second. Then pick a runner off second and third. The pitcher needs to assist in these rundowns after they pick the runner off. Rotate base runners and defense after 5 minutes.

F. 15 minutes – Base Running and Sliding

1. Work on secondary leads from all bases.
2. Progress to Ball-in-Dirt Drill.
3. Put runners at second base and call out number of outs. Hit ground balls and fly balls as runners read situations and play them accordingly.
4. Sliding practice.

OFFENSIVE AND BASE RUNNING PRACTICE (60-90 Minute Practice)

This practice is set up for those coaching 9-12 year olds. If your age group is older or younger, just adjust the drills and game situations to apply to the correct level. This is just a sample of how to set up an offensive practice.

Practice Plan (Ages 9-12)

A. 5 minutes – Stretching Routine

B. 20 minutes – Throwing

Follow same routine, as 9-12 practice except add relay game.

C. 10 minutes – Pepper

Break into three or four groups and play pepper.

D. 5 minutes – Dry Drills of Hitting and Bunting

E. 34 minutes – Batting practice (three groups of four players)

10 minutes each group with 1 minute for rotations. Remember to tell players to get helmets, bats and batting gloves out of bags and in front of dugout so transition between groups is smooth.
Group 1: Soft Toss.

Group 2: Bunting. Practicing both sacrifice and bunting for a base hit.

Group 3: Live hitting group on field. One player hitting live, one is hitting off a tee and the rest shagging. Rotate from Shag to Tee to Live.

F. 15 minutes – Situational Hitting and Bunting

Split the team into three even groups. Set up one group in the outfield, one in the infield and one hitting. Each group hits and runs the bases for 4 1/2 minutes. Then rotate the groups. Outfields go to infield, infield to hitting and hitting to outfield. The coach is throwing batting practice and calls out different situations for the batter to perform. Or play the situational hitting game, line drive game or contact game with your hitters. This is also an opportunity to have a coach at third base giving offensive signs to the hitters for practice.

WHEN COACHING ALONE

This is a situation a coach can find himself in more than once. It is important you are always prepared if your assistant coaches do not show up. Below are drills for an effective practice even if you are alone. It contains drills that can keep all players active. This is just an example of which drills you can use to devise a practice plan. When you are alone this is a great time to work on different team drills and game situations, which will keep all players involved. You can also use this time to scrimmage if you find yourself alone.

A. **Stretching Routine**

B. **Throwing and Receiving Drills and Games**
- Arm-action dry drills
- Extension forward and backward drill
- Block, break, throw dry drill
- Warm-up drill
- Long toss
- Four-corner games
- Four-corner speed game

C. **Infield Drills and Games**
- Partner ground ball drill and game
- Partner short-hop drill
- Triangle-rotation drill
- Four-base tag drill
- Relay-drill and game

D. **Outfield Drills and Games**
- Drop-step drill
- Football drill and game

E. **Pitching Drills**
- All pitching dry drills

F. **Hitting Drills and Games**
- All hitting dry drills
- Shadow swinging drill
- Pepper
- Situation hitting game (Put players in field to play balls live off the bat)
- Coaches batting practice (Put players in field to play balls live off the bat)

G. **Base Running Drills and Games**
- Home-to-first drill
- Making a turn
- Turns reading the play
- Balls in the dirt (catchers can get in work at same time)
- Picking up the coach
- Reading fly balls
- Reading balls at second base
- All sliding drills
- Relay race game
- Stopwatch games

H. **Team Drills and Games**
- Cutoffs and relays
- Infield and outfield practice
- First-and-third defensive drills with base runners
- Bunt play fundamentals with base runners
- Pop-up responsibilities
- Scrimmages
- Six on six baseball

T-Ball (5-6 years Old)

This level obviously stands alone and is a real challenge when it comes to finding out what players are ready for and how to help them with the game. At these ages it is about the activity and introducing players to the game. You want practices and games to be a fun experience. This level is mostly about keeping their attention with some activities of throwing, hitting, fielding and running. Without overdoing it or placing expectations, you can help most of these kids with some very basic body position alignments.

Here are a few thoughts to keep in mind as you prepare to help the players in this age group. First of all, the more parental participation you can get the better. This allows for smaller working groups, which equates to fewer chances for the player to lose interest. Keep all drills short, use your imagination to keep players engaged and utilize different activities often. Play games when performing drills to help maintain their interest and establish some fun routines in the core areas of the game.

During the games, be organized and have coaches assigned to different duties, such as one coach controlling the dugout and another the batting order. Even the task of players putting the catcher's gear on will need some assistance. Pick up some squares of carpet and put each player's name on them. Then set the squares down on the bench as the batting order and a place for players to put their equipment when they come in the dugout. This will help eliminate the confusion of the batting order and help locate someone's hat or glove.

Be patient and don't over coach the players. Let them be kids and enjoy the experience. Lastly, be energetic, positive, patient and enjoy the kids.

PRACTICE PLANNING: AGES 5-6 (75 Minute Practice)

Priority areas for this age group during the year:

1. Throwing skills
2. Receiving ball below and above the waist
3. Ground balls
4. Hitting
5. Base running
6. How to get a force out
7. How to get the ball in from the outfield

Additional areas that need to be covered as the year moves forward:

8. How to tag a runner between bases
9. Base running rules when the ball is hit in the air
10. Catching pop flies

Joe Millette on T-ball Practice

"Recruit as much help as you can get.
Even without an understanding of baseball,
parents can be extremely helpful to you at your practice.
The smaller the working groups the easier the players will be to manage."

Practice Plan (Ages 5-6)

A. **5 minutes – Stretching Routine, Agility & Trivia:** Go over trivia topic of the day.
Example: Show picture of Babe Ruth and give some highlights of his career.

B. **5 minutes – Dry Drills**: Play Simon Says and do dry drills of Ready Position, Target Position (high & low throws), Triangle Fielding Position, Square Up to Throw and Throw. Use down and around to throw for a buzzword. (Players line up in front of a cone)

C. **20 minutes – Station Rotation #1** (Three groups of four players with 6 minute per station and 1 minute to rotate to next station)

1. **Throwing Analysis:** Player throws to coach or into backstop while other coach is next to player making adjustments as needed.
2. **Coach Catch:** Practice catching High-Low and Left & Right throws. Receiver always starts in the Target Position with glove hand outside shoulder away from face.
3. **1st Base Footwork:** Player starts at first base position, runs to base and puts his throwing-hand foot on base. Then Coach throws ball to the player to catch. Make it a game by putting a point value on having the correct foot on the base, catching the ball and making a good throw back to the coach.

D. **20 minutes – Station Rotation #2** (Three groups of four players with 6 minutes per station and 1 minute to rotate to next station)

1. **Tee Hitting Whiffle Balls:** If there are enough coaches, use two tees. With good spacing between tees have one player hitting at each tee and the other two players shagging balls. Make it a game by counting how many line drives the player can hit in a row.
2. **Live Hitting:** Coach pitches to one player at a time while others in group shag.
3. **Game Situation-Ground Balls to Outfield and Throws to 2nd Base:** Put a player in right field, left field, SS and 2nd base position. Roll balls to the outfielders and have opposite-side infielder cover 2nd base and catch ball from outfielder. Once in a while, roll ball to infielder and have them throw ball to 2nd base. Rotate players to each position. Opposite outfielder should be backing up throw to 2nd. All four players should be moving on every play.

Other Game Situations You Need To Cover During the Season

- Getting the force out at 1st base on ball hit to pitcher.
- Getting the force out at 2nd base on ground ball to 2nd & SS.
- Getting the force out at 3rd on ground ball hit to 3rd.
- Tagging runners out between bases.
- Pop fly base running rules.

E. **18 minutes – Team Game Situations/Intra Squad:** Split team into three groups and go over game situations. The three groups are outfield, infield and hitting. The hitting group hits twice each and then rotates. Before pitching to the batters, hit balls to each outfielder and have them throw ball to 2nd base with SS or 2nd baseman covering the bag. (Review whatever your game situation was for the day but now with whole team in a game setting.)

F. **5 minutes – Base Running:** Practice swinging the bat, then setting it down, running through first base and turning to the right. Have some fun by timing the runners to see how fast they can run to first base.

G. **2 minutes – Review:** Go over trivia of the day and highlights of practice. Let parents know what drills they can do at home with their kids.

Coach-Parents Meeting

Take the time to set up a parents-coaches meeting early in your training season. The meeting can be done before practices begin, at one of the coach's homes or at the field after your first practice. You may even want to email your meeting agenda ahead of time so the parents can review and prepare questions. The goal of this meeting is to have all the parents meet each other and to go over your philosophy and your expectations for the season. Hopefully, your philosophy will be similar to the one we laid out in our how-to-teach section.

Listed below are topics of discussion:

- Your philosophy.
- What you want to accomplish this year.
- How you will get information out. Email is the best strategy, so ask for any additional e-mail addresses.
- If you need additional coaching help this is a good time see if anyone can help out.
- Fill volunteer duties that some leagues require. (i.e., Team Mom, snack coordinator, umpire, field Marshall, field prep, etc.)
- Provide a team roster, contact information and schedule if available.
- Ask if there are any medical issues that you should be aware of. Offer to have this conversation in private.
- Give out your practice schedule.
- Go over your particular League or division rules.
- Provide a list of equipment needed and explain that the player's name should be marked on all items (i.e. bat, helmet, cleats, etc.)
- Encourage an environment for positive reinforcement from parents, players and coaches.
- Prohibit harassment of the umpires.
- Encourage parents to practice baseball skills at home with their son or daughter.
- Explain how you will handle discipline. Our recommendation is to give players a warning and if the problem persists then have them go sit or go for a little run.
- Tell parents who want to approach the coach to keep players out of any issues. Seek out a one on one environment.
- Establish that your ultimate goal is for the players to enjoy the season and to want to come back and play next season.
- Open up the meeting to additional questions.

Provide a list of these practice responsibilities:

- If you're not 5 minutes early you're 5 minutes late.
- Bring fluids to drink.
- Bring tennis shoes just in case we need to practice on the blacktop.
- If not going to make the practice let me know via e-mail.
- If practice is cancelled due to bad weather, I will do so at least an hour in advance.

Game day procedure. Let parents know these team policies:

- How early you want the players to arrive. Normally arrive 45 minutes to an hour prior to game time for a mini practice/warm up.
- How to handle an absence. If not going to make the game let me know via e-mail.
- How you handle playing time. Depending on player age and level of the league, playing time may or may not be split evenly.
- How you will determine players position. Where players play, again depending upon the level you are coaching. Explain whether all players will rotate and play all positions or whether player will have two or three different positions.
- How you will make safety a priority. Be clear that you may not put a player in a particular position because of safety concerns.
- How you will develop skills. Goal is to put the players in a position where they have a chance to have success.

GAME COACHING

The game is a time when players' minds should be clear to focus on the competition. During the game, do not fill their thoughts with too many fundamentals that will cloud their concentration. Allow the players a chance to compete confidently. Let them know you believe they can succeed, encourage them, and be there for them when their failures occur.

Attempt to keep all players focused on the game, especially the ones who aren't in the game at the time. A lot can be learned by watching from the bench. Give substitutes small responsibilities to help keep their focus on the game until it is their turn to play. For example, have one player in charge of tossing the first baseman and outfielder a ball as they come off the field. Also, create a competition to see who can pick up a tendency of the pitcher or who can pick up the other teams signs.

It is a coach's responsibility to create an atmosphere that is positive and enjoyable. Encourage players to be supportive of each other by congratulating teammates when they perform well, hustle or give good efforts. Attitude and morale can be improved by giving every player an opportunity to contribute to the team.

Know the league's substitution rules and find ways to put players into situations where they can succeed whenever possible. Remember, parents come to watch their children participate, not to watch you coach or manage.

Treat umpires, the opposing team and the game with respect. Your actions and comments are being watched and heard by your players, parents and fans.

Make notes during the game on areas where individuals and the team need to improve. Address these notes at the next practice.

Expert Advice on Game Coaching

The game is a time when players' minds should be clear to focus on the competition. During the game, do not fill their thoughts with too many fundamentals that will cloud their concentration. Allow the players a chance to compete confidently.

Pre-Game Routine

How well the team plays depends largely on how well the team is prepared, each player's athletic ability and some luck. Preparation definitely outweighs luck. Prior to every game, prepare the team physically and mentally for the competition. Have players arrive at least 1 hour before the game in Majors and AAA (10-12), at least 40 minutes before game for AA, A and Farm (7-10) for a solid pre-game routine. Having players warmed up properly will insure optimum performance early in the game and help prevent injury.

Perform game-specific drills during your pre-game routine. The following routine covers basic skills required during the game. On hot days cut back a little and use common sense. Make sure players get plenty of fluids, such as water, before, during and after games.

40-Minute Pre Game Routine

1. **Jog and stretch: 8 minutes**
2. **Three wind sprints. 1 minute**
3. **Play catch and long toss as a team, concentrating on blocking to throw, then crow-hopping to throw as the distance increases: 8 minutes**
4. **Divide team into three groups, 8-minute rotations.**
   a. **Group 1:** Partner ground balls, 10 each player. Coach hits balls to players after they have finished partner ground ball drill.
   b. **Group 2:** Soft toss into net or short toss with wiffle balls if no net is available. Live batting practice in cages if available.
   c. **Group 3:** Fly balls thrown or hit by a coach with players throwing to the cut-off man or an extra coach
5. **Starting pitcher does not have to do all stations. Let the pitcher hit and then sit down to conserve energy. Starter goes through pitching routine 10-12 minutes before start of game.**
6. **Take infield and outfield practice if available and time permits.**

COACHES CHECK LIST BEFORE GAMES

- Be organized. Have your line up already done and in your coaches bag so you can read it to the team when you have your meeting before you start your pre game routine.
- Have your line-up card completed for umpire and opponent.
- Have your clipboard mapped out with substitutions you are going to make during the game.
- Have pitch count clicker ready for an assistant coach.
- Score book ready for scorekeeper with line up completed.
- Tell your non-starters their role for the game and when you intend to use them if possible.
- Assign a non-starter to warm up the left or right fielder in between innings depending on what dugout you are using.
- Give assistant coaches their roles during the game. Keep these roles consistent from week to week so your coaching staff has continuity.

DYNAMIC WARM-UP/ STRETCHING

Establishing a warm-up and stretching routine is important at all levels of the game. Prior to every practice and game, time should be allotted to properly warm up and stretch the body. First, it sets the tone by bringing the team together and preparing as a unit for the given practice or game. It also gives different players a chance to lead the team. Perhaps a player who doesn't get much recognition would be a good choice to lead. Most importantly, it gets each player physically ready to play the game.

A proper dynamic warm-up should include general mobility and sport specific movements, and it will:

- Increase core temperature.
- Prepare the muscles for baseball.
- Improve joint flexibility and range of motion.
- Take less than 10 minutes.

Begin with a light jog around the field or run two times around the bases. Then have the players stand along the left or right foul line to begin the rest of the warm-up. Walk off 10 to 15 yards, enough to perform 8-10 repetitions of each exercise. Perform one exercise going towards the line and the next one on the way back.

After performing a light jog around the field or two times around the bases, perform the following exercises.

1. **Walking toe grabs:** Take a step forward with the left foot, keeping the left leg straight, and grab the toes with the left hand. Take a step and repeat with the opposite leg. **(picture 17-1)**
2. **Frankenstein walks (straight leg walks):** Keeping the back straight, step forward and kick the opposite leg straight, attempt to touch the outstretched hand. Take a step and repeat with the opposite leg. **(picture 17-2)**
3. **Butt kickers:** Light jog while attempting to bring your heel to your butt with each step. Keep your thighs perpendicular to the ground. **(picture 17-3)**
4. **Knee huggers:** Bring your knee towards your chest, grab it with both arms and hug it towards your chest then lower leg to the ground. Take a step and repeat with the opposite knee. **(picture 17-4)**

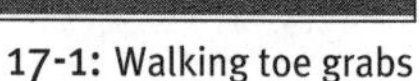

17-1: Walking toe grabs

17-2: Frankenstein walks

17-3: Butt kickers

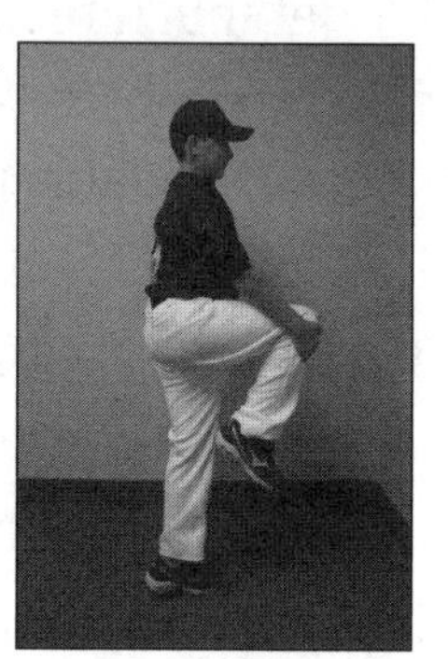

17-4: Knee huggers

5. **Leg cradle:** Grab your right knee with your right hand and your right ankle with your left hand. Bring your lower leg towards your hip. Lower your leg take a step and repeat with your opposite leg. **(picture 17-5)**
6. **High knee skips:** Skip while bringing your knees high and keep your hips and shoulders facing forward. **(picture 17-6)**
7. **Side shuffle with giant arm swings:** (like moving jumping jacks) Stand sideways take a big side step to the right while bringing hands overhead, bring legs together with hands returning to the side and repeat. Then repeat going to the left. Make sure your feet don't cross or touch. **(picture 17-7 and 17-8)**

17-5: Leg cradle

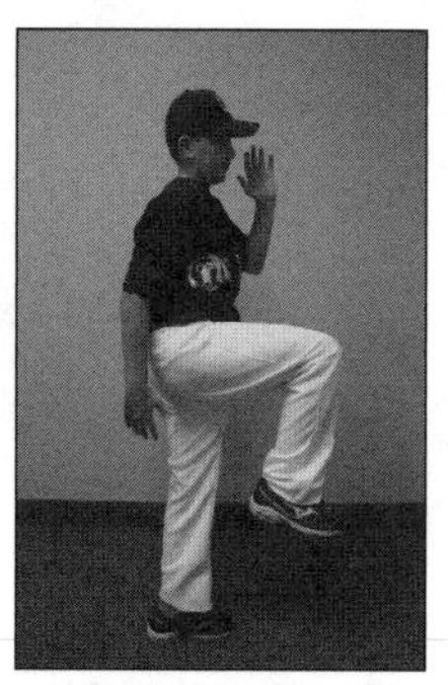

17-6: High knee skips

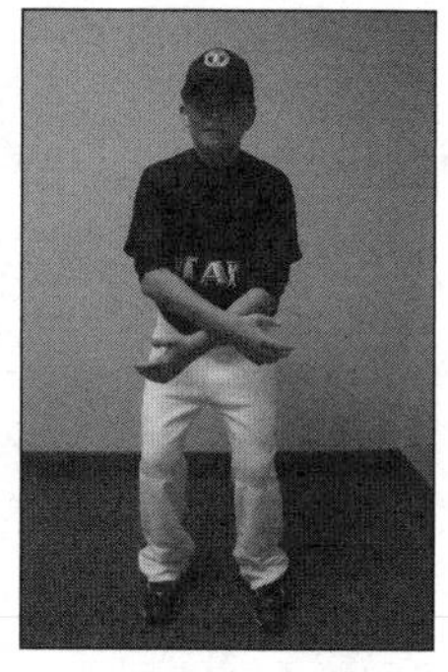

17-7: Side shuffle with giant arm swings

17-8: Side shuffle with giant arm swings

8. **Walking lunges with trunk twist:** Lunge forward with the left leg and rotate your trunk and arms to the left, return to standing and repeat with the right. **(picture 17-9)**
9. **Hug the world/hug yourself:** Swing your arms as open as you can, then swing them closed in a self hug. Repeat 10 times. **(pictures 17-10 and 17-11)**

17-9: Walking lunges with trunk twist

17-10: Hug the world/ hug yourself

17-11: Hug the world/ hug yourself

(These are the minimal recommended dynamic stretches. More can be found on our Web site at www.allprobaseballgroup.com)

POST PRACTICE/GAME STRETCHING

After practice or game, it is important to perform static stretches to enhance muscle recovery and improve flexibility. Have the team line up or form a circle to perform the stretches. Have between one and three players lead the stretch, or have one player responsible for each stretch and go around the circle with a different leader for each stretch. A stretch should be held for 20 to 30 seconds and should be a steady stretch with no bouncing action. The stretches listed below are priority stretches and should be done at every team get-together. These are a minimum. Feel free to add more stretching to the program.

1. Hamstring/Calf
2. Quads
3. Glutes/low back
4. Shoulder
5. Triceps
6. Forearms

Hamstring stretch

Calf Stretch

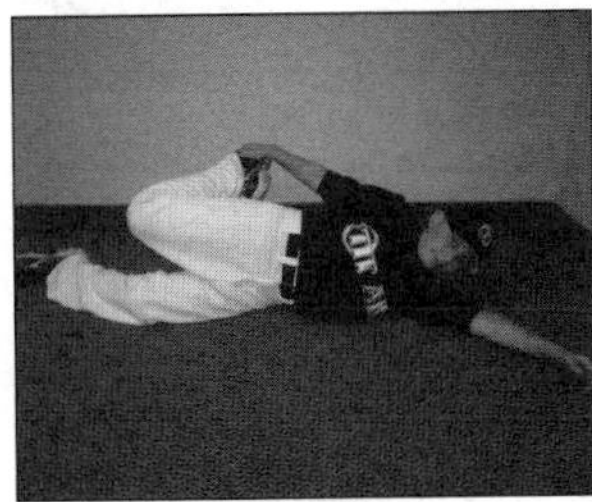

Quadricep stretch

Glute/low back stretch

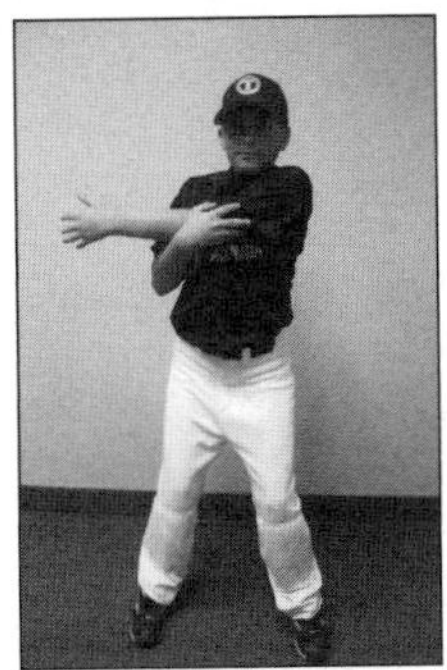

Shoulder stretch

Tricep stretch

Forearm stretch

STRENGTHENING EXERCISES

Youth sports related injuries and surgeries have increased at an alarming rate. Most of the increased injuries have been due to overuse injuries and not because of accidents or contact. There are a few exercises using body weight and exercise tubing that help in conditioning the body for baseball. These exercises offer a foundation. If you are looking for a more personalized exercise program contact a health care provider.

Body weight general conditioning can be done daily with 2 sets to fatigue while keeping good form.

- **Pushups:** Start with push up position with your hands slightly wider than your shoulders, keep your elbows at a 45 degree angle to your body. Keep your abdominal muscles tight so your low back doesn't sag. Keep your shoulders, hips knees and ankles in a straight line as you lower your body to the ground. Only go down until your elbows are in line with your body then push back up. You may have to start with push ups on a stable chair or wall until strong enough to perform a full body push up. **(picture 17-12)**
- **Squats:** Stand with your feet slightly wider than hip width apart. Keep your back straight and squat until your thighs are parallel to the floor. Your knees should not extend past your toes and they should stay in line with your hips and feet. If having difficulty, try sitting on the edge of a chair or bench and stand up without leaning forward and sit back down just touching the edge of the chair. **(picture 17-13)**
- **Curl ups:** Lie on your back with your arms crossed over your chest and your knees bent. Raise your upper body off of the floor by flexing your abdominal muscles until your shoulder blades are off of the ground then slowly lower back down. Keep your chin tucked at all times. Do not let your low back come off the floor at anytime. **(picture 17-14)**

17-12: Push ups

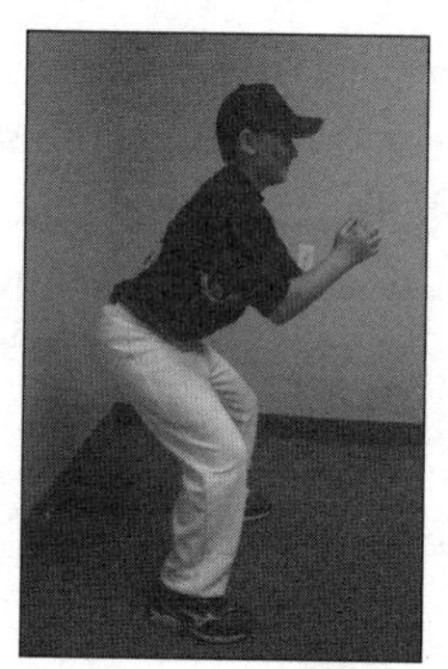
17-13: Squats

17-14:Curl ups

Shoulder exercises with tubing should be done 2-3 times per week

Rotator cuff exercises (2-3 sets of 10-30 reps)

- **Internal Rotation:** Tie or fasten an exercise cord/band to the fence and stand sideways with targeted closest to the fence. Bend your elbow and place your glove or small towel between your elbow and your body. Squeeze your shoulder blades back. With the cord in your hand, your elbow bent and your shoulder in line, bring your hand to your belly button then slowly back in line with your shoulder. **(pictures 17-15 and 17-16)**
- **External Rotation:** Tie or fasten an exercise cord/band to the fence and stand sideways with the shoulder you will NOT be strengthening closest to the fence. Bend your elbow and place your glove or small towel between your elbow and your body, squeeze your shoulder blades back, and hold the cord in your hand. With your hand in front of your belly button, and elbow (bent), bring your hand back in line with your shoulder then slowly back to your belly button. **(pictures 17-17 and 17-18)**
- **90/90:** This exercise should only be performed with players 12 years old and above (with 2 sets of 15 reps or less.) Stand facing the fence with your elbow abducted (away from your body) to 90 degrees in line with your shoulder, with your elbow bent to 90 degrees and holding the band in your hand. Slowly rotate your hand away from the fence and slowly back down so that your forearm goes from parallel to the ground to just below parallel to the fence. (This is a highly skilled exercise and you must keep our shoulder blades stable and retracted back together. If you have any pain or if the exercise is uncomfortable consult an exercise specialist to verify proper form.) **(pictures 17-19 and 17-20)**

17-15: Internal rotation—starting position

17-16: Internal rotation—ending position

17-17: External rotation—starting position

17-18: External rotation—ending position

17-19: 90/90—starting position

17-20: 90/90—ending position

Scapular strength/stability exercises (2-3 sets of 10-15 reps): Tie an exercise band/cord with two ends at about chest height. Stand with feet hip width apart and keep abdominal muscles tight so your low back should not move with each exercise. Take a handle or end in each hand and walk backwards until the cord is under tension.

- **Rows:** Hold the cord in both hands stretched out in front of your body with elbows straight. Keeping your thumb up, squeeze your shoulder blades together without shrugging your shoulders. Bring your elbows to your side, hold for two seconds and slowly return to the starting position. **(picture 17-21)**
- **'I's:** Stand with palms together and arms stretched out in front of your body. Squeeze your shoulder blades together and bring your arms (fully extended) down to your side, hold for two seconds and return to the starting position. **(picture 17-22)**
- **'T's: (also known as reverse fly):** Stand with palms together and arms stretched out in front of your body. Squeeze your shoulder blades together and bring your arms (fully extended) away from your body without letting your elbows or hands pass your body, hold for two seconds and return to the starting position. Should look like you are making a letter T. **(picture 17-23)**
- **'W's:** Stand with palms together and arms stretched out in front of your body. Squeeze your shoulder blades together and bring your arms (45 degree bend at the elbow) away from your body, hold for two seconds and return to the starting position. Should look like you are making a letter W with your body. **(picture 17-24)**

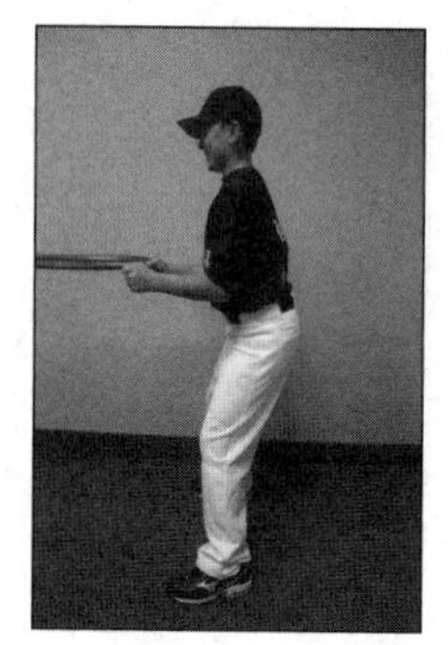
17-21: Rows

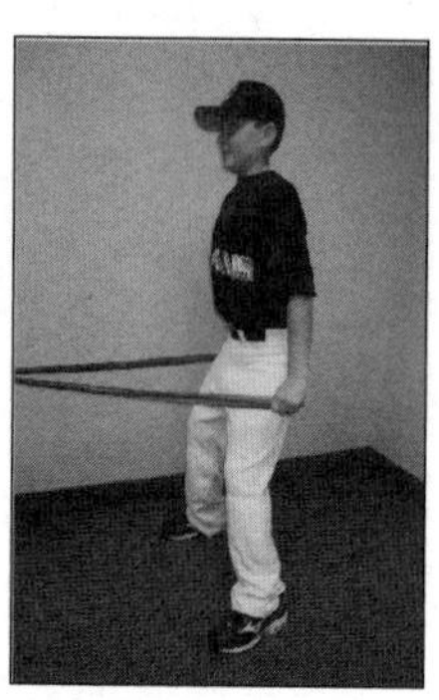
17-22: "I"s

17-23: "T"s

17-24: "W"s

All-Pro Baseball has added a sports medicine staff member in order to offer a more comprehensive resource. Kristy was the perfect fit because of her vast experience and expertise in athletic training, physical therapy, strength-and-conditioning and rehabilitation. Kristy is a long time consultant and has been working with APBG since 2009.

Kristy Illg MPT, ATC, CSCS

Kristy obtained her Bachelor of Science degree from CSU Sacramento and then completed a sports medicine internship with UC Berkeley from 1999-2001. At Cal, she worked mainly with the baseball and volleyball teams. She continued on to Nova Southeastern University to complete her Masters of Physical Therapy degree.

She returned in 2003 to work in the UC Berkeley athletic training room as well as at Diablo Physical Therapy and Sports Medicine. Kristy also worked for UC Davis athletics as the physical therapist in the athletic department from 2007-2008. She specializes in orthopedic and sports physical therapy. She uses her knowledge of biomechanics and sport specific skills to rehabilitate, enhance performance, and prevent overuse injuries.

- Licensed Physical Therapist
- Certified Athletic Trainer (ATC) through the National Athletic Training Association
- Credentialed Active Release Technique (ART) provider.
- Certified Strength and Conditioning Specialist (CSCS) through the National Strength and Conditioning Association.
- Certified golf fitness specialist from Titleist Performance Institute

Jump Rope

Jumping rope is an excellent activity for players at any age and level but is ideal for youths. It helps develop coordination, agility and foot speed. Foot speed is an attribute that all position players should have. The program below is not geared for conditioning but is designed to develop coordination, agility and foot speed. The routine should be done a minimum of three times per week. The length of the exercise isn't as important as the consistency. It's much easier to jump rope on dirt or a hard surface than on grass. Ropes are relatively inexpensive and last a long time. Bring a rope to practice and encourage the players to jump rope at home.

FIVE-MINUTE JUMP ROPE PROGRAM

- Warm-up: Normal jump with feet together, 15 seconds.
- Alternating feet skips: Land on right, land on left, land on right, land on left, etc., 30 seconds.
- Jumping-jack skips: Two feet together, two feet out, two feet together, two feet out, etc., 30 seconds.
- Skiing skips: Two feet together jumping from side to side, 15 seconds.
- Reverse jumping-jack skips: Feet are splitting forward and backward instead of to the side, 30 seconds.
- High-knee jump: Bring knees up as high as possible, 15 seconds
- Butt kicker jump: Kick heels up behind legs as high as possible, 15 seconds.
- Repeat high-knee jump, 15 seconds.

NOTE: Between each different jump pattern, skip rope roughly 10 seconds with the player's easiest jump. That gives him a chance to catch his breath and prepare for the next jump pattern, which the coach yells during this 10-second break. Begin each jump pattern at a regular speed and rhythm. Progress in each jump pattern so the last 5 to 10 seconds of jumping is done as quickly as possible.

Pepper

Pepper is a fun and effective drill for enhancing bat control, fielding and throwing skills. It can be played with as few as 2 players or as many as 6. We recommend playing in groups of 3 for ages 13-16 or advanced players and groups of 6 for ages 10-12 or beginners. This is a challenging drill, and players younger than 10 will have a difficult time performing it. The coach can help in this drill as well. Have the coach hit if the desired result is quality fielding practice. The coach can field if the desired result is hitting and bat control.

HOW IT'S PLAYED

Place one hitter 10 to 15 feet away from the fielders. The fielding players are side-by-side arm's length apart and in ready position to field a ground ball. The hitter is choked up on the bat for control. The drill begins when a fielder throws the ball softly to the batter. The hitter, using a half swing for control, hits the ball back to the fielder. If there are more than two players, the batter should attempt to hit the ball to each fielding player in succession. Fielders should attempt to get in front of every ball, not just reach for them. The drill continues with each player taking 10 swings. **(picture 17-25)**

17-25

Pepper, The Game

The game is set up as stated above. The object of the game is for the hitter to stay at bat as long as possible by hitting ground balls under control back to the fielders.

RULES:

1. If the ball is hit in the air to a fielder, whoever catches the ball becomes the hitter. The batter takes their place in the fielding line farthest to the left. Play continues.
2. Hitters do not have to swing at bad pitches, and there is no penalty to the fielder for a badly thrown ball.
3. If the hitter doesn't swing at a strike or swings and misses, the fielder who is furthest to the right becomes the hitter. The previous hitter takes their place in line farthest to the left. Play continues. Note: For players ages 12 and below allow them 3 swings and misses before they loose their turn at bat.
4. If a ball is not fielded cleanly by a fielder, that player changes position in line with the fielder to their left. Play continues.
5. Fielders are responsible for fielding balls in their area. The hitter will judge who should have caught the ball if it goes between two fielders.

Whiffle Ball Pepper

The game is set up and played as stated above. Instead of a real baseball players use a whiffle ball. Players remove their gloves and work on fielding the ball with their bare hands. It will be difficult to catch the whiffle ball with one bare hand, and will force players to utilize two hands in the fielding process. This is a productive game for all ages, and add an element of safety for younger players.

NOTES